FACT FILE 2011 CONTENTS

Ethnic minorities will make up a fifth of Britain's population by 2051

page 26

32% of teenage girls struggle with their independence while 32% of boys struggle with studies

page 75

Fact File 2011

Statistics brought alive!

Farnham
Sixth Form College

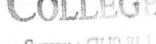

@ **Copiable and online**

Log on: Get instant access to this book by logging on.

Fact File Online: www.carelpress.co.uk/FF

User name: _____

Password: _____

CAREL PRESS
www.carelpress.com

Editor: Christine Shepherd

Fact File is...

... an attractive, fully copiable book

It contains important, interesting and relevant statistics presented in an attractive and stimulating way so that readers will want to look at the figures and engage with the issues behind them.

We've looked at hundreds of sources, uncovering the numbers behind the issues, controversies and news stories. Our chief concern is to select figures which are relevant to the curriculum and, especially, to the lives of young people in Britain today.

The book can take its place on the library shelf – for reference or the sheer pleasure of browsing. It is also fully copiable – for research or classroom use.

... a useful, flexible online resource

As an owner of the book you get single user online access. This means you can log on to Fact File Online, which allows you to instantly download the pages as PDFs. We also provide you with the raw data behind each chart and links to all the sources, making it easy for you, staff or students to take research further and to create your own graphs using our data. You even have access to the archive of previous editions, giving you a wealth of statistics to use. Just typing in a search term will produce all the relevant pages you need.

Online access allows you to display individual pages to a group via a screen or whiteboard, in the library, in the classroom, in assembly – even at home. The single user online access that comes with the book really makes Fact File a flexible and thoroughly usable resource.

Go to: www.carelpress.co.uk/FF/register to register for your online access.

... instantly accessible and usable for everyone with a multi-user site licence

To make Fact File even more usable you can buy an inexpensive multi-user site licence. This makes Fact File Online available to any number of staff and students anywhere, anytime.

If you haven't already purchased a site licence just email us at office@carelpress.co.uk to set up your access.

No more wasting effort on fruitless internet searches yielding unreliable results. Fact File only gives you the most up-to-date, relevant, understandable and suitable material.

And there's more ...

As well as access to Fact File, if you go to
www.carelpress.com/quicksearch

you can search previous editions of both Fact File and Essential Articles. Typing a keyword into our QUICKSEARCH facility will bring you a list of statistics from previous volumes and the matching articles in our Essential Articles series. If you are a registered online user, you can then download the PDFs directly.

This provides you with a complete package of text and figures for whatever topic you choose. This pairing of facts and excellent writing, in copiable formats, makes these resources uniquely adaptable to your needs.

You can find even more useful links in Key Organisations, our annually updated guide to thousands of organisations.

Whether you want to raise an issue in the classroom, or find information for a project, these fantastic publications will certainly provide you with what you need.

Published by Carel Press Ltd
4 Hewson St, Carlisle CA2 5AU
Tel +44 (0)1228 538928, Fax 591816
office@carelpress.co.uk
www.carelpress.com
© Carel Press

Research, design and editorial team:
Jack Gregory, Anne Louise Kershaw, Debbie Maxwell, Christine A Shepherd, Chas White

Cover design: Anne Louise Kershaw

Subscriptions: Ann Batey (Manager), Brenda Hughes, Anne Maclagan

British Library Cataloguing in Publication Data
Fact file 2011 : essential statistics for today's key issues.
1. Great Britain--Statistics.
I. Shepherd, Christine A., 1951-
314.1
ISBN 978-1-905600-24-3

Printed by Finemark, Poland

There were 102,327 cases of identity fraud in 2009

page 136

The floods in Pakistan affected an estimated 20 million people

page 179

Alcohol & drugs

Road to recovery?

More teenagers are receiving help for drug and alcohol problems than ever before

Overall drug and alcohol use among young people may be declining, but making services more available ensures that many more young people who need help are getting it.

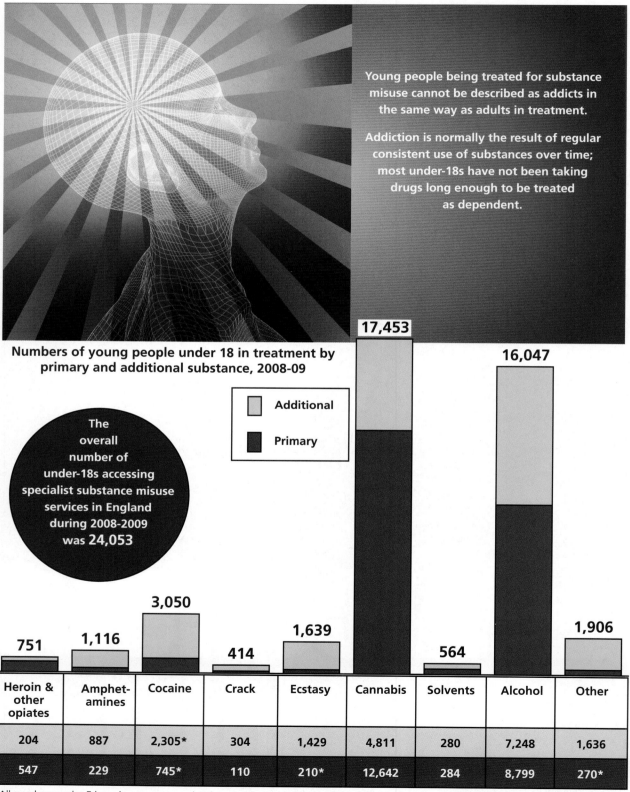

Young people being treated for substance misuse cannot be described as addicts in the same way as adults in treatment.

Addiction is normally the result of regular consistent use of substances over time; most under-18s have not been taking drugs long enough to be treated as dependent.

Numbers of young people under 18 in treatment by primary and additional substance, 2008-09

The overall number of under-18s accessing specialist substance misuse services in England during 2008-2009 was **24,053**

Legend:
- Additional
- Primary

	Heroin & other opiates	Amphet-amines	Cocaine	Crack	Ecstasy	Cannabis	Solvents	Alcohol	Other
Total	751	1,116	3,050	414	1,639	17,453	564	16,047	1,906
Additional	204	887	2,305*	304	1,429	4,811	280	7,248	1,636
Primary	547	229	745*	110	210*	12,642	284	8,799	270*

*All numbers under 5 have been suppressed. Where totals could then be derived, figures have been rounded to the nearest 5

Number of young people accessing services, by age group 2008-09

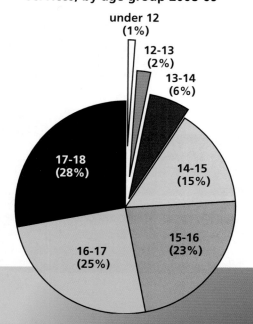

- under 12 (1%)
- 12-13 (2%)
- 13-14 (6%)
- 14-15 (15%)
- 15-16 (23%)
- 16-17 (25%)
- 17-18 (28%)

Number of young people aged under 18 accessing services, by gender 2008-09

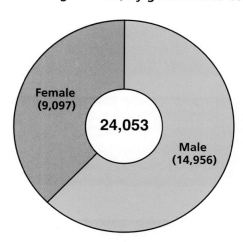

Female (9,097)

24,053

Male (14,956)

Most young people needed help such as counselling, sometimes with families, to address the underlying causes and consequences of substance misuse.

They would also need support for a range of problems from the breakdown of family relationships, social networks and poor school attendance to emotional and physical harms.

% in treatment, by primary substance, 2008-09

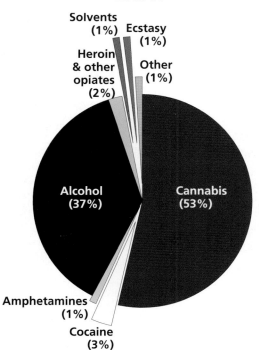

- Solvents (1%)
- Ecstasy (1%)
- Heroin & other opiates (2%)
- Other (1%)
- Alcohol (37%)
- Cannabis (53%)
- Amphetamines (1%)
- Cocaine (3%)

Class A drugs are deemed the most dangerous and so carry the harshest punishment

Numbers in treatment by Class A substance 2008-09

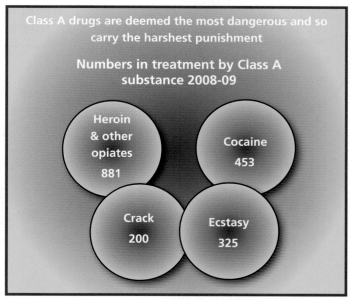

- Heroin & other opiates 881
- Cocaine 453
- Crack 200
- Ecstasy 325

Source: Substance misuse among young people 2008-09, NHS National Treatment Agency for Substance Misuse
www.nta.nhs.uk

Drug deaths

Heroin and morphine deaths declined by 2% in 2009 but are still five times higher than levels seen in 1993

In England and Wales, the number of deaths involving **methadone** increased by **8%**, continuing the upward trend in deaths related to methadone-poisoning seen since 2002.

Deaths involving **cocaine** decreased for the first time since 2000 – a **14%** decrease compared with 2008.

There was an increase of **6%** in deaths from **antidepressants** in 2009 the highest number since 2004.

Males accounted for **73%** of drug poisoning deaths in 2009. From 1996 onwards there have been at least twice as many deaths in males than in females.

There were **46,632** drug-related deaths in England and Wales between 1993 and 2009.

Number of deaths from drug-related poisoning (illegal and legal), by gender, England and Wales

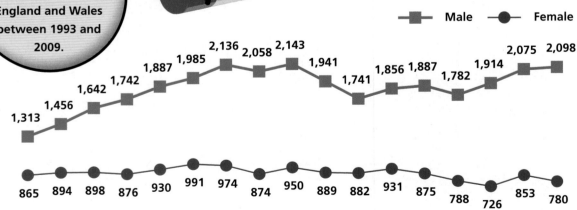

■— Male   ●— Female

Male: 1,313 (1993), 1,456 (1994), 1,642 (1995), 1,742 (1996), 1,887 (1997), 1,985 (1998), 2,136 (1999), 2,058 (2000), 2,143 (2001), 1,941 (2002), 1,741 (2003), 1,856 (2004), 1,887 (2005), 1,782 (2006), 1,914 (2007), 2,075 (2008), 2,098 (2009)

Female: 865 (1993), 894 (1994), 898 (1995), 876 (1996), 930 (1997), 991 (1998), 974 (1999), 874 (2000), 950 (2001), 889 (2002), 882 (2003), 931 (2004), 875 (2005), 788 (2006), 726 (2007), 853 (2008), 780 (2009)

1993 1994 1995 1996 1997 1998 1999 2000 2001 2002 2003 2004 2005 2006 2007 2008 2009

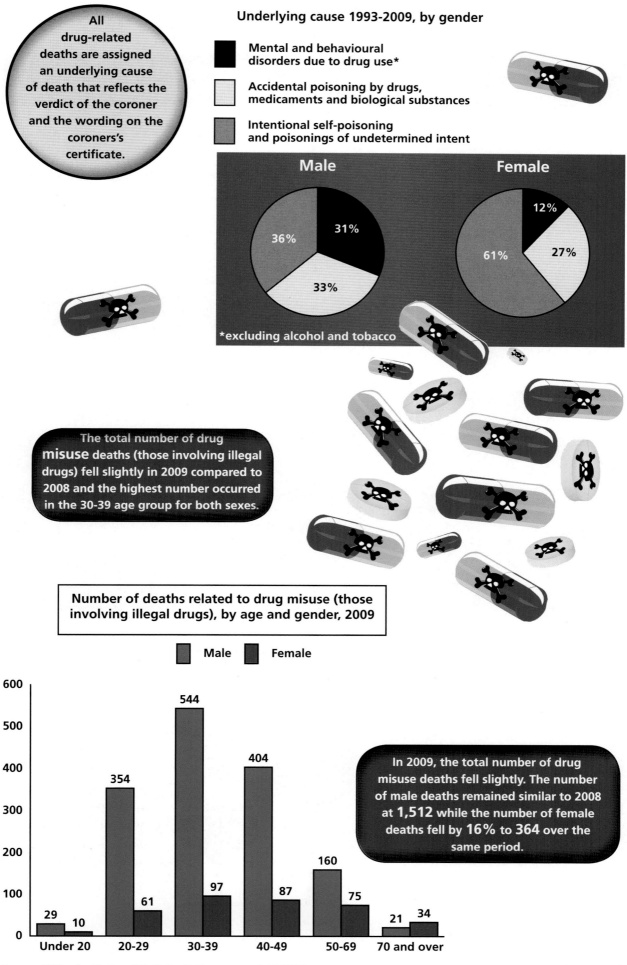

All drug-related deaths are assigned an underlying cause of death that reflects the verdict of the coroner and the wording on the coroners's certificate.

Underlying cause 1993-2009, by gender

■ Mental and behavioural disorders due to drug use*

□ Accidental poisoning by drugs, medicaments and biological substances

▧ Intentional self-poisoning and poisonings of undetermined intent

Male

36%
31%
33%

Female

12%
61%
27%

*excluding alcohol and tobacco

The total number of drug **misuse** deaths (those involving illegal drugs) fell slightly in 2009 compared to 2008 and the highest number occurred in the 30-39 age group for both sexes.

Number of deaths related to drug misuse (those involving illegal drugs), by age and gender, 2009

■ Male   ■ Female

In 2009, the total number of drug misuse deaths fell slightly. The number of male deaths remained similar to 2008 at **1,512** while the number of female deaths fell by **16%** to **364** over the same period.

Age	Male	Female
Under 20	29	10
20-29	354	61
30-39	544	97
40-49	404	87
50-69	160	75
70 and over	21	34

Source: Office for National Statistics © Crown copyright 2010

www.statistics.gov.uk

The cost of a drink

Almost 100,000 people could die over the next ten years as a direct result of their alcohol consumption

The number of deaths in the last decade totalled
80,089 – 52,790 men and **27,299** women

The number of alcohol-related deaths has consistently increased in the UK since the early 1990s. There were **4,023** deaths in 1992 (6.7 per 100,000) and **9,031** in 2008 (13.6 per 100,000).

UK alcohol-related death rate per 100,000, by gender

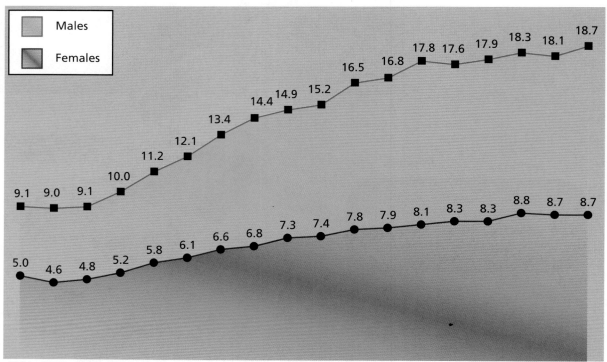

Males

Females

18.7 18.1 18.3 17.9 17.6 17.8 16.8 16.5 15.2 14.9 14.4 13.4 12.1 11.2 10.0 9.1 9.0 9.1

8.7 8.7 8.8 8.3 8.3 8.1 7.9 7.8 7.4 7.3 6.8 6.6 6.1 5.8 5.2 4.8 4.6 5.0

1991 1992 1993 1994 1995 1996 1997 1998 1999 2000 2001 2002 2003 2004 2005 2006 2007 2008

Female rates have increased slightly but alcohol-related deaths in males increased in 2008 and have more than doubled since 1991

Results show alcohol related deaths are significantly associated with trends in alcohol consumption – as average consumption went up by one litre per person per year, there were 928 more deaths in the UK

The figures on alcohol related deaths only include those regarded as being most directly due to alcohol consumption and do not include deaths caused indirectly by alcohol such as those from drink-driving or cancers which have been caused in part by drinking

UK alcohol-related death rates per 100,000, by age and gender, 2008

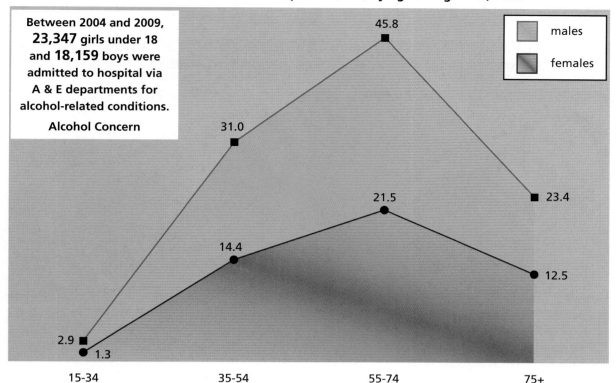

Between 2004 and 2009, **23,347** girls under 18 and **18,159** boys were admitted to hospital via A & E departments for alcohol-related conditions.
Alcohol Concern

males
females

45.8
31.0
21.5
23.4
14.4
12.5
2.9
1.3

15-34   35-54   55-74   75+

Alcohol misuse can be directly related to deaths from certain types of diseases:

Causes of alcohol-related deaths, England	2008
Mental & behavioural disorders	637
Alcoholic cardiomyopathy	80
Alcoholic liver disease	4,400
Chronic hepatitis	62
Fibrosis and cirrhosis of the liver	1,367
Alcoholic induced pancreatitis	48
Accidental poisoning by and exposure to alcohol	153
Other causes	22

Men	4,473
Women	2,296
Total	6,769

The estimated annual cost of alcohol misuse to the NHS in England is £2,704.1 million

A face that should haunt a generation p118-119 in Essential Articles 13 discusses the controversy about who should receive a transplanted organ

"The rise of very cheap, affordable alcohol has led to an increase in consumption and hence a tripling of alcohol-related mortality over the past 25 years ...the worst part is that all of these deaths are avoidable".

Alcohol Concern Chief Executive Don Shenker

Sources: Alcohol Concern, Office for National Statistics – Alcohol-related deaths in the UK 1991-2008 © Crown copyright 2010

www.alcoholconcern.org.uk
www.ons.gov.uk

Much too much...

Half of men and a third of women in Scotland regularly drink above sensible drinking guidelines

Total sales of alcohol units* per adult, per week
(average)
*One unit is 10ml of alcohol

☐ Scotland
■ England & Wales

NHS Health Scotland's report on alcohol sales over these five years confirms that adults in Scotland buy on average **24%** more alcohol than the rest of Britain

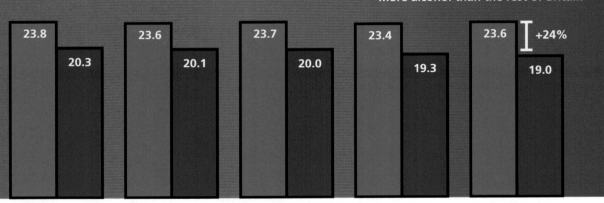

	2005	2006	2007	2008	2009
Scotland	23.8	23.6	23.7	23.4	23.6
England & Wales	20.3	20.1	20.0	19.3	19.0

+24%

275ml
BOTTLE
OF ALCO-POP
1.4 UNITS

500ml
CAN OF LAGER
1.9 UNITS

25ml
SINGLE SPIRIT
AND MIXER
1 UNIT

PINT
OF STRONG BEER/
LAGER/CIDER
3 UNITS

175ml
GLASS OF RED
OR WHITE WINE
2.3 UNITS

PINT
OF LAGER
2.3 UNITS

What is a unit of alcohol?

One unit of alcohol =
half a pint of ordinary strength beer, lager or cider
or
a small pub measure (25ml) of spirits

One and a half units of alcohol =
a small glass (125ml) of ordinary strength wine
or
a standard pub measure (35ml) of spirits

But remember, many wines and beers are stronger than the more traditional 'ordinary' strengths

The annual cost of alcohol misuse in Scotland is estimated to be around **£3.56 billion** in costs to business, NHS, social services, police and courts, which amounts to around one tenth of Scotland's annual budget of **£900** for every adult in Scotland.

On average Scotland sees **115** hospital admissions every day due to alcohol misuse – one Scot dies due to alcohol misuse every three hours.

...much too often

Too many of us are simply drinking much too much, much too often"
Nicola Sturgeon – Cabinet Secretary for Health and Wellbeing, Scotland, 2010

Sales of alcohol units*
per adult, per week,
Scotland (average)
*One unit is 10ml of alcohol

☐ On-trade
■ Off-trade

In England & Wales in 2009 on-trade sales averaged **6.3** units per adult per week and off-trade sales averaged **12.7** units per adult per week

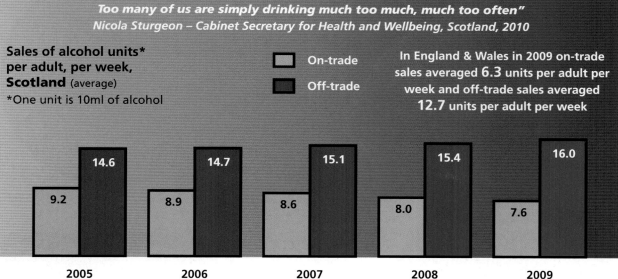

2005	2006	2007	2008	2009
On-trade 9.2 / Off-trade 14.6	8.9 / 14.7	8.6 / 15.1	8.0 / 15.4	7.6 / 16.0

Over the past five years, Scots have shown a preference for drinking at home – with one factor being that alcohol sold in off-licences and supermarkets is three times cheaper per unit than that sold in pubs. The Scottish government is discussing the introduction of minimum pricing for alcohol to deal with the problem.

Over five years, on-trade prices increased from **£1.12** to **£1.31** per unit, an increase of **19p**, much more than the increase in off trade prices – **39p** to **43p** per unit – an increase of only **4p**.

Only **32%** of alcohol sales are on licensed premises (on trade) while **68%** are off-trade.

26% of off-sales cider is sold at just **20p** per unit. At that rate, a man can exceed his weekly maximum recommended amount for **£4.40** while a woman can exceed hers for just **£3.00**.

The NHS recommends that:
men should not regularly drink more than 3-4 units a day
women should not regularly drink more than 2-3 units a day
'Regularly' means drinking these amounts every day or most days of the week

Sources: Analysis of alcohol sales data, 2005-2009,
NHS Health Scotland, Patient UK
www.healthscotland.com

www.drinking.nhs.uk
www.alcohol-focus-scotland.org.uk
www.patient.co.uk/health/Recommended-Safe-Limits-of-Alcohol.htm

Unseen damage

Over 9,000 people in the UK die from alcohol-related causes each year

DRINKING CAUSES DAMAGE YOU CAN'T SEE

SHOULD NOT REGULARLY EXCEED
MEN 3-4 UNITS DAILY
WOMEN 2-3 UNITS DAILY
1 PINT OF STRONG LAGER = 3 UNITS
1 LARGE GLASS OF WINE = 3 UNITS

A YouGov poll of over 2,000 adults in England which coincided with an NHS campaign found that:

55% of those surveyed misguidedly believed that alcohol **ONLY** damages your health if you regularly get drunk or binge drink.

83% of those who regularly drink more than the NHS recommended limits of **2-3 units a day for women** (about one glass of wine) and **3-4 units a day for men** (about one pint of lager) don't think their drinking is putting their long-term health at risk.

Since about **10 million** adults in England drink above the recommended limits, this means that about **8.3 million** people could be unaware of the damage they are doing to themselves.

86% of drinkers surveyed knew that drinking alcohol is related to liver disease.

Only **7%** knew of the link to breast cancer, **25%** to throat cancer, **28%** to mouth cancer, **37%** to stroke and **56%** to heart disease along with other serious conditions.

...but it's not only binge drinking that harms health

Men who regularly drink more than 2 pints of 5.2% lager a day

- are over **3 times** more likely to get mouth cancer
- could be **3 times** more likely to have a stroke

Women who regularly drink 2 large glasses of 13% wine or more a day:

- are **2 times** as likely to have high blood pressure
- are **50%** more likely to get breast cancer

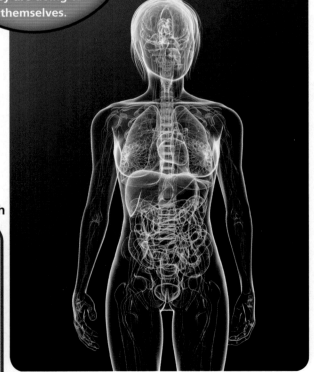

Source: NHS
www.nhs.uk/drinking

Animals

Animal rights... and wrongs

71% of us can accept animal research as long as there is no unnecessary suffering ... but not all of us trust that this is the case

How strongly do you agree or disagree with the following statements about the rules and regulations governing animal experimentation?

Legend: Strongly disagree | Tend to disagree | Neither agree nor disagree | Tend to agree | Strongly agree | Don't know

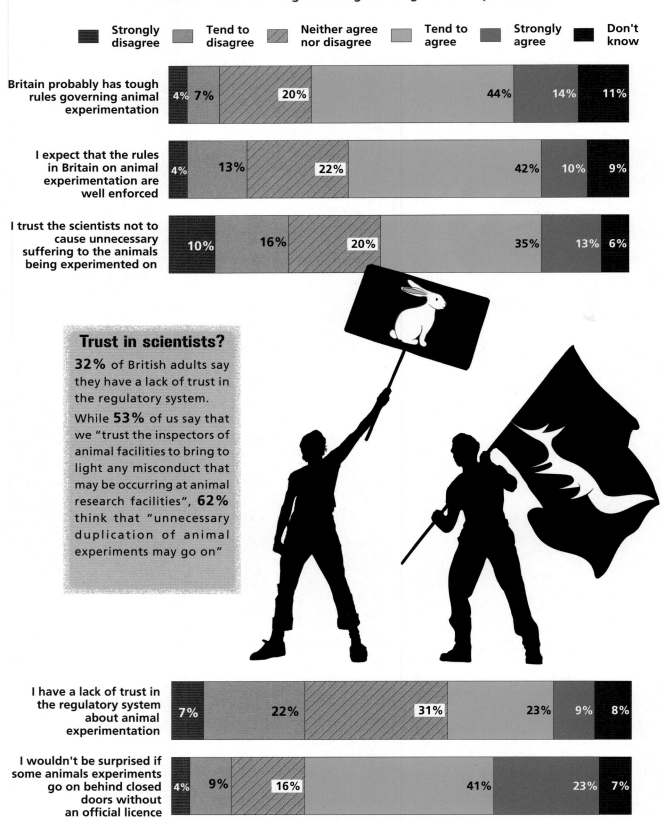

Britain probably has tough rules governing animal experimentation
4% | 7% | 20% | 44% | 14% | 11%

I expect that the rules in Britain on animal experimentation are well enforced
4% | 13% | 22% | 42% | 10% | 9%

I trust the scientists not to cause unnecessary suffering to the animals being experimented on
10% | 16% | 20% | 35% | 13% | 6%

Trust in scientists?

32% of British adults say they have a lack of trust in the regulatory system.

While **53%** of us say that we "trust the inspectors of animal facilities to bring to light any misconduct that may be occurring at animal research facilities", **62%** think that "unnecessary duplication of animal experiments may go on"

I have a lack of trust in the regulatory system about animal experimentation
7% | 22% | 31% | 23% | 9% | 8%

I wouldn't be surprised if some animals experiments go on behind closed doors without an official licence
4% | 9% | 16% | 41% | 23% | 7%

Is animal experimentation acceptable and when?

70% can **accept animal experimentation** so long as it is for medical research purposes.

50% agree that animal experimentation **for medical research purposes** should only be conducted for life-threatening diseases.

68% agree with animal experimentation **for all types of medical research**, where there is no alternative.

29% do not support the use of animals in **any experimentation** because of the importance they place on animal welfare.

19% think the Government should **ban all experiments on animals** for any form of research.

People are generally more likely to **accept** experimentation for testing chemicals that could harm people **(48%)**, rather than for testing chemicals that could harm wildlife or the environment **(39%)**.

Is protest against animal experimentation acceptable and how?

Top 5 ACCEPTABLE things for an animal rights organisation to do if it were protesting about the use of animals in research

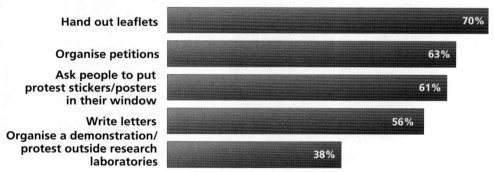

- Hand out leaflets — 70%
- Organise petitions — 63%
- Ask people to put protest stickers/posters in their window — 61%
- Write letters — 56%
- Organise a demonstration/protest outside research laboratories — 38%

Top 5 UNACCEPTABLE things for an animal rights organisation to do if it were protesting about the use of animals in research

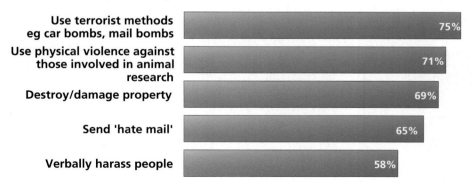

- Use terrorist methods eg car bombs, mail bombs — 75%
- Use physical violence against those involved in animal research — 71%
- Destroy/damage property — 69%
- Send 'hate mail' — 65%
- Verbally harass people — 58%

Source: Views on Animal Experimentation, Department for Business, Innovation and Skills, Ipsos-mori, March 2010
www.ipsos-mori.com/

Animal research

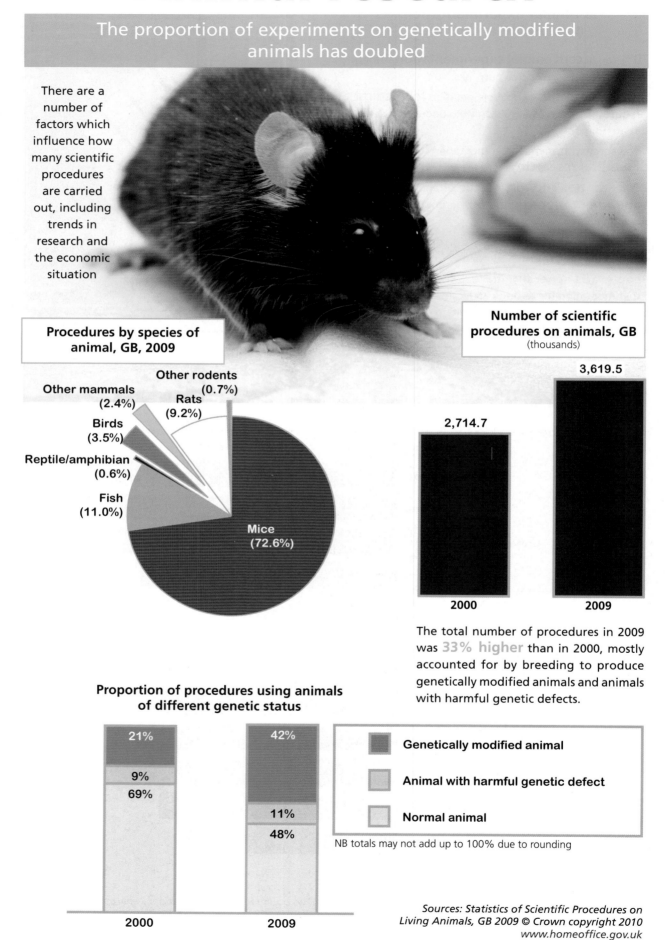

There are a number of factors which influence how many scientific procedures are carried out, including trends in research and the economic situation

Procedures by species of animal, GB, 2009

Other mammals (2.4%)

Other rodents (0.7%)

Birds (3.5%)

Rats (9.2%)

Reptile/amphibian (0.6%)

Fish (11.0%)

Mice (72.6%)

Number of scientific procedures on animals, GB (thousands)

2,714.7 — 2000

3,619.5 — 2009

The total number of procedures in 2009 was 33% higher than in 2000, mostly accounted for by breeding to produce genetically modified animals and animals with harmful genetic defects.

Proportion of procedures using animals of different genetic status

2000:
21%
9%
69%

2009:
42%
11%
48%

Genetically modified animal

Animal with harmful genetic defect

Normal animal

NB totals may not add up to 100% due to rounding

Sources: Statistics of Scientific Procedures on Living Animals, GB 2009 © Crown copyright 2010 www.homeoffice.gov.uk

Acting for animals

...this may have been because 2008 was an unusually busy year for
the RSPCA or perhaps the Animal Welfare Act has made the public
more aware of the duty of care they owe their animals

The RSPCA received more than **1.25 million** phone calls during 2009

On average, every 30 seconds someone in England and Wales phones the RSPCA's 24 hour cruelty line for help

CRUELTY LINE:
Tel:
0300 1234 999

Ignorant owner causes suffering

Labradors fed on pizza

"The thinnest horse I've ever seen, alive or dead"
Andy Shipp, RSPCA Prosecution Case Manager

Dog left dying as owners celebrate Christmas

240 animals in one house

During 2009 the RSPCA...

rescued and collected **135,293** animals and
investigated **141,280** cruelty complaints

Of those people brought before the court,
2,579 convictions were obtained and **20**
defendants had all their charges dismissed –
a **98.3%** success rate

There were **69** prison sentences and
98 suspended prison sentences imposed for cruelty

Top five most mistreated animals

Dog	1,808
Cat	341
Horse	212
Rabbit	61
Snake	22

The Animal Welfare Act has been described as the single most important piece
of animal welfare legislation for nearly 100 years – the Act places a legal obligation
on owners and keepers of animals to care for them properly.

Source: RSPCA

www.rspca.org.uk

Home and astray

There has been a rapid increase in the number of stray dogs

Decade of strays!

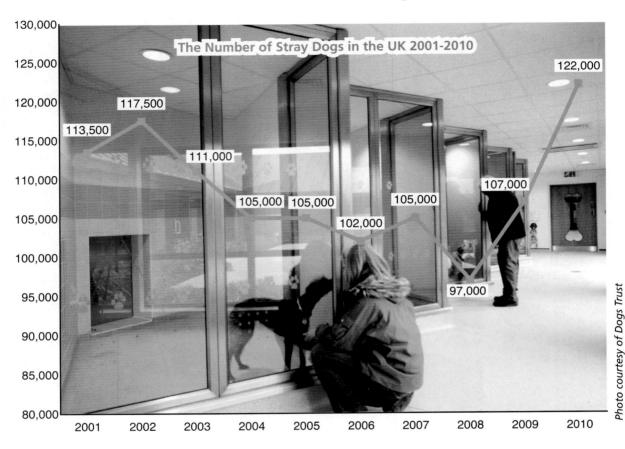

The Number of Stray Dogs in the UK 2001-2010

- 113,500
- 117,500
- 111,000
- 105,000
- 105,000
- 102,000
- 97,000
- 105,000
- 107,000
- 122,000

(y-axis: 80,000 to 130,000)
(x-axis: 2001 2002 2003 2004 2005 2006 2007 2008 2009 2010)

Photo courtesy of Dogs Trust

Photo courtesy of Dogs Trust

Prevention

The Dogs Trust is calling for the introduction of a compulsory microchipping system for all dogs in the UK. It believes this will help reunite even more owners with their lost pets, trace abandoned pets back to irresponsible owners and ultimately reduce the number of healthy dogs unnecessarily put to sleep in the UK.

The RSPCA, on the other hand, would like to see a dog licence scheme saying it would help to curb problems such as puppy farms and stray, stolen or abandoned animals and that the money raised could be used to provide services such as dog wardens. In their recent survey, 76% of all people asked and 66% of dog owners were in favour of a dog licence.

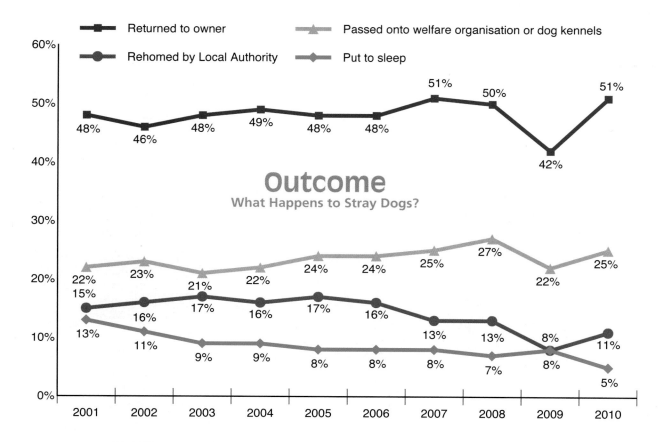

Outcome
What Happens to Stray Dogs?

Returned to owner: 48%, 46%, 48%, 49%, 48%, 48%, 51%, 50%, 42%, 51%

Passed onto welfare organisation or dog kennels: 22%, 23%, 21%, 22%, 24%, 24%, 25%, 27%, 22%, 25%

Rehomed by Local Authority: 15%, 16%, 17%, 16%, 17%, 16%, 13%, 13%, 8%, 11%

Put to sleep: 13%, 11%, 9%, 9%, 8%, 8%, 8%, 7%, 8%, 5%

2001, 2002, 2003, 2004, 2005, 2006, 2007, 2008, 2009, 2010

Success?

An encouraging 51% of stray dogs picked up by Local Authorities in the UK were reunited with their owners according to the 2010 Dogs Trust Stray Dog Survey. This is only the second time the figure has gone through the 50% barrier since survey records began in 1997.

Where we know the method used, the proportion of dogs returned through microchipping was 35%.

There has been a considerable decline in the number of dogs being put to sleep by Local Authorities due to ill health, aggression (under the Dangerous Dogs Act) or simply for want of a home – down from 9,310 in last year's survey to 6,404 this year.

Photo courtesy of Dogs Trust

Source: Stray dog survey, Prepared for the Dogs Trust, GfK NOP
www.dogstrust.org.uk
www.rspca.org.uk

For more information about the dogs trust and what they do go to:
www.dogstrust.org.uk

Alright pet

We are a nation of animal lovers – or half of us are!

In 2010 the percentage of households owning a pet in the UK was broken down as follows

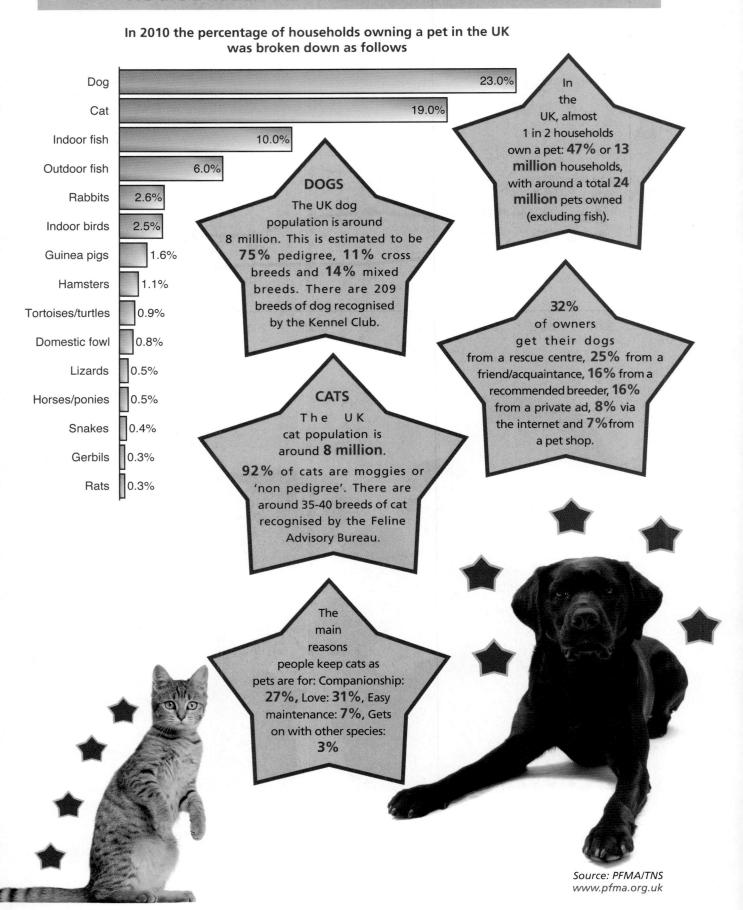

Pet	Percentage
Dog	23.0%
Cat	19.0%
Indoor fish	10.0%
Outdoor fish	6.0%
Rabbits	2.6%
Indoor birds	2.5%
Guinea pigs	1.6%
Hamsters	1.1%
Tortoises/turtles	0.9%
Domestic fowl	0.8%
Lizards	0.5%
Horses/ponies	0.5%
Snakes	0.4%
Gerbils	0.3%
Rats	0.3%

In the UK, almost 1 in 2 households own a pet: **47%** or **13 million** households, with around a total **24 million** pets owned (excluding fish).

DOGS
The UK dog population is around 8 million. This is estimated to be **75%** pedigree, **11%** cross breeds and **14%** mixed breeds. There are 209 breeds of dog recognised by the Kennel Club.

32% of owners get their dogs from a rescue centre, **25%** from a friend/acquaintance, **16%** from a recommended breeder, **16%** from a private ad, **8%** via the internet and **7%** from a pet shop.

CATS
The UK cat population is around **8 million**.
92% of cats are moggies or 'non pedigree'. There are around 35-40 breeds of cat recognised by the Feline Advisory Bureau.

The main reasons people keep cats as pets are for: Companionship: **27%**, Love: **31%**, Easy maintenance: **7%**, Gets on with other species: **3%**

Source: PFMA/TNS
www.pfma.org.uk

Britain & its citizens

Who do you think you are?

As the population rises, the make-up of Britain changes

Photo by Wootang01

The UK Population – On the rise

The UK population was estimated at 61.4 million in 2008.

It is projected to increase by over 4 million to 65.6 million in 2018.

It is expected to exceed 70 million by 2029 rising to to 71.6 million by 2033.

Photo by Hiten Mistry

Births, deaths and migration

Of the 10.2 million projected increase in population over the next 25 years, 55% is likely to be natural increase (more births than deaths) and 45% is projected net migration (the difference between people leaving and entering the country).

However, future numbers of births and deaths are themselves partly dependent on future migration. Taking this into account, just over two-thirds of the projected total increase in population between 2008 and 2033 is expected to be either directly or indirectly due to future migration.

Photo by Alamez

Ethnic shift

Ethnic minorities will make up a fifth of Britain's population by 2051, compared with 8% in 2001, according to new projections published by the University of Leeds.

Researchers found striking differences in the respective growth rates of the 16 ethnic groups studied. White British and Irish groups are expected to grow the most slowly, while the so-called 'other' white group is projected to grow the fastest, driven by immigration from Europe, the US and Australasia. Traditional immigrant groups of south Asian origin (Indian, Pakistani and Bangladeshi) will also grow rapidly.

Trends and prediction in the UK population, 2001-2031 by ethnic group, In thousands

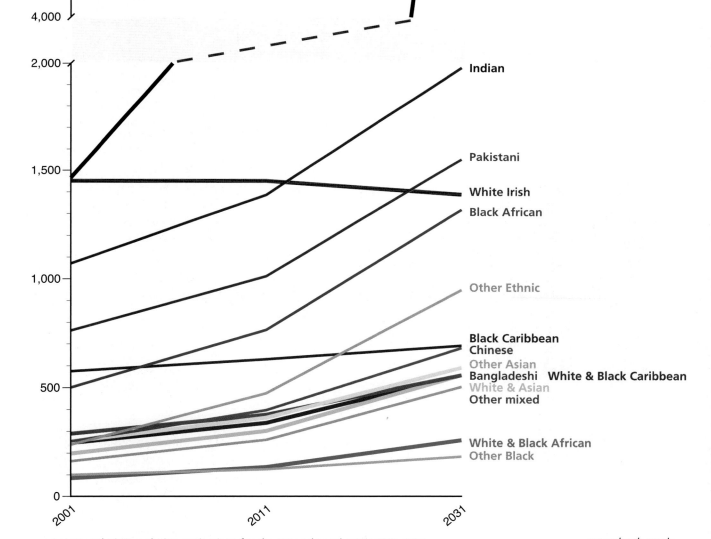

"It is impossible to predict exactly how people will move into, out of and within the country in the coming decades" said Professor Philip Rees of Leeds University.

"However, our results suggest that overall we can look forward to being not only a more diverse nation, but one that is far more spatially integrated than at present."

	White British
2001	51,469
2011	50,613
2031	47,290

The figures for White British are in a table of their own as their numbers would distort the graph

White Other

Indian

Pakistani

White Irish

Black African

Other Ethnic

Black Caribbean
Chinese
Other Asian
Bangladeshi   White & Black Caribbean
White & Asian
Other mixed

White & Black African
Other Black

Source: Ethnic Population Projections for the UK and Local Areas 2001-2051, Leeds University; Office for National Statistics © Crown Copyright 2010

www.leeds.ac.uk
www.ons.gov.uk

UK growth

Estimated population of UK countries

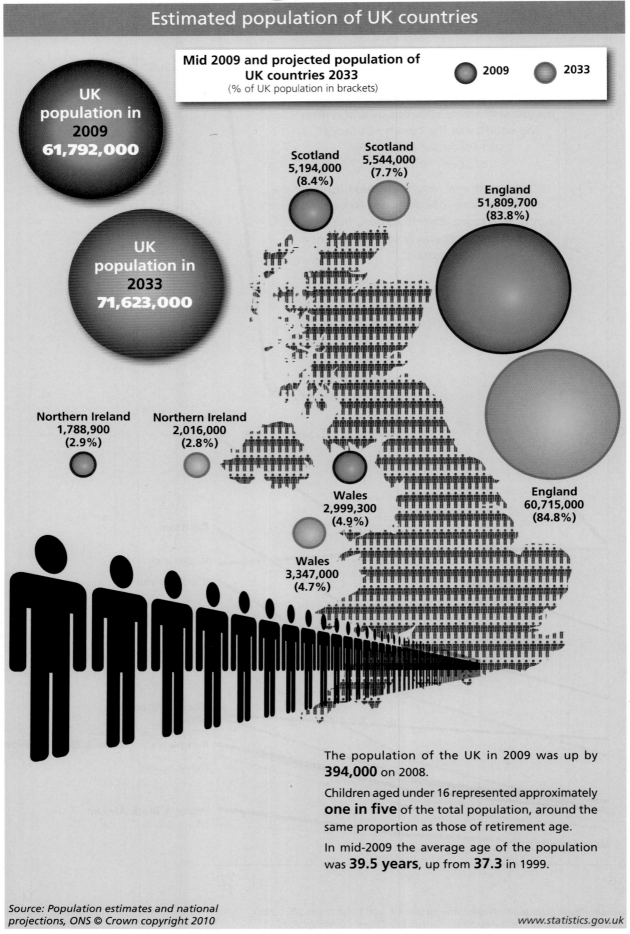

Mid 2009 and projected population of UK countries 2033
(% of UK population in brackets)

2009   2033

UK population in 2009
61,792,000

UK population in 2033
71,623,000

Scotland 5,194,000 (8.4%)

Scotland 5,544,000 (7.7%)

England 51,809,700 (83.8%)

Northern Ireland 1,788,900 (2.9%)

Northern Ireland 2,016,000 (2.8%)

Wales 2,999,300 (4.9%)

Wales 3,347,000 (4.7%)

England 60,715,000 (84.8%)

The population of the UK in 2009 was up by **394,000** on 2008.

Children aged under 16 represented approximately **one in five** of the total population, around the same proportion as those of retirement age.

In mid-2009 the average age of the population was **39.5 years**, up from **37.3** in 1999.

Source: Population estimates and national projections, ONS © Crown copyright 2010

www.statistics.gov.uk

Migrant workers

Many thousands of European migrants are working below their ability

IMMIGRATION

Enlargement of the European Union (EU) has changed migration patterns to the UK. Over the past five years, it has brought hundreds of thousands of new EU citizens into the UK's society and labour market. The new migration poses distinctive new challenges.

LABOUR MARKET

An estimated 1.5 million workers have come to the UK from new EU member states since May 2004, and the number of eastern European nationals resident in the UK has increased to about 700,000.

Eastern Europeans have made up about half of labour immigration in recent years and differ substantially from the UK's previous immigrant groups.

EXPLOITATION

On average, these individuals (and especially Polish people) are young and despite often high levels of education, receive low wages and work in unskilled jobs. In many cases the new migrants have unreliable employment and housing arrangements and are easily exploited due to a lack of support networks and access to information.

WHO?

Every year from 2004/05 onwards Polish migrants have obtained the highest number of National Insurance numbers. However in 2009/10 their numbers dropped to almost half and Indian migrants were the highest group.

National Insurance number allocations 2009/10, thousands

Country	Thousands
India	75.38
Poland	69.94
Rep of Lithuania	23.42
Rep of Latvia	23.20
Pakistan	22.96
Bangladesh	21.18
Romania	17.68
France	16.45
Nigeria	16.23
Nepal	14.59

WHAT NEXT?

The recent migration has added to UK 's existing diversity. Eastern European workers have been relatively well received by the public and by employers - but attitudes to both EU and non-EU migration may have hardened to some extent during recent economic turmoil.

Source: The UK's new Europeans, Equality and Human Rights Commission © crown copyright; Department for Work and Pensions
www.equalityhumanrights.com/
www.dwp.gov.uk/

National Insurance numbers allocated to Polish nationals 2004/05-2009/10, thousands

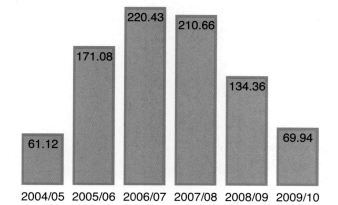

Year	Thousands
2004/05	61.12
2005/06	171.08
2006/07	220.43
2007/08	210.66
2008/09	134.36
2009/10	69.94

Gay UK?

For the first time national statistics have investigated sexual orientation

How were people asked?

The Office for National Statistics asked a sample of 450,000 UK residents about their sexual identity. They asked all household members aged 16 and above who were present in the household at the time of interview or were interviewed by phone. From a total of 247,623 eligible adults 238,206 (96%) provided valid responses.

What are the categories?

The 'Other' option on the sexual identity question was included to address the fact that not all people will fall in the three categories of heterosexual, gay/lesbian or bisexual and that some people may feel no sense of sexual identity at all. In addition, individuals who disagree with a simple male/female gender division, or who were against categorisation based on gender, could also choose to identify as 'other'.

General profiles

Those who identified as being LGB (Lesbian, Gay or Bisexual) tended to be younger than heterosexuals – 64.9% were aged under 45 compared with 48.6%.

A higher proportion of men than women identified themselves as LGB (54.6% compared with 45.4%). Of those who identified themselves as gay/lesbian, only one-third were women (33.8%) and two-thirds were men (66.2%), whereas more than two-thirds (68.2%) of bisexuals were women, and one-third (31.8%) were men.

One-third (33.5%) of LGB respondents said that they did not identify with a religion. This compares with one-fifth (20.4%) of heterosexual or straight respondents.

Educational profile

38.1% of gay/lesbian respondents were educated to degree level or higher, compared with 23.5% of bisexuals and 21.9% of heterosexuals. 11.8% of gay/lesbian respondents had qualifications above 'A' level or equivalent but below degree level. This compares with 9.5% of heterosexual respondents and 8.6% of bisexual respondents.

At the other end of the educational scale, heterosexuals were more likely to have no formal qualifications - 13.2% compared with 12.3% of bisexuals and just 5.7% of gay/lesbian respondents.

Sexual identity, UK 2010

2.8%
0.5%
0.5%
0.5%
1.0%
94.8%

■ Non response

■ Don't know/refusal

■ Other

■ Bisexual

■ Gay/Lesbian

■ Heterosexual/Straight

Figures may not add up to 100% due to rounding

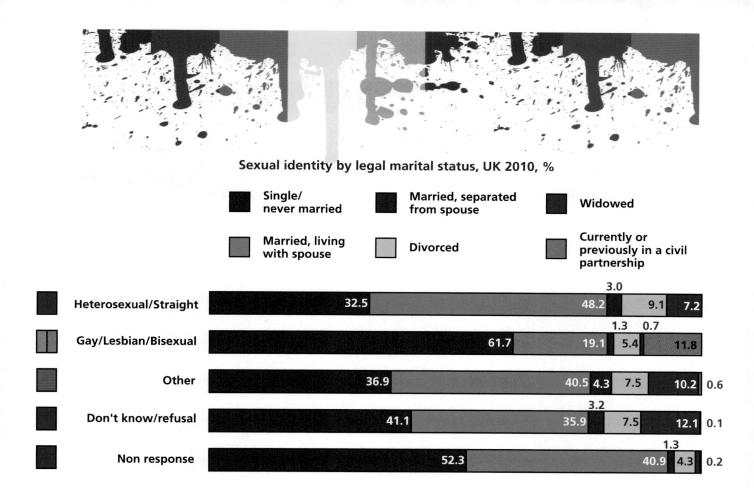

Sexual identity by legal marital status, UK 2010, %

Legend:
- Single/never married
- Married, separated from spouse
- Widowed
- Married, living with spouse
- Divorced
- Currently or previously in a civil partnership

	Single/never married	Married, living with spouse	Married, separated from spouse	Divorced	Widowed	Currently or previously in a civil partnership
Heterosexual/Straight	32.5	48.2	3.0	9.1	7.2	
Gay/Lesbian/Bisexual	61.7	19.1	1.3	0.7	5.4	11.8
Other	36.9	40.5	4.3	7.5	10.2	0.6
Don't know/refusal	41.1	35.9	3.2	7.5	12.1	0.1
Non response	52.3	40.9	1.3	4.3		0.2

Those who were NOT married and living with their spouse or NOT in a current civil partnership were then asked whether or not they were living with another person as part of a couple.

Sexual identity by cohabitation status, UK 2010, %

Legend:
- Cohabiting
- Not cohabiting

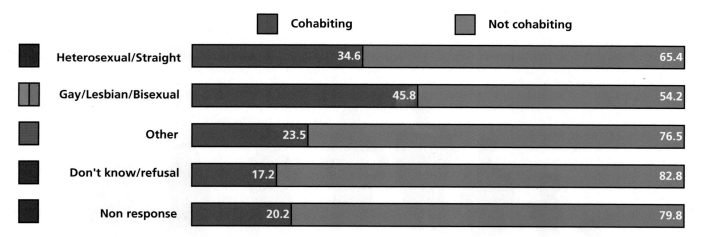

	Cohabiting	Not cohabiting
Heterosexual/Straight	34.6	65.4
Gay/Lesbian/Bisexual	45.8	54.2
Other	23.5	76.5
Don't know/refusal	17.2	82.8
Non response	20.2	79.8

Source: Measuring Sexual Identity: An Evaluation Report,
Office for National Statistics © Crown Copyright
www.statistics.gov.uk

Age of reason

Do you agree with these legal age restrictions?

The British public generally agrees with existing UK laws about the ages at which you can smoke, drink, vote, have sex, or be sent to prison, but a significant minority feels that certain activities should be restricted until **21** or even **25**

Age that largest percentage of people questioned believed limit should be set at, 2010

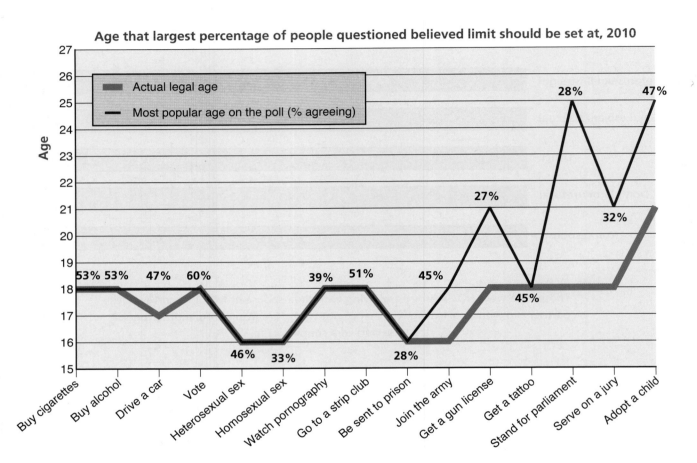

Legend:
- Actual legal age
- Most popular age on the poll (% agreeing)

Y-axis: Age (15 to 27)

Categories (x-axis): Buy cigarettes, Buy alcohol, Drive a car, Vote, Heterosexual sex, Homosexual sex, Watch pornography, Go to a strip club, Be sent to prison, Join the army, Get a gun license, Get a tattoo, Stand for parliament, Serve on a jury, Adopt a child

Data labels: 53%, 53%, 47%, 60%, 46%, 33%, 39%, 51%, 28%, 45%, 27%, 45%, 28%, 32%, 47%

18?

The age of **18** – the most common age at which many activities become legal in the UK – receives the most support among the public. However, **18** is also a popular choice for many activities whose age 'limits' are higher or lower. While nearly **1** in **6** (**15%**) agrees that **17** should be the legal driving age (which it is), nearly half (**47%**) think that it should be higher, at **18**. A cautious **22%** think it should be as high as **21**.

Sex

The age of consent in the UK is **16**. **46%** think that this is correct for heterosexual sex but **33%** would choose **18** and **1%** would raise it to **21**. The picture changes with regard to homosexual sex – **33%** agree it should be **16**, and **28%** think it should be **18** while **8%** think **21** is more appropriate.

Prison

A prison sentence usually only becomes a long-term option from the age of **16** onwards. While a seemingly harsh **24%** would allow under-**14s** to go to prison, **21%** think that **18**-plus would be better. **28%** agree with the current age of **16**.

Too young?

However, for some activities, even 18 seems too young for a proportion of people. **18** year olds can serve on a jury but **32%** think **21** would be a better age and a sizeable **25%** think it should be **25** years or above. Only **28%** feel **18** is the right age. Equally, when it comes to standing for Parliament, just **26%** think that **18** is the right age, compared to **28%** who feel it should be **21**, and **28%** who feel that it should be **25** or over.

And while **16** is the current age at which someone (albeit with parental consent) can join the army, only **29%** agree with this age compared to **45%** who would prefer **18**.

Older is best

27% think **21** should be the right age after which one can get a gun licence, while a similar **26%** think **25** and over would be more apt. The current legal age is **21**.

The highest age restriction though, is left to those people looking to adopt a child. This currently stands at **21** years, but a significant **47%** feel that the age limit should be raised to **25** and over, compared to just **26%** who agree with the law as it currently stands.

Source: YouGov; The Age of Reason
http://today.yougov.co.uk

Religious matters

How religious we are affects our opinions on the BIG issues

Religious rise and fall

Between 1983 and 2008 there was a sharp fall in the proportion of people saying they belong to a particular religion from **69%** to **56%** and in the numbers who attend religious services frequently from **13%** to **10%.** Belief in God has also declined, from **64%** in 1991 to **48%** in 2008.

Immigration and population change has led to a rise in numbers belonging to other world religions and pentecostal Christianity. There also seems to be more interest in religion among second and subsequent generations of immigrants.

The British Social Attitudes Survey grouped people as follows:

THE RELIGIOUS: Those who believe in God, belong to a religious group and attend religious services at least sometimes – **28%** of respondents. We might expect this group to have attitudes which are distinct from the rest of the population.

THE FUZZY FAITHFUL: Those who show some evidence of religious belief, belonging or practice, either through belief in God, reporting that they belong to a religion, or at least some attendance (but not all three). This group covers **39%** of respondents.

THE UNRELIGIOUS: Those who neither believe in God nor belong to any religious group – **33%** of respondents.

The survey examined how opinions on a variety of moral issues varied according to religious belief.

Attitudes towards some personal relationship issues...

Legend:
- Religious
- Fuzzy faithful
- Un-religious
- All

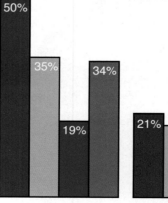
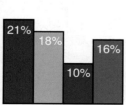

Pre-marital sex is always or almost always wrong
- 29%
- 10%
- 3%
- 13%

A married person having sex outside marriage is always or almost always wrong
- 90%
- 84%
- 80%
- 84%

Homosexual sex is always or almost always wrong
- 50%
- 35%
- 19%
- 34%

Agree that men should earn money, women stay at home
- 21%
- 18%
- 10%
- 16%

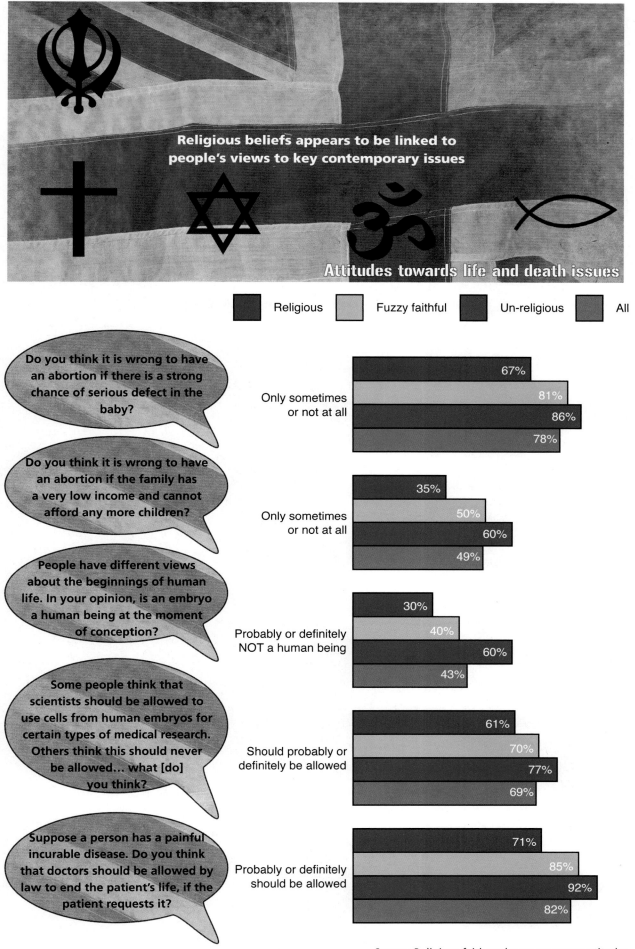

Religious beliefs appears to be linked to people's views to key contemporary issues

Attitudes towards life and death issues

Religious | Fuzzy faithful | Un-religious | All

Do you think it is wrong to have an abortion if there is a strong chance of serious defect in the baby?

Only sometimes or not at all
- 67%
- 81%
- 86%
- 78%

Do you think it is wrong to have an abortion if the family has a very low income and cannot afford any more children?

Only sometimes or not at all
- 35%
- 50%
- 60%
- 49%

People have different views about the beginnings of human life. In your opinion, is an embryo a human being at the moment of conception?

Probably or definitely NOT a human being
- 30%
- 40%
- 60%
- 43%

Some people think that scientists should be allowed to use cells from human embryos for certain types of medical research. Others think this should never be allowed... what [do] you think?

Should probably or definitely be allowed
- 61%
- 70%
- 77%
- 69%

Suppose a person has a painful incurable disease. Do you think that doctors should be allowed by law to end the patient's life, if the patient requests it?

Probably or definitely should be allowed
- 71%
- 85%
- 92%
- 82%

Source: Religious faith and contemporary attitudes
From British Social Attitudes 2009-2010

Charitable giving

How people give and how much

In 2008-09 74% of people living in England had given money to charity in the four weeks before interview.

Most common methods of giving
(Respondents could mention more than one method. Base: 8,768)

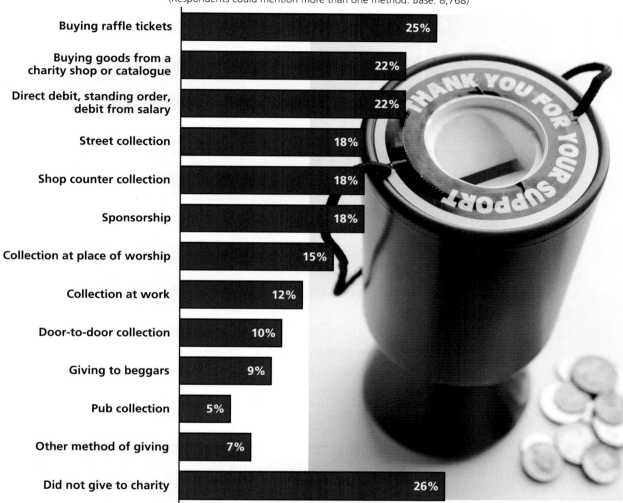

Method	%
Buying raffle tickets	25%
Buying goods from a charity shop or catalogue	22%
Direct debit, standing order, debit from salary	22%
Street collection	18%
Shop counter collection	18%
Sponsorship	18%
Collection at place of worship	15%
Collection at work	12%
Door-to-door collection	10%
Giving to beggars	9%
Pub collection	5%
Other method of giving	7%
Did not give to charity	26%

Average amount given to charity, by ethnic group

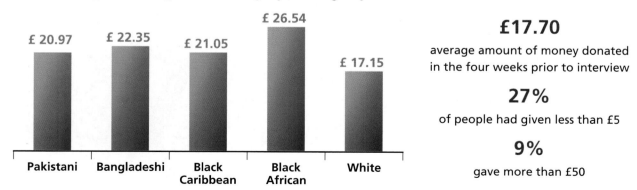

Pakistani	Bangladeshi	Black Caribbean	Black African	White
£ 20.97	£ 22.35	£ 21.05	£ 26.54	£ 17.15

£17.70

average amount of money donated in the four weeks prior to interview

27%

of people had given less than £5

9%

gave more than £50

Source: Citizenship Survey 2008-09 – Volunteering and Charitable Giving, Department for Communities and Local Government © Crown Copyright 2010

www.communities.gov.uk

Charitable trust

 Q: Firstly, thinking about how much trust and confidence you have in charities overall, on a scale of 0-10 where 10 means you trust them completely and 0 means you don't trust them at all, how much trust and confidence do you have in charities?

| 0-4 | 5-7 | 8-10 | Don't know |

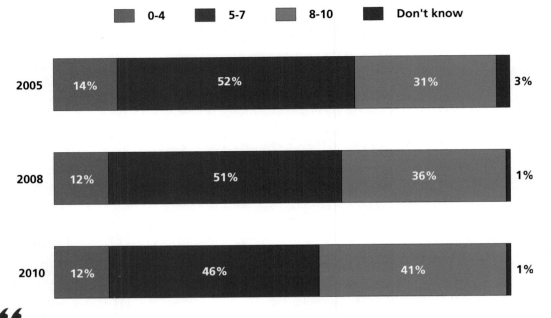

2005 — 14% | 52% | 31% | 3%

2008 — 12% | 51% | 36% | 1%

2010 — 12% | 46% | 41% | 1%

" How much of this money is actually going to do what they say it's going to do, and how much money's getting sliced off in administration. "

 Q: Which one, if any, of these qualities is most important to your trust and confidence in charities overall?

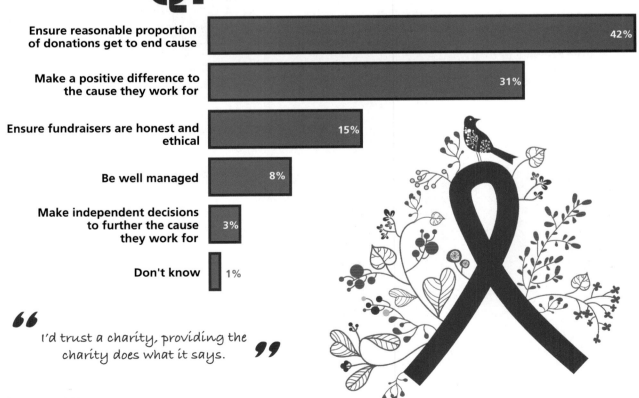

Ensure reasonable proportion of donations get to end cause — 42%

Make a positive difference to the cause they work for — 31%

Ensure fundraisers are honest and ethical — 15%

Be well managed — 8%

Make independent decisions to further the cause they work for — 3%

Don't know — 1%

" I'd trust a charity, providing the charity does what it says. "

Most people (61%) can name a specific charity or type of charity that they trust more than others. The charities mentioned most often tend to be larger, well-known ones, which suggests that the public are more likely to trust charities that are familiar brands such as Cancer Research UK (12%); NSPCC (6%); the British Heart Foundation (5%) and Oxfam (4%).

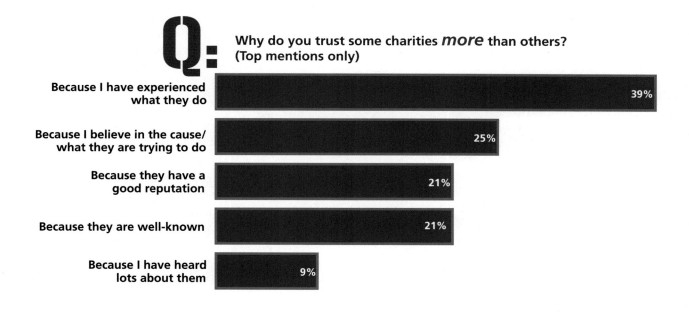

Q: **Why do you trust some charities *more* than others?**
(Top mentions only)

Because I have experienced what they do	39%
Because I believe in the cause/ what they are trying to do	25%
Because they have a good reputation	21%
Because they are well-known	21%
Because I have heard lots about them	9%

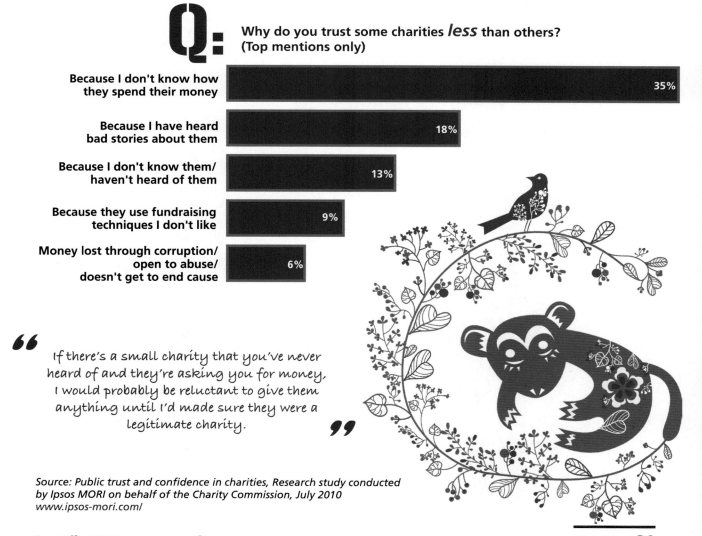

Q: **Why do you trust some charities *less* than others?**
(Top mentions only)

Because I don't know how they spend their money	35%
Because I have heard bad stories about them	18%
Because I don't know them/ haven't heard of them	13%
Because they use fundraising techniques I don't like	9%
Money lost through corruption/ open to abuse/ doesn't get to end cause	6%

" *If there's a small charity that you've never heard of and they're asking you for money, I would probably be reluctant to give them anything until I'd made sure they were a legitimate charity.* "

Source: Public trust and confidence in charities, Research study conducted by Ipsos MORI on behalf of the Charity Commission, July 2010
www.ipsos-mori.com/

Helping hands

People who volunteer regularly are volunteering more...

...those who volunteered at least once a month in 2008-09 were giving, on average, 12.6 hours in the previous four weeks, a big increase on the 11 hours in 2007-08

Formal volunteering	Informal volunteering
Unpaid help given as part of a group, club or organisation to benefit others or the environment	Unpaid help given as an individual to someone who is not a relative

Regular FORMAL volunteering activities, England
(Respondents could mention more than one activity. Base: 2,271)

- Organising or helping to run an activity or event — **59%**
- Raising or handling money/sponsored events — **52%**
- Other practical help — **37%**
- Leading the group/ member of committee — **36%**
- Providing transport/driving — **26%**
- Giving information/ advice/counselling — **25%**
- Visiting people — **23%**
- Secretarial, clerical or admin work — **21%**
- Befriending or mentoring people — **21%**
- Representing — **17%**
- Any other activities — **11%**
- Campaigning — **10%**

In 2008-09, 26% of people in England participated regularly (at least once a month in the year before interview) in formal volunteering and 35% of people participated regularly in informal volunteering.

Regular INFORMAL volunteering activities, England
(Respondents could mention more than one activity. Base: 3,104)

- **45%** Giving advice
- **37%** Keeping in touch with someone
- **36%** Transporting or escorting someone
- **33%** Looking after property or pet
- **31%** Doing shopping, collecting pension
- **30%** Babysitting or caring for children
- **25%** Writing letters, filling in forms
- **23%** Cooking, cleaning, laundry
- **17%** Decorating, home improvement
- **10%** Representing someone
- **8%** Sitting with, providing personal care
- **5%** Any other activities

The 16-25 age group were less likely than older people to participate regularly in formal volunteering, but were more likely to participate regularly in informal volunteering.

People in older age groups tended to volunteer because the cause was important to them or there was a need in the community. People aged 16-25 were more likely to volunteer in order to 'get on' in their careers or learn new skills.

Volunteers were asked why they started.
They were allowed to select up to five reasons from a card

Motivations for volunteering for regular FORMAL volunteers, England
(Base: 2,271)

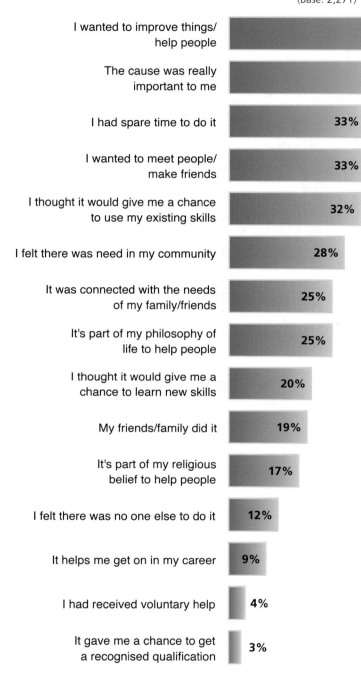

Motivation	%
I wanted to improve things/ help people	62%
The cause was really important to me	40%
I had spare time to do it	33%
I wanted to meet people/ make friends	33%
I thought it would give me a chance to use my existing skills	32%
I felt there was need in my community	28%
It was connected with the needs of my family/friends	25%
It's part of my philosophy of life to help people	25%
I thought it would give me a chance to learn new skills	20%
My friends/family did it	19%
It's part of my religious belief to help people	17%
I felt there was no one else to do it	12%
It helps me get on in my career	9%
I had received voluntary help	4%
It gave me a chance to get a recognised qualification	3%

Barriers to volunteering

People who had done some volunteering – but said they would like to do more – were given a list of barriers and asked which ones applied to them.

They could choose as many reasons as applicable.

Work commitments were the most common reason – **58%** gave this reason.

Time commitments generally were a major barrier to taking part – people having homes/children to look after **31%** and doing other things with their spare time **29%**.

Study commitments were mentioned as a barrier by **14%**.

Lack of information – not having heard about opportunities to help out **18%**

The 16-25 age group were most likely to say they had never thought about volunteering and hadn't heard about opportunities to help.

Source: Citizenship Survey 2008-09 – Volunteering and Charitable Giving, Department for Communities and Local Government © Crown Copyright 2010

www.communities.gov.uk
www.volunteering.org.uk

Global giving

Charitable behaviour differs immensely across the globe...

...An act that is considered charitable in one country may be seen as a regular, everyday activity in another

The **World Giving Index** is based on research carried out in 153 countries that together represent around 95% of the world's population.

The Index is based upon three types of charitable behaviour – **giving money** to an organisation, **volunteering time** to an organisation and helping a stranger.

There is enormous variation in how countries 'give'. **Giving money** to charity ranges from as low as **4%** in Lithuania to as high as **83%** in Malta. **Volunteering** lies in a range from **2%** in Cambodia to **61%** in Turkmenistan. In Liberia, just **8%** of the population give money to charity every month, yet **76%** of Liberians help a stranger every month.

Women are marginally more likely to give money than men

Men, however, are marginally more likely to volunteer, and to help a stranger

Being charitable is about more than simply giving money

The older we are the more we tend to give

We are least likely to help a stranger when over 50

Overall, **20%** of the world's population had volunteered time in the month prior to interview, **30%** had given money, and **45%** had helped a stranger.

The country rankings are based on an average of their giving of money, volunteering and helping strangers.

We might expect prosperous countries to be high in the rankings, but around **half** of the top **20** countries seem to rank higher in charity than in prosperity, for example Guinea (ranked 18th), Guyana (16th) and Turkmenistan (14th).

Top five ranked countries and UK ranking, by overall World Giving Index score, 2009

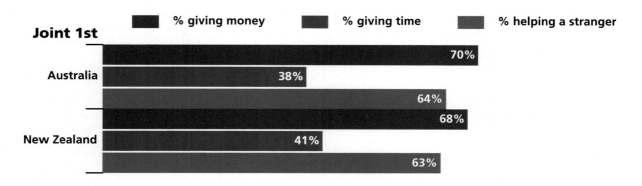

■ % giving money   ■ % giving time   ■ % helping a stranger

Joint 1st

Australia
- 70%
- 38%
- 64%

New Zealand
- 68%
- 41%
- 63%

Joint 3rd

Canada
- 64%
- 35%
- 68%

Ireland
- 72%
- 35%
- 60%

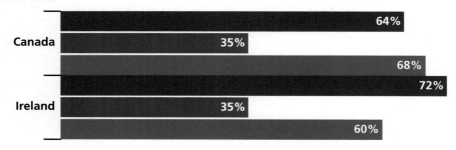

Joint 5th

Switzerland
- 71%
- 34%
- 60%

USA
- 60%
- 39%
- 65%

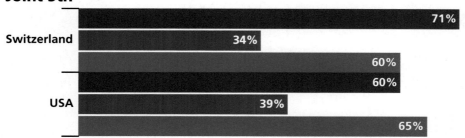

THE UNITED KINGDOM RANKS 8TH OVERALL

UK
- 73%
- 29%
- 58%

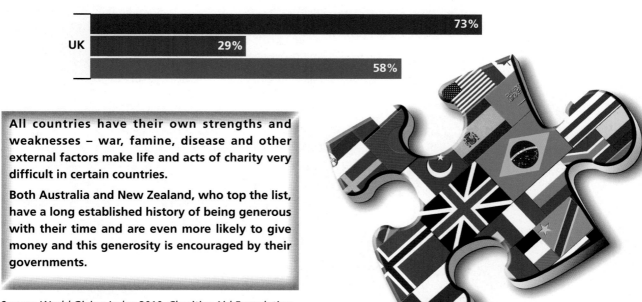

All countries have their own strengths and weaknesses – war, famine, disease and other external factors make life and acts of charity very difficult in certain countries.

Both Australia and New Zealand, who top the list, have a long established history of being generous with their time and are even more likely to give money and this generosity is encouraged by their governments.

Source: World Giving Index 2010, Charities Aid Foundation
www.cafonline.org

Education

Bottom of the class

Pupil-teacher ratio in primary education, EU member states
(average number of pupils per teacher)

● 2007 ● 2002 ← Countries with Worsening ratios

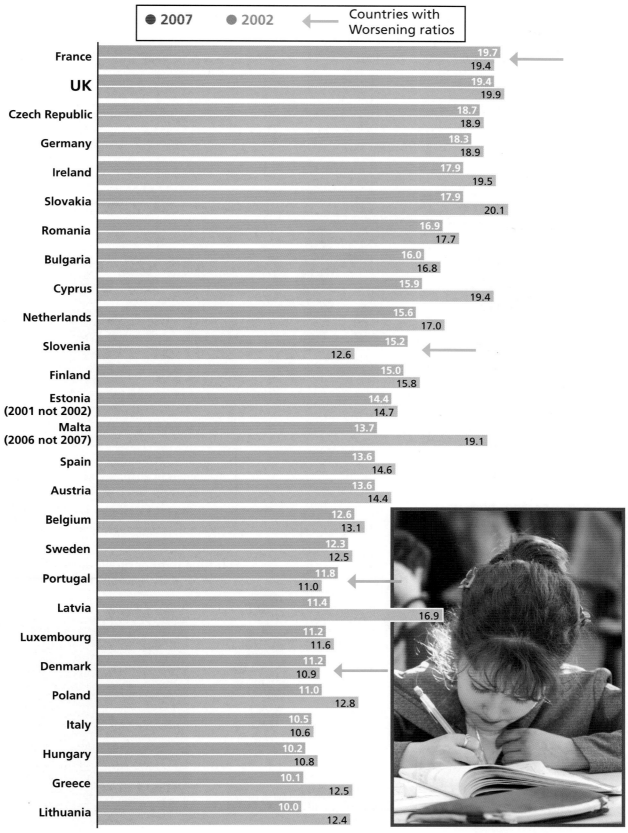

Country	2007	2002
France	19.7	19.4
UK	19.4	19.9
Czech Republic	18.7	18.9
Germany	18.3	18.9
Ireland	17.9	19.5
Slovakia	17.9	20.1
Romania	16.9	17.7
Bulgaria	16.0	16.8
Cyprus	15.9	19.4
Netherlands	15.6	17.0
Slovenia	15.2	12.6
Finland	15.0	15.8
Estonia (2001 not 2002)	14.4	14.7
Malta (2006 not 2007)	13.7	19.1
Spain	13.6	14.6
Austria	13.6	14.4
Belgium	12.6	13.1
Sweden	12.3	12.5
Portugal	11.8	11.0
Latvia	11.4	16.9
Luxembourg	11.2	11.6
Denmark	11.2	10.9
Poland	11.0	12.8
Italy	10.5	10.6
Hungary	10.2	10.8
Greece	10.1	12.5
Lithuania	10.0	12.4

Source: Eurostat, 2010

http://epp.eurostat.ec.europa.eu

Those who can...

Full time equivalent number of teachers and support staff, secondary schools, England
(thousands)

➤ **All regular teachers** ▲ **Total support staff**

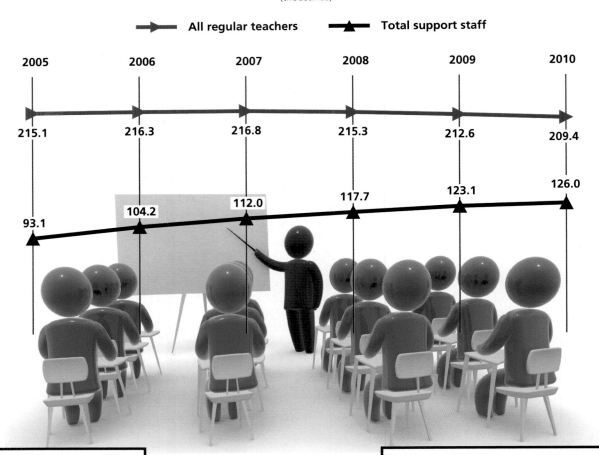

	2005	2006	2007	2008	2009	2010
All regular teachers	215.1	216.3	216.8	215.3	212.6	209.4
Total support staff	93.1	104.2	112.0	117.7	123.1	126.0

In 2000, regular teachers stood at **193,200** and support staff at **51,200**

In City Technology Colleges and academies in 2010, the total numbers of teachers stood at **15,200** and support staff at **11,300**.

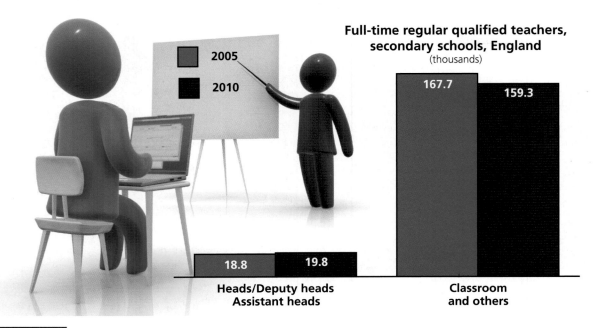

2005
2010

Full-time regular qualified teachers, secondary schools, England
(thousands)

	2005	2010
Heads/Deputy heads Assistant heads	18.8	19.8
Classroom and others	167.7	159.3

Full-time equivalent support staff, secondary schools, 2010
(thousands)

39.9	Teaching assistants (inc. special needs & minority ethnic pupil support)
38.1	Admin staff (inc. secretaries & bursars)
21.5	Technicians
26.5	Other support staff (inc. matrons/ nurses/medical staff & child care)

Pupil:teacher ratios (PTR) and pupil:adult ratios (PAR), secondary schools

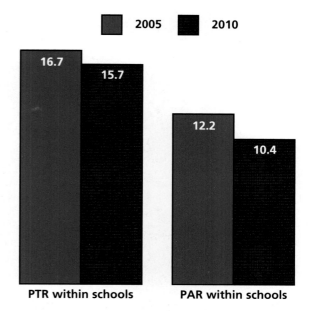

■ 2005　■ 2010

16.7　15.7　12.2　10.4

PTR within schools　　PAR within schools

Numbers of secondary pupils aged up to and including 15 started to decline after 2004 and they are expected to decline further until around 2015 (when the increases in primary pupil numbers start to flow through).

Numbers in maintained nursery and primary schools have started to rise and are expected to continue to rise until by 2018 they reach levels last seen in the late 1970s.

By 2014, all regions in England are likely to have an increase in their primary aged population (aged 5 to 10), ranging from **7%** in the South West to **16%** in London. The secondary populations are projected to recover from 2014 for London, and from 2015 onwards for most of the other regions.

There were **760** full-time classroom teacher vacancies in secondary schools in 2010.
More than half of these were from three subjects:

Maths	170
Sciences	120
English	120

NB 2010 figures are provisional
*Source: Department for Education ©
Crown Copyright 2010*
www.education.gov.uk

Exam cheats

In June 2009:

Over **1 million** AS qualification awards were made

840,000 A levels

nearly **5.5 million** GCSE and

over **16 million** exam scripts were marked.

Although **4,415 penalties** for malpractice were issued – this is just **0.03%** of the total examinations taken by candidates.

Number of penalties issued to candidates by category of malpractice
(An individual candidate may be penalised more than once and by more than one awarding organisation)

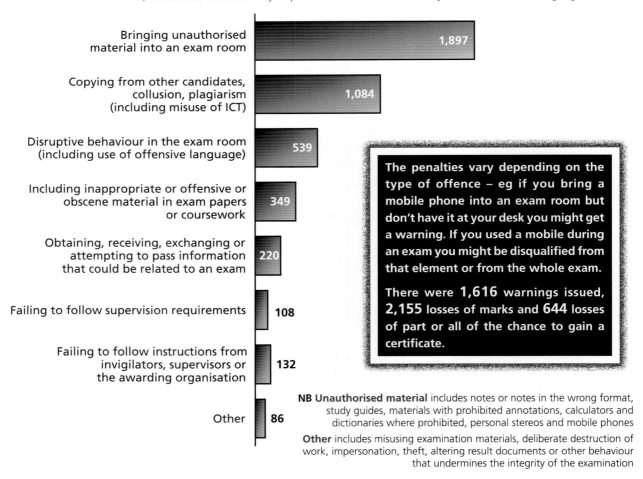

Bringing unauthorised material into an exam room — 1,897

Copying from other candidates, collusion, plagiarism (including misuse of ICT) — 1,084

Disruptive behaviour in the exam room (including use of offensive language) — 539

Including inappropriate or offensive or obscene material in exam papers or coursework — 349

Obtaining, receiving, exchanging or attempting to pass information that could be related to an exam — 220

Failing to follow supervision requirements — 108

Failing to follow instructions from invigilators, supervisors or the awarding organisation — 132

Other — 86

The penalties vary depending on the type of offence – eg if you bring a mobile phone into an exam room but don't have it at your desk you might get a warning. If you used a mobile during an exam you might be disqualified from that element or from the whole exam.

There were **1,616** warnings issued, **2,155** losses of marks and **644** losses of part or all of the chance to gain a certificate.

NB Unauthorised material includes notes or notes in the wrong format, study guides, materials with prohibited annotations, calculators and dictionaries where prohibited, personal stereos and mobile phones

Other includes misusing examination materials, deliberate destruction of work, impersonation, theft, altering result documents or other behaviour that undermines the integrity of the examination

Centre Staff and Centres

Centre **staff** and **centres** are sometimes found guilty of malpractice too – ranging from actions that are intended to give an unfair advantage to candidates, to not knowing or not properly following regulations.

In the June 2009 exams there were **88 penalties** issued to centre **staff** and **70 penalties** issued to **centres**

Number of penalties issued to staff, by category of malpractice
(more than one penalty may have been imposed for an individual case)

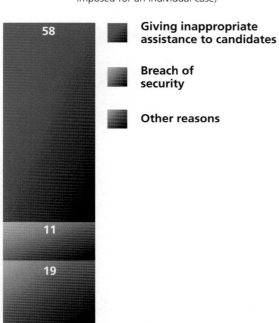

58

11

19

■ Giving inappropriate assistance to candidates

■ Breach of security

■ Other reasons

Number of penalties issued to centres, by category of malpractice
(more than one penalty may have been imposed for an individual case)

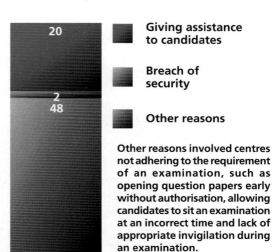

20

2
48

■ Giving assistance to candidates

■ Breach of security

■ Other reasons

Other reasons involved centres not adhering to the requirement of an examination, such as opening question papers early without authorisation, allowing candidates to sit an examination at an incorrect time and lack of appropriate invigilation during an examination.

Penalties issued to centre **staff** were:	Penalties issued to **centres** were:
27 written warnings	**44** written warnings
14 requirements for training or mentoring of staff	**16** required the Head of the centre to review and provide a report on an incident of malpractice
17 staff suspensions from involvement in exams or assessments and	**7** imposed an increased level of inspection and monitoring of a centre and
30 cases of special conditions to an individual's future involvement in exams and assessments	**3** led to a restriction on centres' access to examination materials

Source: Malpractice in GCSE and GCE: June 2009 examinations, Ofqual on behalf of the regulators in England Wales and Northern Ireland © Crown copyright 2010

http://www.ofqual.gov.uk

Star students

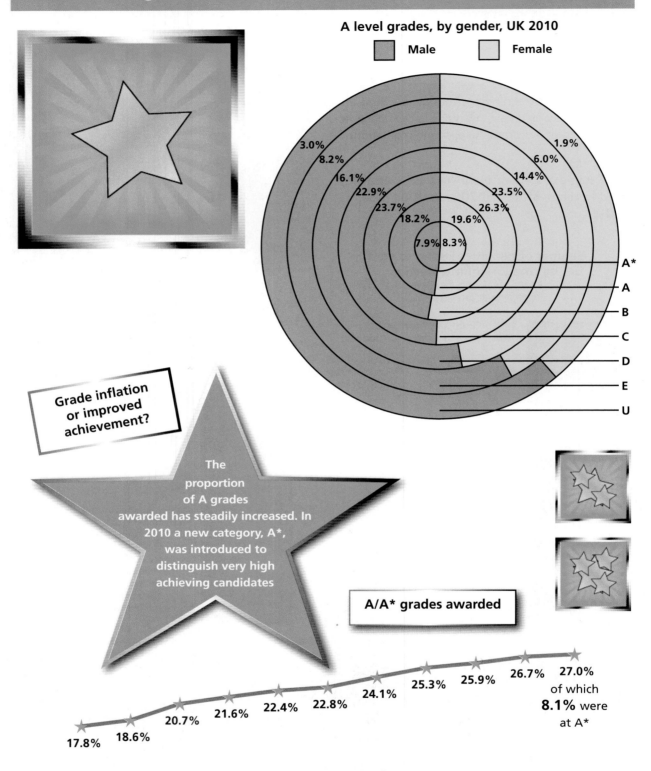

A level grades, by gender, UK 2010

Male   Female

	Male	Female
A*	3.0%	1.9%
A	8.2%	6.0%
B	16.1%	14.4%
C	22.9%	23.5%
D	23.7%	26.3%
E	18.2%	19.6%
U	7.9%	8.3%

Grade inflation or improved achievement?

The proportion of A grades awarded has steadily increased. In 2010 a new category, A*, was introduced to distinguish very high achieving candidates

A/A* grades awarded

17.8% 18.6% 20.7% 21.6% 22.4% 22.8% 24.1% 25.3% 25.9% 26.7% 27.0% of which **8.1%** were at A*

2000 2001 2002 2003 2004 2005 2006 2007 2008 2009 2010

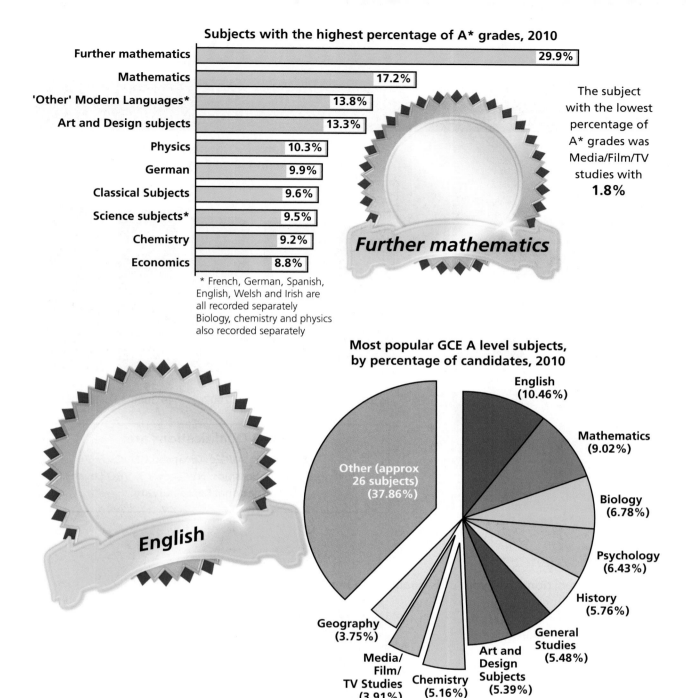

Subjects with the highest percentage of A* grades, 2010

Subject	Percentage
Further mathematics	29.9%
Mathematics	17.2%
'Other' Modern Languages*	13.8%
Art and Design subjects	13.3%
Physics	10.3%
German	9.9%
Classical Subjects	9.6%
Science subjects*	9.5%
Chemistry	9.2%
Economics	8.8%

The subject with the lowest percentage of A* grades was Media/Film/TV studies with **1.8%**

Further mathematics

* French, German, Spanish, English, Welsh and Irish are all recorded separately
Biology, chemistry and physics also recorded separately

English

Most popular GCE A level subjects, by percentage of candidates, 2010

- Other (approx 26 subjects) (37.86%)
- English (10.46%)
- Mathematics (9.02%)
- Biology (6.78%)
- Psychology (6.43%)
- History (5.76%)
- General Studies (5.48%)
- Art and Design Subjects (5.39%)
- Chemistry (5.16%)
- Media/Film/TV Studies (3.91%)
- Geography (3.75%)

Most popular GCE A level subjects, by number of candidates, 2010

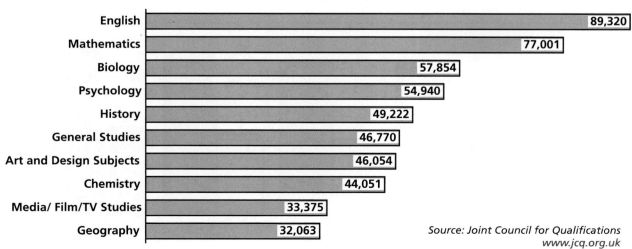

Subject	Number
English	89,320
Mathematics	77,001
Biology	57,854
Psychology	54,940
History	49,222
General Studies	46,770
Art and Design Subjects	46,054
Chemistry	44,051
Media/ Film/TV Studies	33,375
Geography	32,063

Source: Joint Council for Qualifications
www.jcq.org.uk

Levelling out

Proportion of students in England achieving level 3 by age 19

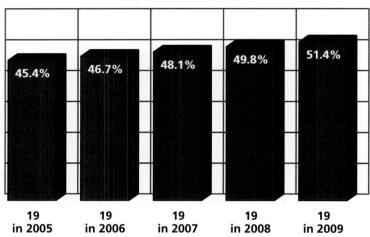

19 in 2005	19 in 2006	19 in 2007	19 in 2008	19 in 2009
45.4%	46.7%	48.1%	49.8%	51.4%

Level 3 Qualifications are:

AS, A levels, AVCEs Advanced GNVQs,
Advanced Apprenticeships, NVQ Level 3, VRQ Level 3,
International Baccalaureate

Proportion of 19 year olds qualified to level 3

Eligibility for Free School Meals (FSM) is taken as a rough indicator of relative deprivation. Although more students in this category are achieving level 3, so are the rest of their age group and the achievement gap between the two groups has reduced by less than **2%** over 5 years.

by FSM uptake

FSM

No FSM

% gap

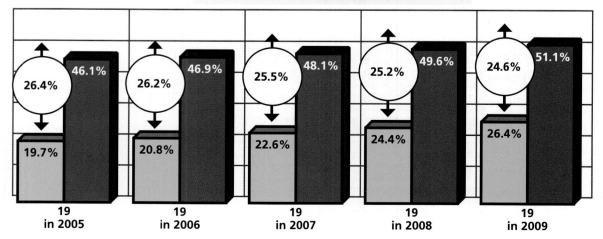

	19 in 2005	19 in 2006	19 in 2007	19 in 2008	19 in 2009
No FSM	46.1%	46.9%	48.1%	49.6%	51.1%
% gap	26.4%	26.2%	25.5%	25.2%	24.6%
FSM	19.7%	20.8%	22.6%	24.4%	26.4%

Ethnicity also appears to have a part to play in achievement

by ethnic group, 2009

Proportion of young people achieving level 3, at age 19

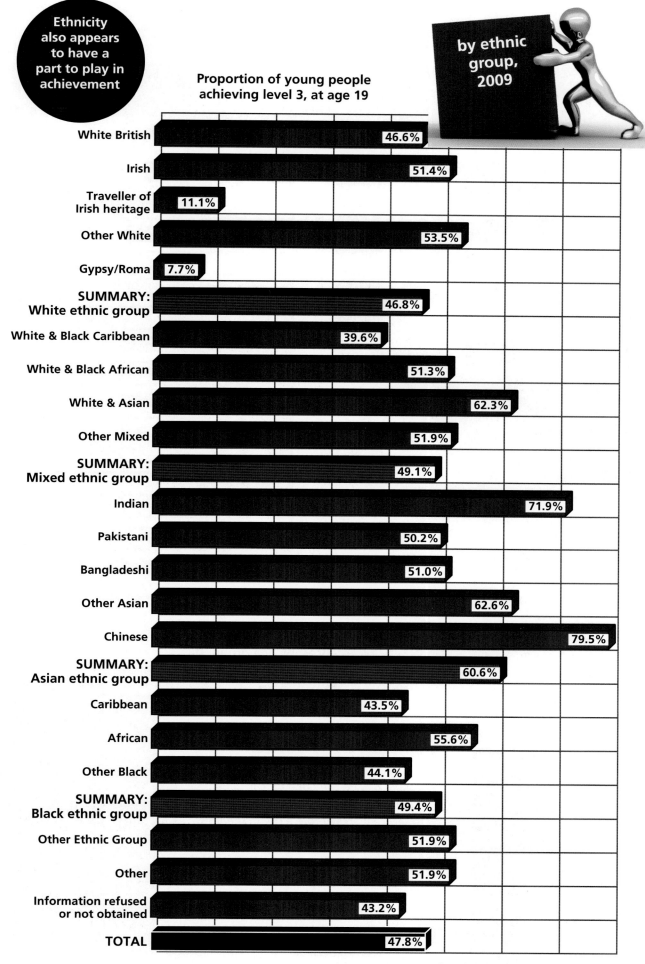

Ethnic group	Percentage
White British	46.6%
Irish	51.4%
Traveller of Irish heritage	11.1%
Other White	53.5%
Gypsy/Roma	7.7%
SUMMARY: White ethnic group	46.8%
White & Black Caribbean	39.6%
White & Black African	51.3%
White & Asian	62.3%
Other Mixed	51.9%
SUMMARY: Mixed ethnic group	49.1%
Indian	71.9%
Pakistani	50.2%
Bangladeshi	51.0%
Other Asian	62.6%
Chinese	79.5%
SUMMARY: Asian ethnic group	60.6%
Caribbean	43.5%
African	55.6%
Other Black	44.1%
SUMMARY: Black ethnic group	49.4%
Other Ethnic Group	51.9%
Other	51.9%
Information refused or not obtained	43.2%
TOTAL	47.8%

Source: Department for Education © Crown copyright 2010
www.education.gov.uk

Take your place

With more applicants than ever some university places are well oversubscribed

Number of university applications and acceptances, UK

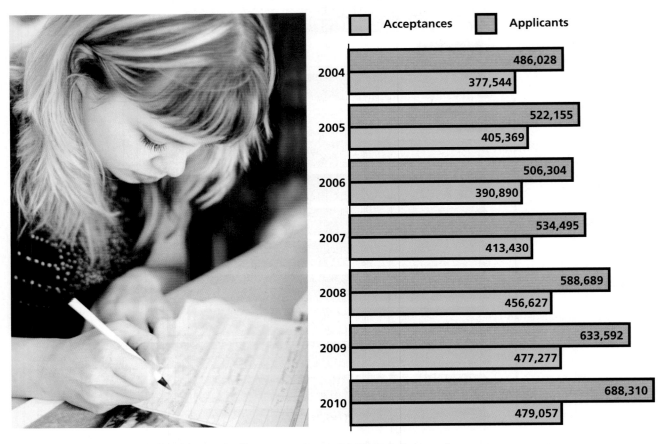

| Acceptances | Applicants |

Year	Applicants	Acceptances
2004	486,028	377,544
2005	522,155	405,369
2006	506,304	390,890
2007	534,495	413,430
2008	588,689	456,627
2009	633,592	477,277
2010	688,310	479,057

The gap between applicants and acceptances is increasing year on year

University acceptances, by age group, UK

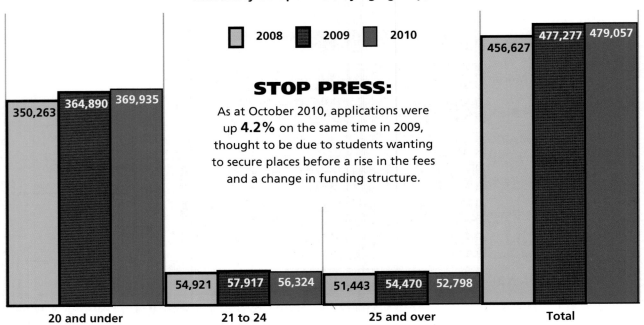

| | 2008 | 2009 | 2010 |

STOP PRESS:

As at October 2010, applications were up **4.2%** on the same time in 2009, thought to be due to students wanting to secure places before a rise in the fees and a change in funding structure.

Age group	2008	2009	2010
20 and under	350,263	364,890	369,935
21 to 24	54,921	57,917	56,324
25 and over	51,443	54,470	52,798
Total	456,627	477,277	479,057

There has also been an increase in overseas students

Acceptance of overseas applicants into UK universities
Top 5 countries, 2010
(% change between 2009 & 2010 in brackets)

Country	Value
China (13.8%)	6,909
Ireland (5.6%)	3,015
Hong Kong (9.8%)	2,812
Cyprus (0.1%)	2,614
France (-18.5%)	2,410

Acceptance of overseas applicants Total 57,769 (4.7%)

What's the hardest subject to get in to?
Top ten ratios of acceptances to applications (2009)

	Ratio
Pre-clinical dentistry	9.7
Pre-clinical medicine	9.1
Pre-clinical veterinary medicine	8.5
Materials Science	8.5
Biotechnology	7.1
Economics	7.0
Architecture	6.6
Drama	6.5
Training Teachers	6.5
Combinations of Social Studies/law with business	6.4

Only those courses with 100+ acceptances have been included because the subjects with very small numbers distort the picture for example Classical Greek studies has the very highest ratio at 23 because there were 23 applications for just one place.

NB All 2010 data is provisional

Source: UCAS
www.ucas.com

Grad-ual slip

...between 2000 and 2008, it fell from third highest to fifteenth among top
industrialised nations for the proportion of young people graduating

**Countries with the highest percentage of population
graduating from Tertiary (degree level) education, 2008**

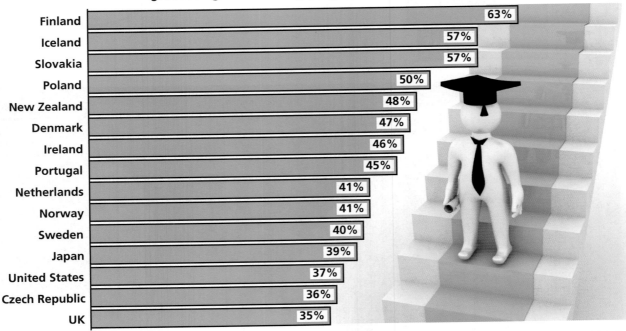

Country	%
Finland	63%
Iceland	57%
Slovakia	57%
Poland	50%
New Zealand	48%
Denmark	47%
Ireland	46%
Portugal	45%
Netherlands	41%
Norway	41%
Sweden	40%
Japan	39%
United States	37%
Czech Republic	36%
UK	35%

The proportion of young people getting degrees in OECD countries doubled between 1995 and 2008, from **20%** to **40%**.

The UK has been increasing the number of students, but the OECD report says that it has failed to keep pace with the even more rapid growth elsewhere.

The UK lags behind countries including Poland, Australia, Ireland, the Slovak Republic, Portugal and the Czech Republic – as well as the traditional high performers such as Finland, Iceland, Sweden and Norway.

Finland has the highest graduation rate among young people – **46%** of men and **80%** women – compared with **30%** of men and **40%** of women in the UK, with these latest OECD figures drawn from 2008.

**Trends in tertiary graduation rates Finland & UK,
percentage graduating**

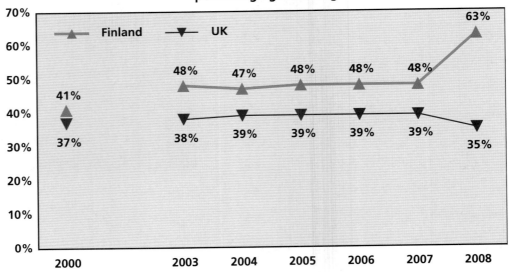

The OECD's report, which looks at education from an economic perspective, argues that both individuals and the wider economy gain an advantage from increasing graduate numbers

Employment rates (25-64 year olds) by level of education, UK, 2008

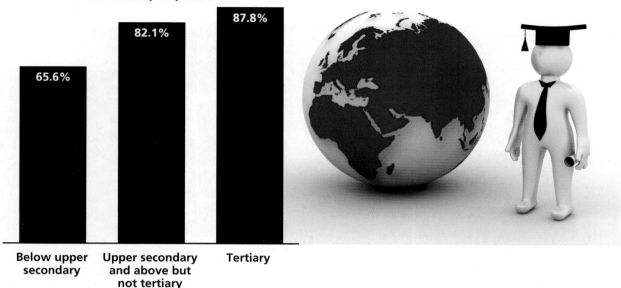

- **Below upper secondary** — 65.6%
- **Upper secondary and above but not tertiary** — 82.1%
- **Tertiary** — 87.8%

Taxpayers benefit from investing in higher education, says the OECD. Even though the government subsidises students, this is outweighed by the increased revenue from higher tax from better-paid jobs.

The OECD says that in the UK each extra graduate brings $89,000 (£58,000) to the taxpayer over a working life – the picture is similar to elsewhere.

Net cost & benefit of tertiary education, UK
(equivalent US$)

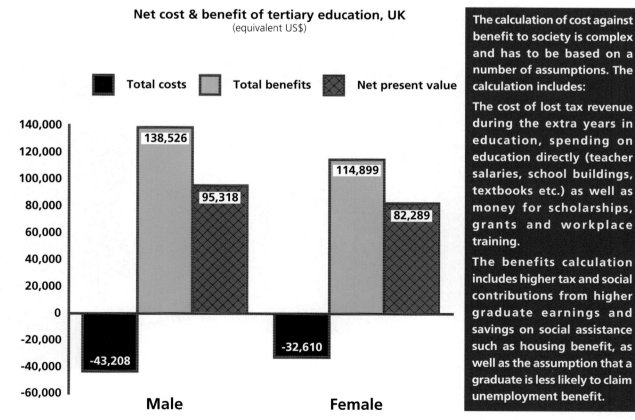

Total costs ▪ Total benefits ▪ Net present value

Male: -43,208 (Total costs), 138,526 (Total benefits), 95,318 (Net present value)
Female: -32,610 (Total costs), 114,899 (Total benefits), 82,289 (Net present value)

The calculation of cost against benefit to society is complex and has to be based on a number of assumptions. The calculation includes:

The cost of lost tax revenue during the extra years in education, spending on education directly (teacher salaries, school buildings, textbooks etc.) as well as money for scholarships, grants and workplace training.

The benefits calculation includes higher tax and social contributions from higher graduate earnings and savings on social assistance such as housing benefit, as well as the assumption that a graduate is less likely to claim unemployment benefit.

Source: Education at a Glance 2010 – OECD indicators, BBC
www.oecd.org
www.bbc.co.uk

Speaking my language?

Do we continue to use the languages we learn in school?

What students learn

In the EU, **60%** of students in upper secondary education **studied** two or more foreign languages, a **third** studied one and **6%** did not study any

español **english** *deutsch*

In all Member States where data is available, **English** is the **most studied** foreign language in upper secondary education, except for **Luxembourg** where **English, French** and **German** are equal, and in the **UK** and **Ireland** where **French** is the most common.

51% of students in the **UK did not study** any foreign language.

italiano

100% of upper secondary students in the **Czech Republic, Luxembourg,** the **Netherlands** and **Finland** **studied** two or more languages

français

What adults speak

Among the EU adult population, **64%** said they could **speak** at least one foreign language and **36%** said they couldn't speak any

speak sproche parlo parle hablo

In two-thirds of Member States, **English** is the most commonly **spoken** foreign language. **65%** of UK adults said that they **spoke** one or more foreign languages

Source: Eurostat – European Day of Languages 2009
http://ec.europa.eu/eurostat

Environmental issues

Citylife

There's huge scope for all UK cities to improve...

...but they have a long way to go to match the best European cities such as Copenhagen or Stockholm

The Sustainable Cities Index

The Sustainable Cities Index ranks Britain's 20 largest cities according to social economic and environmental performance.

Each city is analysed according to **three** criteria

- its **environmental performance** – resource use and pollution;
- its **quality of life** – what the city is like to live in for all its citizens; and
- **future-proofing** – how well the city is addressing issues such as climate change, recycling and biodiversity.

Newcastle is leading the way in the UK and has remained Britain's most sustainable city, widening the gap with the other cities. It has placed itself at the centre of an increasingly vibrant clean-tech cluster in the North East and it aims to become a world-class centre of science and innovation, benefiting economically and socially from the emerging green economy and aspires to be the UK's electric car capital.

	Overall ranking 2010 (2009 ranking in brackets)
Newcastle	1 (1)
Leicester	2 (4)
Brighton	3 (3)
Bristol	4 (2)
London	5 (5)
Leeds	6 (6)
Coventry	7 (11)
Plymouth	8 (12)
Edinburgh	9 (7)
Sheffield	10 (9)
Cardiff	11 (10)
Nottingham	12 (8)
Manchester	13 (14)
Liverpool	14 (15)
Birmingham	15 (17)
Sunderland	16 (13)
Derby	17 (*)
Bradford	18 (16)
Glasgow	19 (19)
Hull	20 (20)

*Derby is a new entrant this year having overtaken Wolverhampton to become Britain's 20th largest city

The top five cities have remained the same as 2009, with **Brighton** and **Bristol** having been in this group since 2007.

The two biggest climbers, **Coventry** and **Plymouth** have both moved up four places overall since 2009.

Nottingham had the biggest fall since 2009, dropping four places.

Hull remains the lowest ranking city in the Index for the third year in a row. It ranks near the bottom for business start-ups and comes last on employment, with **7.4%** of residents claiming Jobseekers' Allowance.

There's a marked difference also in the rate of improvement. Those cities making slower progress are slipping down the rankings and the gap between the top and bottom performers is widening.

Despite an ambition to be European Green Capital, **Glasgow** has been unable to improve on 2009's 19th place.

Newcastle has four rivals with similar scores but their strengths and weaknesses lie in different areas:

Leicester performs best on the environment and does well on **future-proofing**, but falls behind on quality of life.

Brighton is also strong on **future-proofing** and **quality of life**, but has a high environmental impact.

Bristol is the best city for **quality of life** and doing well on the economy, but is falling behind on environmental performance and future-proofing.

London scores best on its **future-proofing**, with strong plans to reduce emissions and adapt to climate change and the greatest number of business start-ups per person.

Environmental performance

The quality of the cities' natural environment is important not just because they should be pleasant places to live, but because it has an important bearing on the health and wellbeing of their inhabitants and on wider global concerns such as resource use and climate change.

Indicators measure:

Air quality

Biodiversity

Household waste

Ecological footprint

Quality of life

This reflects the social and human aspects of sustainability.

Indicators measure:

Employment

Transport

Education

Health

Green space

Future-proofing

Looks at how cities are preparing for climate change, how well they can cope with change to their food supply chain, dynamism and innovation in the local economy.

Indicators measure:

Climate change

Local food

Economy

Recycling

Environmental performance	Overall ranking	Quality of life	Overall ranking	Future-proofing	Overall ranking
Leicester	1	Bristol	1	London	1
Newcastle	2	Brighton	2	Newcastle	2
Coventry	3	Plymouth	3	Leicester	3
Nottingham	4=	London	4	Brighton	4
Sheffield	4=	Sheffield	5	Bristol & Cardiff	5=

Overall, Britain's 20 largest cities are clearly becoming more sustainable. Since the first index in 2007, their performance has improved on 11 of the 13 indicators. Only employment and provision of allotments have fallen.

Source: Forum for the Future – Sustainable Cities Index www.forumforthefuture.org.

Water waste

We use water as if it will never run out

The water we drink and which is used by farming and industry comes from three main sources: reservoirs, rivers and underground aquifers.

Every year around **18 billion tonnes** of water are taken from these sources in England – of this about **6 billion tonnes** are put in the public water supply.

Photo: Debbie Maxwell

Why is it a problem?

In the coming years there will be less water and more people in the UK. The demand for water will increase by **5%** by 2020 – that's **800 million** extra litres of water a day and some areas of England are already classified as seriously water-stressed.

Despite being an island – and our reputation for wet weather – the UK actually has less available water per head than many European countries including France, Italy and Greece. London, for example, has less annual rainfall than Rome, Paris or Naples.

Generally, people don't see wasting water as an issue – because they don't yet see or feel the consequences of this waste.

We don't appreciate how much water we use every day and we don't see how easy it would be to change this.

The target is to reduce daily water consumption by **20 litres** per person by 2030.

What we use per day (litres)

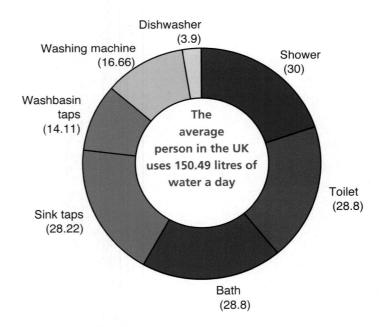

- Dishwasher (3.9)
- Washing machine (16.66)
- Washbasin taps (14.11)
- Sink taps (28.22)
- Shower (30)
- Toilet (28.8)
- Bath (28.8)

The average person in the UK uses 150.49 litres of water a day

The average family uses **500 litres** of water a day – producing **1.5 tonnes** of greenhouse gases per year.

What do we think about it?

2,009 adults aged 16 and over were interviewed about their attitudes and behaviour towards the environment:

 25% did not pay much attention to the amount of water they used at home

 87% agreed that we should all try to save water

 74% only washed full loads of laundry

 69% were making an effort to cut down on water usage

 68% took showers instead of baths

 66% turned the tap off whilst brushing their teeth.

We could save an average of **42 litres** per property, per day by installing water-efficient products such as dual-flush toilets, aerated showerheads, shower timers and using water butts in the garden

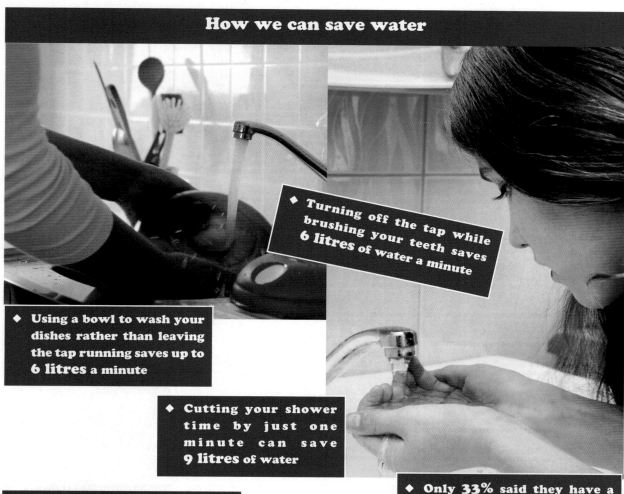

How we can save water

Turning off the tap while brushing your teeth saves 6 litres of water a minute

◆ **Using a bowl to wash your dishes rather than leaving the tap running saves up to 6 litres a minute**

◆ **Cutting your shower time by just one minute can save 9 litres of water**

◆ **Using a watering can or a bucket in the garden or for washing the car instead of a hosepipe, saves 16 litres a minute**

◆ **Only 33% said they have a water meter, but on average, households reduce their water consumption by around 10% after a meter is fitted**

Source: Future Water, Public attitudes and behaviours towards the environment, Defra © Crown copyright 2009, Waterwise

www.defra.gov.uk
www.waterwise.org.uk

What a waste

On average, half a tonne of waste is generated per person, per year in the EU

EU27 comparison of municipal* waste generated
(kg per person, 2008)

1 tonne = 1,000 kg

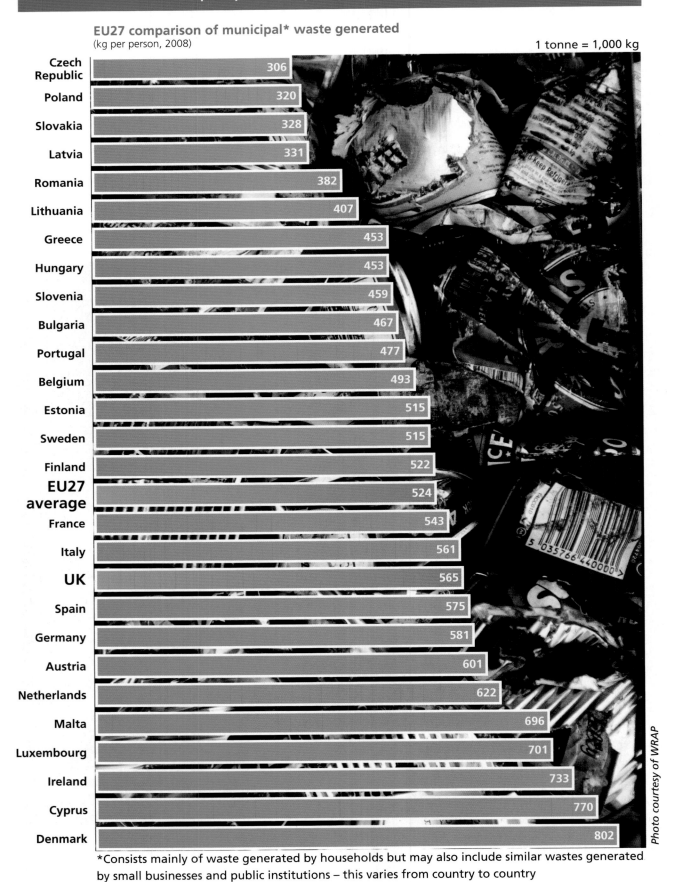

Country	kg per person
Czech Republic	306
Poland	320
Slovakia	328
Latvia	331
Romania	382
Lithuania	407
Greece	453
Hungary	453
Slovenia	459
Bulgaria	467
Portugal	477
Belgium	493
Estonia	515
Sweden	515
Finland	522
EU27 average	524
France	543
Italy	561
UK	565
Spain	575
Germany	581
Austria	601
Netherlands	622
Malta	696
Luxembourg	701
Ireland	733
Cyprus	770
Denmark	802

Photo courtesy of WRAP

*Consists mainly of waste generated by households but may also include similar wastes generated by small businesses and public institutions – this varies from country to country

European comparison of how the waste is treated, %
Figures do not add up to 100% due to rounding

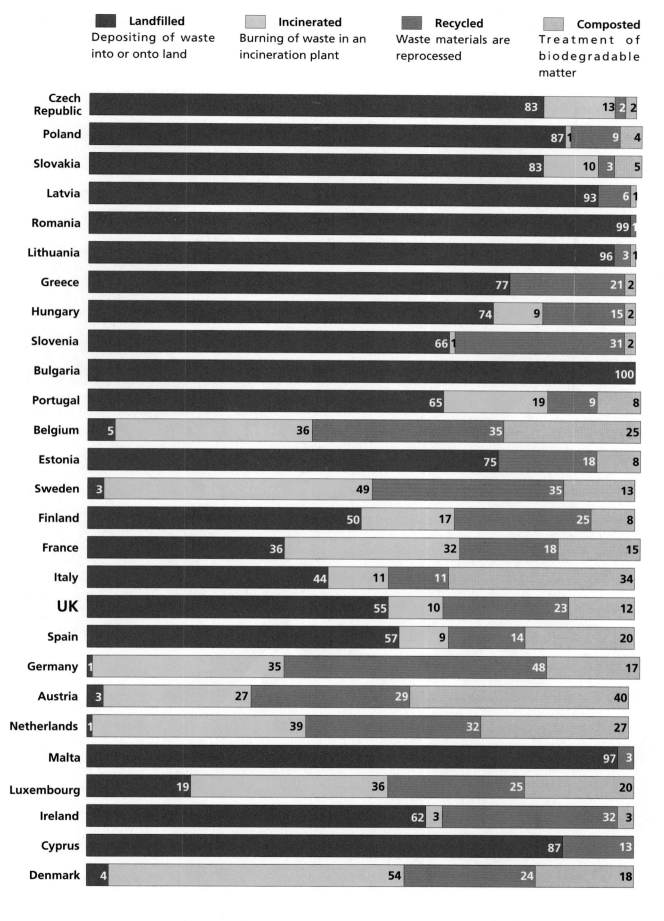

Landfilled
Depositing of waste into or onto land

Incinerated
Burning of waste in an incineration plant

Recycled
Waste materials are reprocessed

Composted
Treatment of biodegradable matter

Country	Landfilled	Incinerated	Recycled	Composted
Czech Republic	83	13	2	2
Poland	87	1	9	4
Slovakia	83	10	3	5
Latvia	93		6	1
Romania	99		1	
Lithuania	96		3	1
Greece	77		21	2
Hungary	74	9	15	2
Slovenia	66	1	31	2
Bulgaria	100			
Portugal	65	19	9	8
Belgium	5	36	35	25
Estonia	75		18	8
Sweden	3	49	35	13
Finland	50	17	25	8
France	36	32	18	15
Italy	44	11	11	34
UK	55	10	23	12
Spain	57	9	14	20
Germany	1	35	48	17
Austria	3	27	29	40
Netherlands	1	39	32	27
Malta	97		3	
Luxembourg	19	36	25	20
Ireland	62	3	32	3
Cyprus	87		13	
Denmark	4	54	24	18

Source: Eurostat, Wrap

http://ec.europa.eu/eurostat
www.wrap.org.uk

Tip-off

Fly-tipping or illegal dumping of waste is anti-social behaviour which affects our environment

Fly-tipping has declined in England in the past year suggesting that tougher action by local authorities is paying off

Local authorities dealt with nearly 947,000 incidents of fly-tipping in 2009-10, an 18.7% decrease from 2008-09

63% of fly-tips was household black bags and other household waste

8% of incidents in 2009-10 were commercial black bags or other commercial waste (a 35.5% reduction from 2008-09)

6% were construction, demolition and excavation waste

58% of the fly-tips was made up of amounts that would fit into a car boot or a small van

49% of all fly-tips that were cleared came from the roadside, 33% were cleared from council land and footpaths & bridleways

The four groups who fly-tip are:

- Organised criminal fly-tippers who gain financially

- Commercial fly-tippers wanting to avoid waste disposal charges

- Domestic fly-tippers for whom legal disposal methods are inconvenient

- Travellers who leave a lot of waste on their sites

There were 154 incidents of serious organised waste crime in England in 2009-10 dealt with by the Environment Agency.

In addition, the Environment Agency dealt with a total of **1,047** illegal waste dumping incidents in 2009-10 (a rise from **676** in 2008-09).

Fly-tipping can lead to serious pollution of the environment and harm to human health. It can cost innocent victims and local authorities large amounts of money to remove the waste.

The cost of fly-tipping

The estimated cost of clearing illegally dumped waste in 2009-10 was **£45.8 million...**

...a reduction of **£9.2 million (16.7%)** compared to 2008-09

Local authorities increased their action against fly-tipping in 2009-10 by **2.3%** over 2008-09

It is estimated that they spent **£19.1 million** an increase of around **4.3%** over 2008-09

116,500 warning letters, 37,200 statutory notices and **2,100 formal cautions** were issued about fly-tipping

There were **2,460 prosecutions** against waste offenders (23.2% more than in 2008-09)...

...of which **97%** achieved a successful outcome

The Environment Agency also took **165 prosecutions** forward in relation to illegal waste, resulting in over **£500,000** in fines.

The average fine per prosecution was **£5,022**.

Offenders prosecuted by the Environment Agency for waste crime offences have received a range of penalties from **custodial sentences, curfew orders** and in some cases had their **assets seized**.

"The statistics only deal with fly-tipping on public land. The bill for dealing with fly-tipping would be significantly higher if you added the costs incurred by farmers and other private landowners who have to clear up fly-tipping at their own expense"

Samantha Harding, Campaign to Protect Rural England

Source: Defra – Flycapture database © Crown copyright 2010, Campaign to Protect Rural England
www.defra.gov.uk
www.cpre.org.uk

Light up the world

In the modern world, electricity is essential – but many people don't have access to it

Well over one-fifth of the world's population does not have access to electricity. **85%** of those people live in rural areas, mainly in Sub-Saharan Africa and South Asia.

It is impossible to operate a factory, run a shop, grow crops or deliver goods to consumers without using some form of energy. Access to electricity is crucial to human development. It is vital for lighting, refrigeration and the running of household appliances. It cannot easily be replaced by other forms of energy.

Number of people without access to electricity (millions)

Key
- 2008
- 2030

China & East Asia
- 195.1m
- 72.5m

South Asia
- 613.9m
- 488.6m

Middle East
- 21.4m
- 5.1m

North Africa
- 1.7m
- 1.6m

Latin America
- 34.1m
- 12.8m

Sub-Saharan Africa
- 587.1m
- 698.3m

World population without access to electricity:

2008
1.5 billion

2030
1.3 billion

16% of the world's population will still have no electricity in 2030... despite more widespread prosperity and more advanced technology

Source: World Energy Outlook 2009 – International Energy Agency
www.iea.org/weo/electricity.asp

Family & relationships

Who's having babies?

The total number of live births in England and Wales fell to **706,248** in 2009 compared with **708,711** in 2008 (a decrease of **0.3%**).

Between 2004 and 2009, the proportion of women of child-bearing age who were born outside the UK grew from **13%** to **17%**.

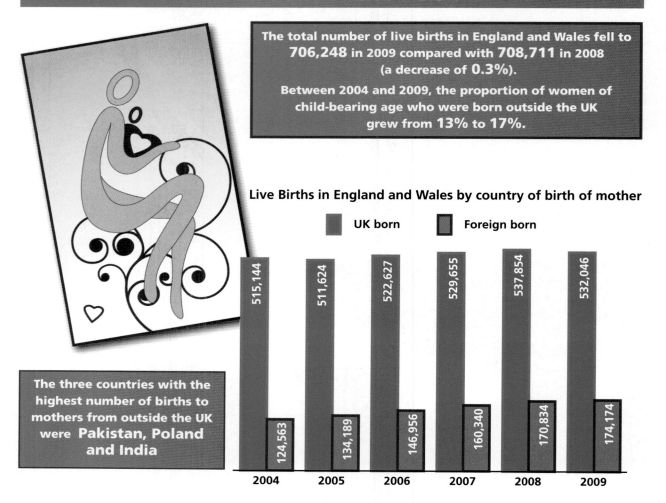

Live Births in England and Wales by country of birth of mother

UK born   **Foreign born**

	2004	2005	2006	2007	2008	2009
UK born	515,144	511,624	522,627	529,655	537,854	532,046
Foreign born	124,563	134,189	146,956	160,340	170,834	174,174

The three countries with the highest number of births to mothers from outside the UK were **Pakistan, Poland and India**

In 2009, **23.0%** of all live births were babies born to non-UK born fathers. **24.7%** of births were to non-UK mothers. **17.3%** of babies born had both a non-UK born mother and non-UK born father.

Babies born to families where only one parent was born outside the UK constituted **12.1%** of all births.

Information for fathers is not available for births registered solely by the mother (**6.2%** of all live births in 2009).

Live births by country of birth of father, 2009

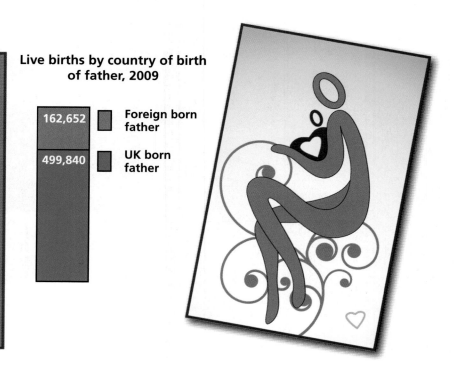

162,652 — Foreign born father

499,840 — UK born father

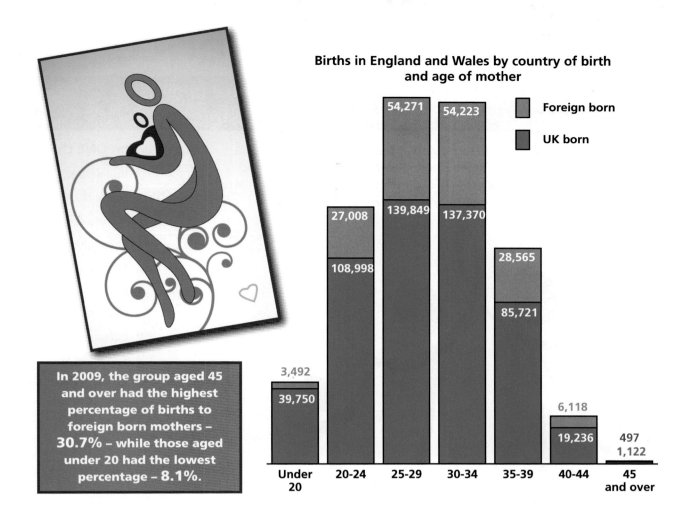

Births in England and Wales by country of birth and age of mother

Legend:
- Foreign born
- UK born

Age group	Foreign born	UK born
Under 20	3,492	39,750
20-24	27,008	108,998
25-29	54,271	139,849
30-34	54,223	137,370
35-39	28,565	85,721
40-44	6,118	19,236
45 and over	497	1,122

In 2009, the group aged 45 and over had the highest percentage of births to foreign born mothers – **30.7%** – while those aged under 20 had the lowest percentage – **8.1%**.

In 2009, the Total Fertility Rate (TFR) for England and Wales was 1.96 children per woman, representing a small decrease over 2008. However, fertility remains at a high level – in 2008 the TFR was at its highest point in 35 years.

Foreign born mothers have a higher fertility on average than those born in the UK – the increasing population share of this group has pushed the estimated overall Total Fertility Rate (TFR) upwards, even though their fertility is fairly stable.

Estimated total fertility rates for UK born and foreign born women living in England and Wales

	2004	2005	2006	2007	2008	2009	
Foreign born	2.50	2.48	2.43	2.55	2.53	2.48	
UK born	1.68	1.69	1.76	1.80	1.85	1.84	

Source: Office for National Statistics © Crown copyright 2010

www.statistics.gov.uk

Sizeable difference

Women of child-bearing age (15 to 39) were asked their own personal ideal family size. The charts show the ten countries with the highest preference for **ONE**, **TWO** or **THREE** children. The figures in brackets show the actual number of households in the country with that number of children.

% preferring ONE child

22	Romania (29.3)
20	Malta (23.9)
19	Austria (26.1)
18	Slovak Rep (22.1)
15	Mexico (18.4)
14	Czech Rep (24.7)
14	Italy (29.5)
13	Portugal (35.1)
13	Spain (30.3)
12	Bulgaria (36.9)
11	**UK (21.3)**

% preferring TWO children

Bulgaria (51.3)	72
Romania (44.1)	70
Czech Rep (55.4)	69
Australia (n/a)	68
Hungary (42.1)	68
Lithuania (45.4)	67
Portugal (48.0)	67
Estonia (41.5)	66
Germany (48.2)	66
Italy (53.7)	64
UK (45.3)	**50**

% preferring THREE children

64	New Zealand (n/a)
57	Cyprus (n/a)
46	Sweden (n/a)
45	Finland (45.4)
45	France (31.8)
45	Ireland (n/a)
42	Mexico (47.4)
41	Denmark (n/a)
36	Belgium (35.3)
36	**UK (33.4)**

n/a = figs not available

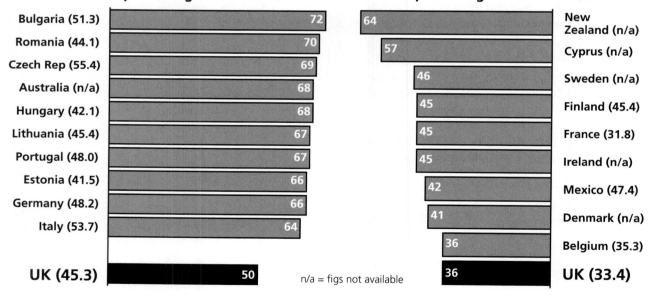

In most OECD countries, the **actual** average family size is around **2.25** children, slightly above the population replacement rate level of **2.1** children per woman.

Attitudes to family size are affected by many factors including social norms, personal circumstances, age, and the number of children already in the family.

In addition, people can have a different opinion of their own **personal** ideal family size and what is the **generally** ideal size.

The country with the highest preference for **NO** children was Austria, where **11%** said this was the ideal family size. Only **3%** of women in the UK opted for this.

NB Mid 2000s latest available figures

Source: OECD Family Database
www.oecd.org

Family matters

Two parent families are still the norm in developed countries

The OECD consists of 31 democratic countries. The 25 in this study show national differences in family structure.

There is a lot of concern about the effects of living in a single parent household because some studies show that children living with a single parent have worse outcomes on a range of measures. However, most of the results show only a small difference between one and two parent families.

Structure of families in which children live
(% of 11, 13 and 15 year olds)

	Both parents	Step-family	Single parent	Other (inc. foster homes and non-parental family members)

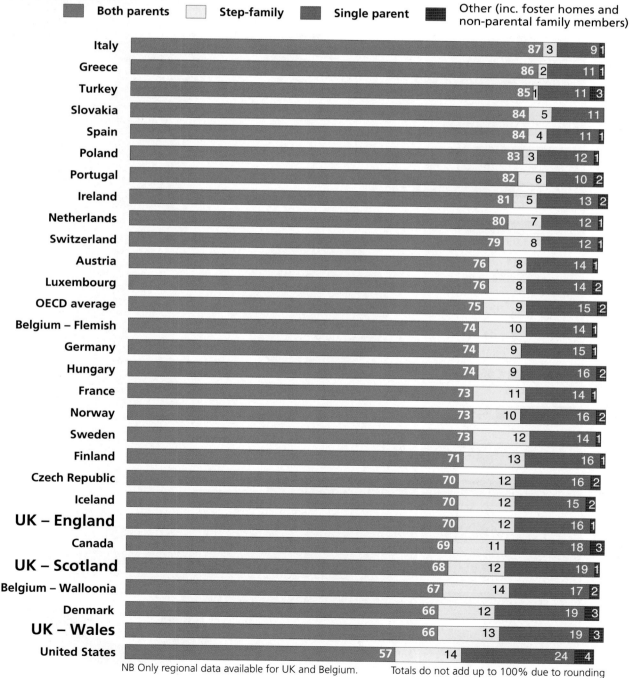

Country	Both parents	Step-family	Single parent	Other
Italy	87	3	9	1
Greece	86	2	11	1
Turkey	85	1	11	3
Slovakia	84	5	11	
Spain	84	4	11	1
Poland	83	3	12	1
Portugal	82	6	10	2
Ireland	81	5	13	2
Netherlands	80	7	12	1
Switzerland	79	8	12	1
Austria	76	8	14	1
Luxembourg	76	8	14	2
OECD average	75	9	15	2
Belgium – Flemish	74	10	14	1
Germany	74	9	15	1
Hungary	74	9	16	2
France	73	11	14	1
Norway	73	10	16	2
Sweden	73	12	14	1
Finland	71	13	16	1
Czech Republic	70	12	16	2
Iceland	70	12	15	2
UK – England	70	12	16	1
Canada	69	11	18	3
UK – Scotland	68	12	19	1
Belgium – Walloonia	67	14	17	2
Denmark	66	12	19	3
UK – Wales	66	13	19	3
United States	57	14	24	4

NB Only regional data available for UK and Belgium.   Totals do not add up to 100% due to rounding

Source: Doing Better For Children – OECD 2009

www.oecd.org

Parents' perspective

Boys are a nightmare at age 15 and girls are a handful at 14 – according to parents

A study of 2,000 parents for TheBabyWebsite.com shows two distinct 'difficult' phases in a child's life. The general consensus is that the teenage years are beyond doubt the worst.

Many toddler traits surface again when children become teenagers, but often become even more difficult to deal with.

Q **If you have a son/daughter, what was his/her most difficult age?** (Perhaps they gave you the most grief, were most difficult to look after or refused to communicate with you)?

- Son
- Daughter

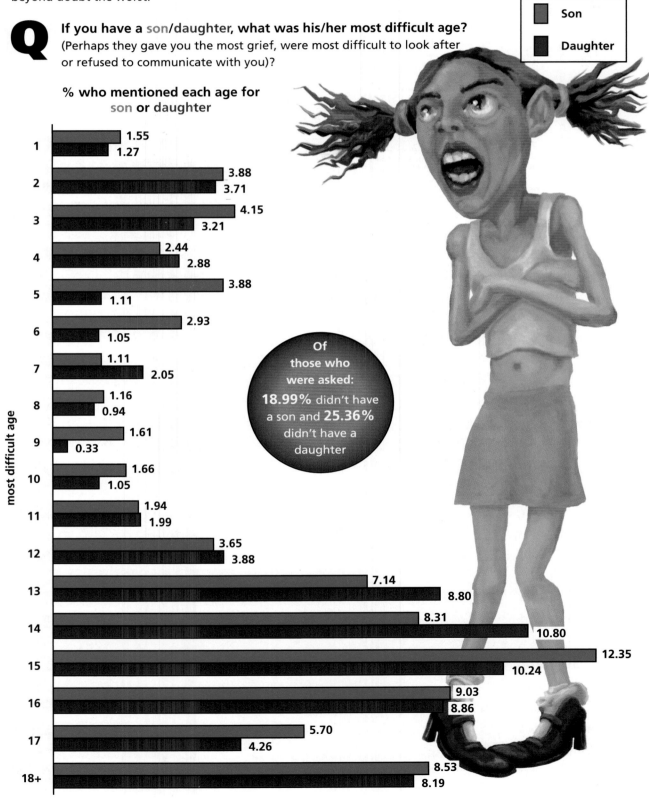

% who mentioned each age for son or daughter

most difficult age	Son	Daughter
1	1.55	1.27
2	3.88	3.71
3	4.15	3.21
4	2.44	2.88
5	3.88	1.11
6	2.93	1.05
7	1.11	2.05
8	1.16	0.94
9	1.61	0.33
10	1.66	1.05
11	1.94	1.99
12	3.65	3.88
13	7.14	8.80
14	8.31	10.80
15	12.35	10.24
16	9.03	8.86
17	5.70	4.26
18+	8.53	8.19

Of those who were asked: **18.99%** didn't have a son and **25.36%** didn't have a daughter

What do you think your son struggled most with when growing up?
(percentages)

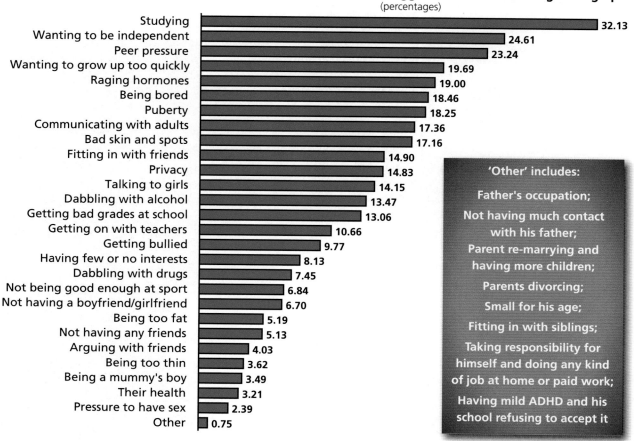

Category	%
Studying	32.13
Wanting to be independent	24.61
Peer pressure	23.24
Wanting to grow up too quickly	19.69
Raging hormones	19.00
Being bored	18.46
Puberty	18.25
Communicating with adults	17.36
Bad skin and spots	17.16
Fitting in with friends	14.90
Privacy	14.83
Talking to girls	14.15
Dabbling with alcohol	13.47
Getting bad grades at school	13.06
Getting on with teachers	10.66
Getting bullied	9.77
Having few or no interests	8.13
Dabbling with drugs	7.45
Not being good enough at sport	6.84
Not having a boyfriend/girlfriend	6.70
Being too fat	5.19
Not having any friends	5.13
Arguing with friends	4.03
Being too thin	3.62
Being a mummy's boy	3.49
Their health	3.21
Pressure to have sex	2.39
Other	0.75

'Other' includes:

Father's occupation;

Not having much contact with his father;

Parent re-marrying and having more children;

Parents divorcing;

Small for his age;

Fitting in with siblings;

Taking responsibility for himself and doing any kind of job at home or paid work;

Having mild ADHD and his school refusing to accept it

What do you think your daughter struggled most with when growing up?
(percentages)

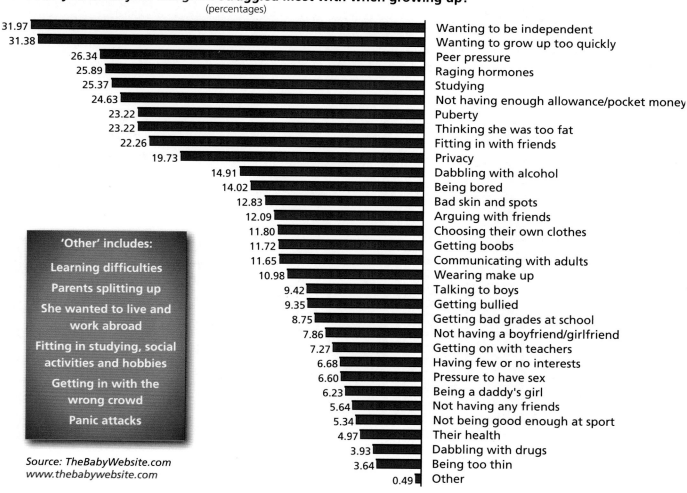

Category	%
Wanting to be independent	31.97
Wanting to grow up too quickly	31.38
Peer pressure	26.34
Raging hormones	25.89
Studying	25.37
Not having enough allowance/pocket money	24.63
Puberty	23.22
Thinking she was too fat	23.22
Fitting in with friends	22.26
Privacy	19.73
Dabbling with alcohol	14.91
Being bored	14.02
Bad skin and spots	12.83
Arguing with friends	12.09
Choosing their own clothes	11.80
Getting boobs	11.72
Communicating with adults	11.65
Wearing make up	10.98
Talking to boys	9.42
Getting bullied	9.35
Getting bad grades at school	8.75
Not having a boyfriend/girlfriend	7.86
Getting on with teachers	7.27
Having few or no interests	6.68
Pressure to have sex	6.60
Being a daddy's girl	6.23
Not having any friends	5.64
Not being good enough at sport	5.34
Their health	4.97
Dabbling with drugs	3.93
Being too thin	3.64
Other	0.49

'Other' includes:

Learning difficulties

Parents splitting up

She wanted to live and work abroad

Fitting in studying, social activities and hobbies

Getting in with the wrong crowd

Panic attacks

Source: TheBabyWebsite.com
www.thebabywebsite.com

Partners

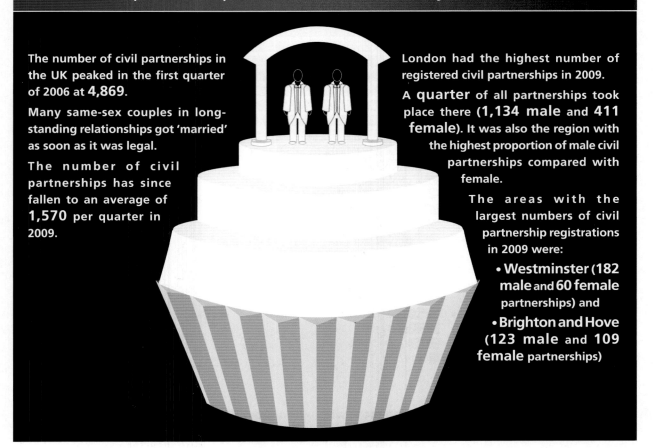

The number of civil partnerships in the UK peaked in the first quarter of 2006 at **4,869**.

Many same-sex couples in long-standing relationships got 'married' as soon as it was legal.

The number of civil partnerships has since fallen to an average of **1,570** per quarter in 2009.

London had the highest number of registered civil partnerships in 2009.

A **quarter** of all partnerships took place there (**1,134 male and 411 female**). It was also the region with the highest proportion of male civil partnerships compared with female.

The areas with the largest numbers of civil partnership registrations in 2009 were:

- **Westminster (182 male** and **60 female** partnerships) and
- **Brighton and Hove (123 male** and **109 female** partnerships)

Number of civil partnerships, by year and gender, UK

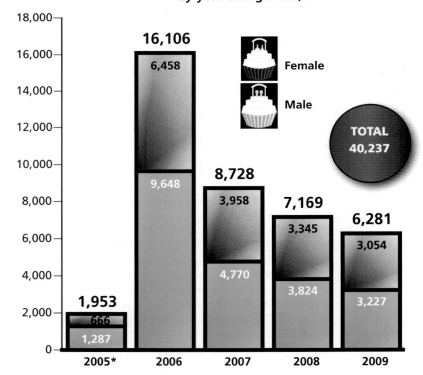

In England, **52%** of partnerships formed in 2009 were male compared with **46%** in Wales, **44%** Scotland and **48%** in Northern Ireland.

The UK average was **51%**.

17% of people entering a partnership in both Wales and Scotland in 2009 had previously been in a marriage or civil partnership, compared with **16%** in England and **11%** in Northern Ireland.

The UK average was **11%** for men and **21%** for women.

*The Civil Partnership Act 2004 came into force on 5 December 2005 in the UK, the first day couples could give notice of their intention to form a civil partnership.

Number of civil partnerships, by age, UK, 2009

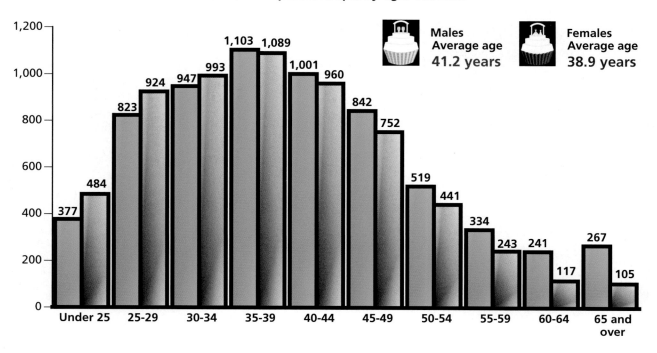

Males Average age **41.2 years**

Females Average age **38.9 years**

Under 25	377 / 484	
25-29	823 / 924	
30-34	947 / 993	
35-39	1,103 / 1,089	
40-44	1,001 / 960	
45-49	842 / 752	
50-54	519 / 441	
55-59	334 / 243	
60-64	241 / 117	
65 and over	267 / 105	

Dissolutions

To obtain a civil partnership dissolution in the UK, a couple must have been in either a registered civil partnership or a recognised foreign same-sex relationship for 12 months. There were **351** civil partnership dissolutions granted in the UK in 2009, compared with **180** in 2008 (a **95%** increase). Of these, **327** were in England and Wales and **24** were in Scotland while there were none in Northern Ireland.

There were **more women than men** dissolving a civil partnership in both England and Wales and in Scotland in 2009.

In **England and Wales, 63%** of civil partnerships dissolved were **female** couples and only **37%** were **male** couples.

The corresponding figures for **Scotland** were **71% female** couples and **29% male** couples.

By the end of 2009, **0.9%** of male civil partnerships and **2.1%** of all female partnerships in the UK had ended in dissolution.

The average age at dissolution of partnership for **men** in the UK was **39.9 years** in 2009 and **38.7 years** for **women**.

15% of men and **21%** of women dissolving a civil partnership in the UK had been in a previous marriage or civil partnership.

Source: Office for National Statistics, General Register Office for Scotland, Northern Ireland Statistics and Research Agency © Crown copyright 2010

www.statistics.gov.uk

Financial issues

Filthy rich

The fortunes of the richest people in the UK have increased by 30%...

...much of this increase is a result of the rebound in stock markets and property values after the government injected hundreds of billions of pounds into banks and the wider economy to stave off collapse

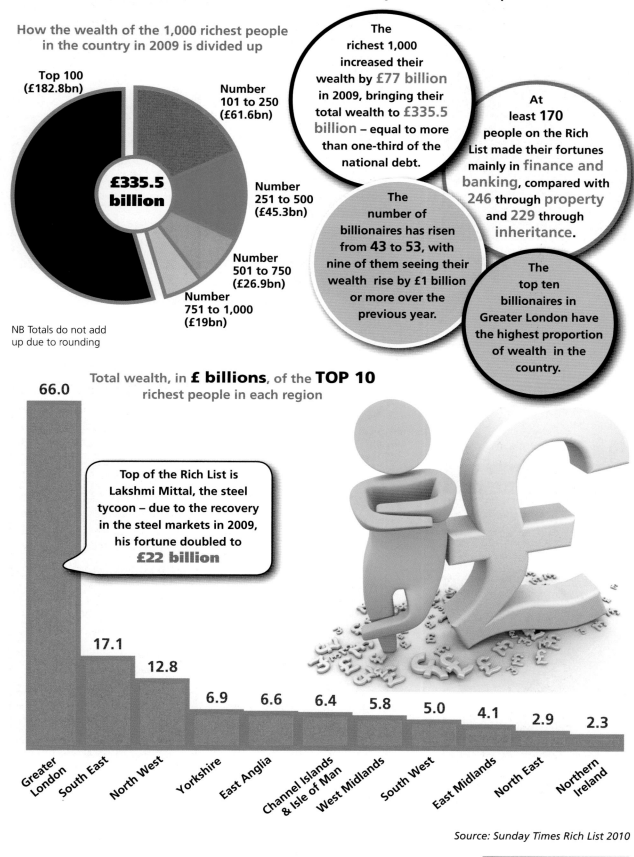

How the wealth of the 1,000 richest people in the country in 2009 is divided up

Top 100 (£182.8bn)

Number 101 to 250 (£61.6bn)

£335.5 billion

Number 251 to 500 (£45.3bn)

Number 501 to 750 (£26.9bn)

Number 751 to 1,000 (£19bn)

NB Totals do not add up due to rounding

The richest 1,000 increased their wealth by **£77 billion** in 2009, bringing their total wealth to **£335.5 billion** – equal to more than one-third of the national debt.

At least **170** people on the Rich List made their fortunes mainly in **finance and banking**, compared with **246** through **property** and **229** through **inheritance**.

The number of billionaires has risen from **43** to **53**, with nine of them seeing their wealth rise by £1 billion or more over the previous year.

The top ten billionaires in Greater London have the highest proportion of wealth in the country.

Total wealth, in **£ billions**, of the **TOP 10** richest people in each region

Top of the Rich List is Lakshmi Mittal, the steel tycoon – due to the recovery in the steel markets in 2009, his fortune doubled to **£22 billion**

Region	£bn
Greater London	66.0
South East	17.1
North West	12.8
Yorkshire	6.9
East Anglia	6.6
Channel Islands & Isle of Man	6.4
West Midlands	5.8
South West	5.0
East Midlands	4.1
North East	2.9
Northern Ireland	2.3

Source: Sunday Times Rich List 2010

Great divide

Pensions

Calculating the value of private pensions is complicated because there are many types, and this makes it difficult to compare.

Unlike the other forms of wealth, pension wealth is not immediately accessible for most people. Most cannot draw directly on this money until they reach at least age 50.

Bricks and mortar

Home ownership:

31.9%
of households do not own their own home

37.7%
Owned with mortgage

30.1%
owned their home outright

0.3%
Part rent and part owned with mortgage

Makeup of household wealth

Pension wealth (39%)

Property wealth (net) (39%)

%

Physical wealth (11%)

Financial wealth (11%)

Bank accounts and savings

Main **formal** financial assets were current account held by **92%** of households; savings accounts held by **62%**; and ISAs held by **42%** of households.

Nearly a **quarter** had a National Savings Certificate or bond, **15%** owned UK shares. A **tenth** had insurance products (excluding life insurance policies).

Informal financial assets means money saved in cash at home, money given to someone to look after or money paid into a savings and loans club.

10% of households had informal assets of more that £250, **6%** in savings and **4%** in loans to others which they expected to be repaid.

Contents and valuables

Makeup of household physical wealth

77%
Household contents (main residence)

16%
Vehicles (inc. number plates)

4%
Collectibles and valuables

4%
Household contents (other property)

Figures may not add up to 100% due to rounding

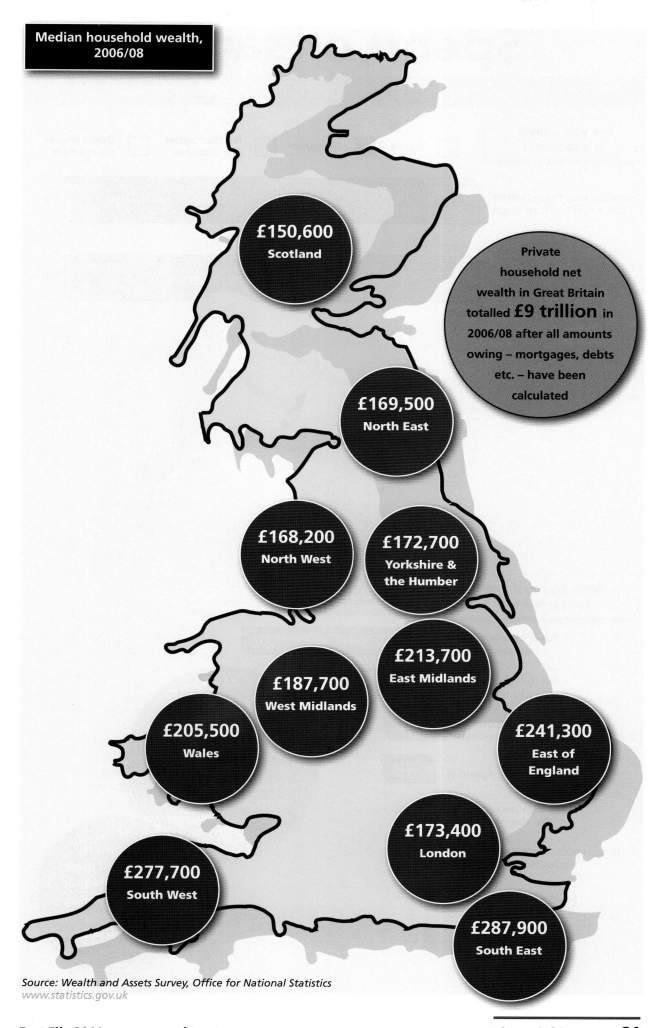

Median household wealth, 2006/08

£150,600
Scotland

Private household net wealth in Great Britain totalled **£9 trillion** in 2006/08 after all amounts owing – mortgages, debts etc. – have been calculated

£169,500
North East

£168,200
North West

£172,700
Yorkshire & the Humber

£213,700
East Midlands

£187,700
West Midlands

£205,500
Wales

£241,300
East of England

£173,400
London

£277,700
South West

£287,900
South East

Source: Wealth and Assets Survey, Office for National Statistics
www.statistics.gov.uk

Spend or save?

Attitudes towards different aspects of people's financial lives

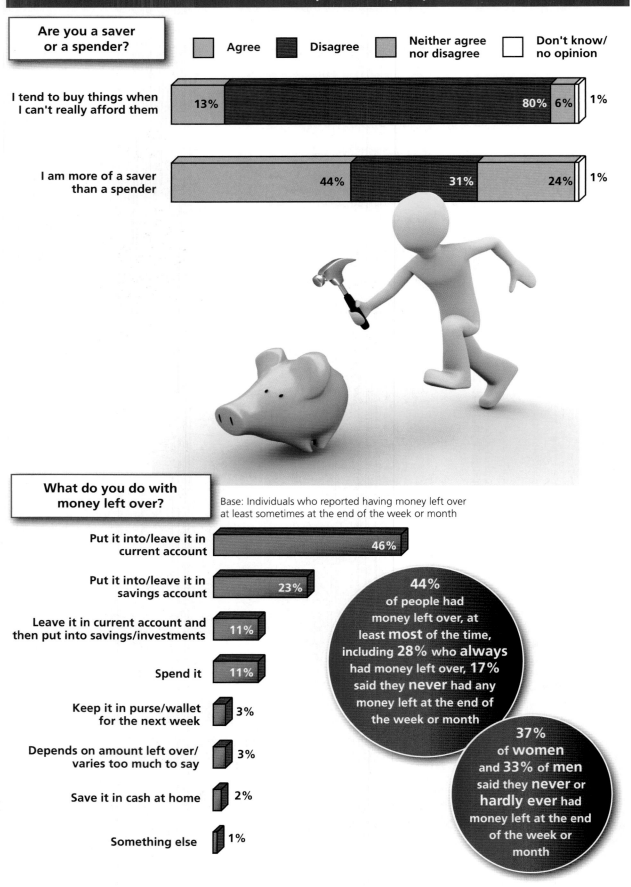

Are you a saver or a spender?

| | Agree | Disagree | Neither agree nor disagree | Don't know/ no opinion |

I tend to buy things when I can't really afford them
13% | 80% | 6% | 1%

I am more of a saver than a spender
44% | 31% | 24% | 1%

What do you do with money left over?

Base: Individuals who reported having money left over at least sometimes at the end of the week or month

- Put it into/leave it in current account — 46%
- Put it into/leave it in savings account — 23%
- Leave it in current account and then put into savings/investments — 11%
- Spend it — 11%
- Keep it in purse/wallet for the next week — 3%
- Depends on amount left over/ varies too much to say — 3%
- Save it in cash at home — 2%
- Something else — 1%

44% of people had money left over, at least **most** of the time, including **28%** who **always** had money left over, **17%** said they **never** had any money left at the end of the week or month

37% of **women** and **33%** of **men** said they **never** or **hardly ever** had money left at the end of the week or month

Why do you save?

Base: All individuals who had saved in the last 12 months

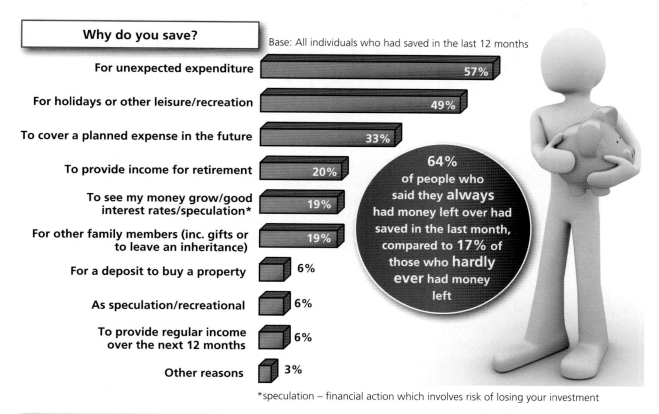

For unexpected expenditure	57%
For holidays or other leisure/recreation	49%
To cover a planned expense in the future	33%
To provide income for retirement	20%
To see my money grow/good interest rates/speculation*	19%
For other family members (inc. gifts or to leave an inheritance)	19%
For a deposit to buy a property	6%
As speculation/recreational	6%
To provide regular income over the next 12 months	6%
Other reasons	3%

64% of people who said they **always** had money left over had saved in the last month, compared to **17%** of those who **hardly ever** had money left

*speculation – financial action which involves risk of losing your investment

Why don't you save?

Base: All individuals who had never saved or had not saved in the last 12 months

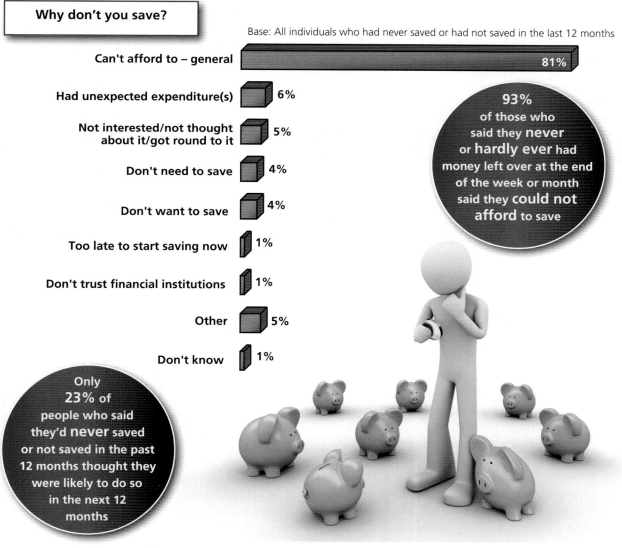

Can't afford to – general	81%
Had unexpected expenditure(s)	6%
Not interested/not thought about it/got round to it	5%
Don't need to save	4%
Don't want to save	4%
Too late to start saving now	1%
Don't trust financial institutions	1%
Other	5%
Don't know	1%

93% of those who said they **never** or **hardly ever** had money left over at the end of the week or month said they **could not afford** to save

Only **23%** of people who said they'd **never** saved or not saved in the past 12 months thought they were likely to do so in the next 12 months

Sample size: 30,595 private households

Source: Wealth in Great Britain – Wealth & Assets Survey 2006/08
www.statistics.gov.uk

The way we pay...

The Payments Council has announced that cheques will be phased out by 2018 (but only if adequate alternatives are developed).

Although cheque use has been in decline since 1990, there are still plenty of situations where cheques are used, including payments to sole traders, small business, clubs, charities and schools.

Timeline	Key facts
1990	Peak year for number of cheques – **11 million** cheques written per day.
2000	Cheques represented **less than a quarter** of all non-cash transactions.
2007-8	Vast majority of major UK retailers begin to stop accepting cheques.
2008	**3.8 million** cheques written per day, compared to **14.8 million** debit card payments. Cheques were used for less than **3%** of non-cash retail transactions. **45,000** trees were cut down to make cheques. **26 million people** write cheques. Among those who write cheques, **50%** write cheques less often than once per month.
2009	350th birthday of the cheque. Those under 25 receive on average only **two** cheques a year whilst those over 65 receive **four** - the rest of us receive **five** cheques a year. Decision taken on closing the Cheque Guarantee Card Scheme.
2011	Cheque Guarantee Card Scheme to close on 30th June.
2016	Payments Council to take go/no-go decision on closing cheque clearings.
2018	31st October. Target for closing the central cheque clearing. The Payments Council's goal is to ensure that by 2018 there is no scenario where customers, individuals or businesses still need to use a cheque.

But can we live without cheques?

YES

In Germany there are no cheques. Older people seem to manage fine. You can go to your local bank and do a transfer by filling out a little transfer form.
SH, Germany

Cheques disappeared in the Netherlands more than ten years ago! In shops you use your debit card or cash (or credit card). If you get a bill by post it has a tear-off slip at the bottom where you add your bank account number and signature and post it to your bank. You can also pay the same bill via internet banking. Although virtually all regular bills are paid by direct debit.
Paul, Rotterdam

NO

How on earth would I send money to my grandchildren if there were no cheques?
VS, Shropshire

When children need to take money to school to pay for trips, photographs, lunches, etc. a cheque is by far the safest way.
GH, Wales

My usage of cheques has increased since I started buying things through Ebay. I am not at all happy with the idea that the cheque will disappear.
SM, England

...is changing

"Payment habits have evolved to take advantage of new technology and to meet the needs of our ever more demanding lifestyles"

Sandra Quinn, Director of Communications, Payments Council

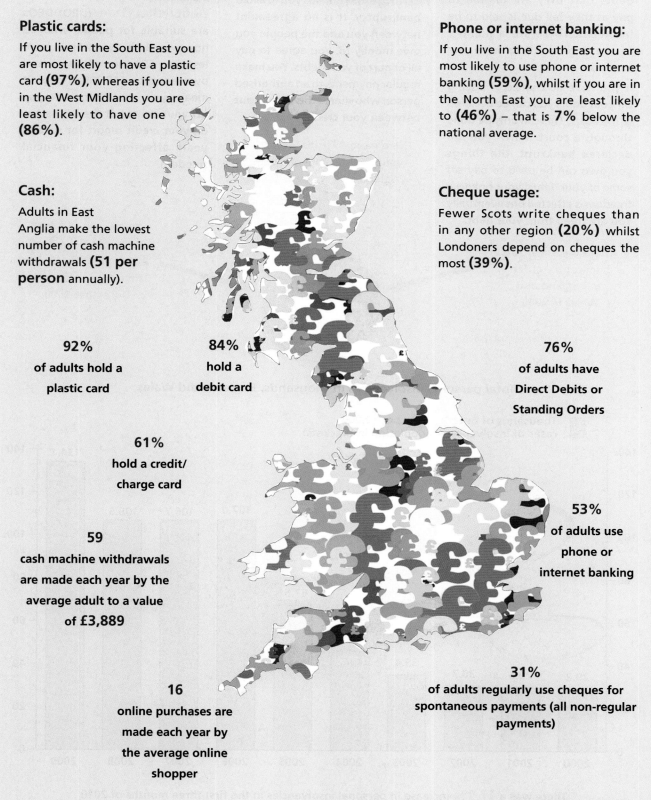

Plastic cards:

If you live in the South East you are most likely to have a plastic card **(97%)**, whereas if you live in the West Midlands you are least likely to have one **(86%)**.

Cash:

Adults in East Anglia make the lowest number of cash machine withdrawals **(51 per person** annually).

Phone or internet banking:

If you live in the South East you are most likely to use phone or internet banking **(59%)**, whilst if you are in the North East you are least likely to **(46%)** – that is **7%** below the national average.

Cheque usage:

Fewer Scots write cheques than in any other region **(20%)** whilst Londoners depend on cheques the most **(39%)**.

92%
of adults hold a plastic card

84%
hold a debit card

76%
of adults have Direct Debits or Standing Orders

61%
hold a credit/ charge card

59
cash machine withdrawals are made each year by the average adult to a value of £3,889

16
online purchases are made each year by the average online shopper

53%
of adults use phone or internet banking

31%
of adults regularly use cheques for spontaneous payments (all non-regular payments)

Base: 3,859 adults in Britain
Source: Payments Council, 2009, BBC
www.paymentscouncil.org.uk
www.bbc.co.uk

Gone bust

More people are unable to pay their debts

A company or individual with debts that they are unable to pay as they fall due is said to be insolvent. There are a number of ways of dealing with the situation.

If you have no chance of paying off your debts you can be declared **bankrupt**. This can only be done through a court. When you are declared bankrupt, the things you own can be used to pay off some of your debts, your financial freedom is affected but eventually you are freed from your debt.

There were **74,600** bankruptcy orders in England and Wales in 2009.

An **Individual voluntary arrangement** helps you to avoid bankruptcy. It is an agreement between you and the people you owe money to. You agree to pay all or part of your debts. You make regular payments to an authorised person who shares this money out between your creditors.

There were **47,600** individual voluntary arrangements in England and Wales in 2009.

Another way to avoid bankruptcy is with a **Debt Relief Order** (DRO). DROs are suitable for people who do not own their own home, have less than £50 a month spare, and owe less than £15,000 of debt. It means you do not have to pay off your debts but the DRO stays on your credit report for several years affecting your financial freedom.

There were **11,800** DROs between April 2009, when they were first introduced, and December 2009.

Total personal insolvencies 134,100

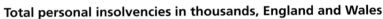

Total personal insolvencies in thousands, England and Wales

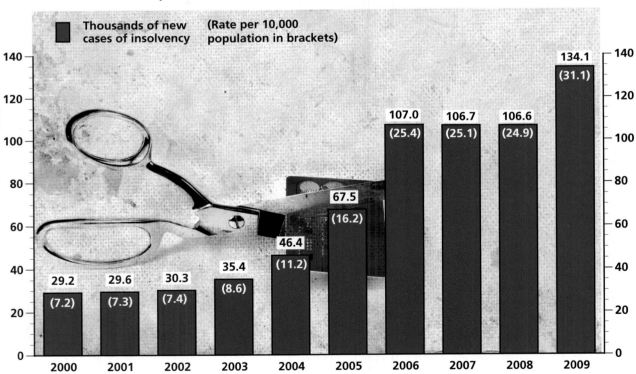

Thousands of new cases of insolvency (Rate per 10,000 population in brackets)

Year	Cases	Rate
2000	29.2	(7.2)
2001	29.6	(7.3)
2002	30.3	(7.4)
2003	35.4	(8.6)
2004	46.4	(11.2)
2005	67.5	(16.2)
2006	107.0	(25.4)
2007	106.7	(25.1)
2008	106.6	(24.9)
2009	134.1	(31.1)

There was a **17.9%** increase in personal insolvencies in the first three months of 2010 – a total of **35,682**. These were made up of: **18,256** bankruptcies, **11,782** Individual Voluntary Arrangements and **5,644** Debt Relief Orders.

Company crisis

Businesses can go bust too

Liquidation

Some people say that a business has gone bankrupt, but in fact only a person can go bankrupt. When a business fails it goes into liquidation.

Insolvency

A company is insolvent if it has more debts than it can pay off even with all its assets taken into account. When a company becomes insolvent it may be forced into liquidation. This means the company ceases to exist and everything it owns is sold to pay off its debts.

This can be done through the courts – **compulsory liquidation** or without involving the courts – **creditors' voluntary liquidation**.

There were **4,082** compulsory liquidations and creditors' voluntary liquidations in England & Wales in the first quarter of 2010. This was a decrease of **17.8%** on the same period a year before.

Company liquidations, England & Wales

- ■ Total
- ● Compulsory Liquidations
- ▲ Creditors' Voluntary Liquidations

5,041
4,357
3,451
4,082
3,561
2,768
2,289
1,163
1,314

2000 2001 2002 2003 2004 2005 2006 2007 2008 2009 2010

Source: The Insolvency Service

www.insolvency.gov.uk

Food & drink

Bad taste

55% of males and 63% of females are concerned about food safety issues

Concerns about specific food issues, 2010, %

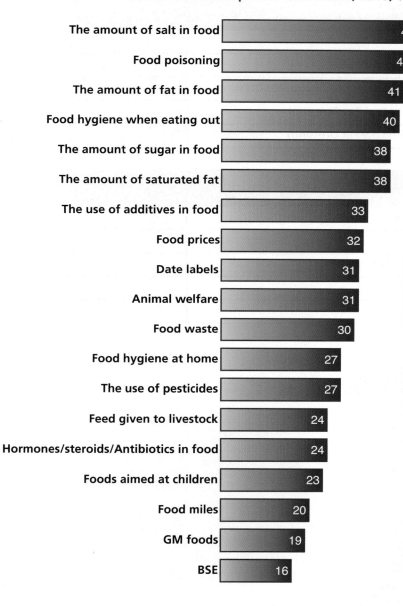

The amount of salt in food	44
Food poisoning	43
The amount of fat in food	41
Food hygiene when eating out	40
The amount of sugar in food	38
The amount of saturated fat	38
The use of additives in food	33
Food prices	32
Date labels	31
Animal welfare	31
Food waste	30
Food hygiene at home	27
The use of pesticides	27
Feed given to livestock	24
Hormones/steroids/Antibiotics in food	24
Foods aimed at children	23
Food miles	20
GM foods	19
BSE	16

Concerns about food issues seem to increase with age. For example only 35% of those aged 16-25 were concerned about salt in their food, compared with 43% of 26-35 year olds, 50% of 36-49 year olds, 55% of 50-65 year olds and 50% of those aged 66+

Similarly only 26% of those aged 16-25 were concerned about the amount of saturated fat in their food compared to 36% of those aged 26-35, 38% of those aged 36-49, 48% of those aged 50-65 and 37% of those aged 66+

Source: Public Attitudes Tracker 2010, Food Standards Agency © crown copyright www.food.gov.uk

Salad with your salt?

One in 10 takeaway salads contains more salt than a Big Mac

A survey of **270 salad and pasta bowls** from supermarkets, high street cafes and fast food chains found that whilst we should eat less than **6 grams of salt a day**, a salad can unexpectedly give you more than **half of your daily maximum intake.**

The new research, carried out by Consensus Action on Salt and Health (CASH), has found surprisingly high levels of salt hidden in salads.

WORST AND BEST 5 TAKEAWAY SALADS:

Take away outlet	Top 5 most salty salads	Salt (g) per portion
EAT	Spicy Crayfish Noodles	3.51
Pret A Manger	Super (Duper) Humous Salad (with dressing)	3.2
KFC	Zinger Salad (with Caesar Dressing or Low Fat Vinaigrette Dressing)	3.1
KFC	Original Recipe Chicken Salad (with Low Fat Dressing)	2.9
McDonalds	Crispy Chicken & Bacon Salad (with Low Fat Dressing)	2.6

Take away outlet	Bottom 5 least salty salads	Salt (g) per portion
Burger King	Garden Salad (with French Dressing)	0.15
Pret A Manger	No Bread Tricolore (with dressing)	0.2
Burger King	Garden Salad (with Honey and Mustard dressing)	0.47
Café Nero	Chicken & Orzo Pasta Salad	0.5
Starbucks	Chicken with Red Pesto Pasta Salad	0.5

Photo: Litandmore

CASH estimates that at least 15,000 people in the UK die early each year as a result of eating too much salt, most of which is processed foods.

Its latest survey has found that in addition to major sources such as bread and breakfast cereals, there was heavy salting of salads by sandwich shops, fast food chains and supermarkets

Photo: FotoosVanRobin

❝ It is absurd that only **6** salads assessed contained less salt than a packet of crisps. Manufacturers still have a long way to go if we are to reduce our salt intake to **6g a day** and save the maximum number of lives.

Every gram of salt removed from our diet is estimated to prevent **6,000 deaths** from heart attacks, heart disease and strokes per year, creating potential healthcare savings of **£1.5billion per year. ❞**

Professor Graham MacGregor of the Wolfson Institute of Preventive Medicine and Chairman of CASH

WORST AND BEST 5 SUPERMARKET SALADS

Supermarkets	Top 5 most salty salads	Salt (g) per portion
Marks & Spencer	A Taste of Asia + four others	2.85
Marks & Spencer	Pasta with British Chicken, Bacon & Sweetcorn in a Chive Mayonnaise Dressing	3.2
Marks & Spencer	Avocado & Feta with a Mint & Crème Fraiche Dressing	2.40
Tesco	Prawn Layered Salad	2.3
Waitrose	Special Edition King Prawn Thai Rice Salad	2.25

Supermarkets	Bottom 5 least salty salads	Salt (g) per portion
Sainsbury's	Be Good To Yourself Orzo Sunbaked Tomato Salad	0.26
Marks & Spencer	Noodles with Sweet Chilli British Chicken with a Sweet Chilli Dressing	0.43
Sainsbury's	Moroccan Chicken Cous Cous	0.47
ASDA	Tomato and Chicken Pasta	0.5
ASDA	Pesto Pasta	0.5

TOP TIPS:

- Avoid salty ingredients such as ham, bacon and cheese, swapping them for chicken, tuna or vegetables instead
- Don't use the whole pot of dressing provided with a ready-made salad
- Olive oil, lemon juice, pepper, balsamic vinegar and herbs can all make a salad taste great without the need for salty dressings and sauces
- Make sure you read the labels carefully and check the recommended portion sizes
- For a more filling salad try one based around pasta or mixed beans

Source: Consensus Action on Salt & Health
www.actiononsalt.org.uk/

Bad breakfast

A nourishing breakfast is the most important meal of the day...

... but a shocking number of 7-14 year olds have bad breakfast habits

 Every day **190,000** 7-14 year olds leave for school without eating breakfast.

 Only **71%** of British schoolgirls have breakfast at home every day compared to **80%** of boys. **9%** of all 7-14 year old girls either never eat breakfast before school or do so only once a week or less.

 Around **1.27m** children - **24%** of this age group will have a bad breakfast. The top 5 'bad' breakfast items are:

1	Biscuits
2	Cakes & pastries
3	Bag of crisps
4	Chocolate bar
5	Can of fizzy drink

 16% of kids are given money to get their own breakfast on the way to school. This rises to one in four 13-14 yr olds.

 7% of dads and **3%** of mums often give their kids breakfast money. **19%** of dads and **11%** of mum occasionally do this.

 Parents aged under 24 are more likely to hand out breakfast money – **49%** do this sometimes or often.

 14% of kids get their breakfast from off-licences, (**24%** of 13-14 yr olds). Around **69%** go to the corner shop, **38%** buy from a supermarket, and **8%** from garages.

 While kids themselves say they spend around half the money on sugary and salty snacks, only **35%** of parents think this is the case.

How much breakfast money do kids get?

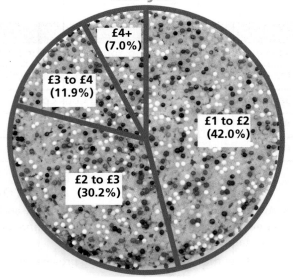

£4+ (7.0%)
£3 to £4 (11.9%)
£1 to £2 (42.0%)
£2 to £3 (30.2%)

Base: A study of 1,000 children aged 7-14 and 1,000 parents of children aged 7-14

Source: A Look at Kids' Bad Breakfast Habits in 21st Century Britain, Kelloggs

School dinners

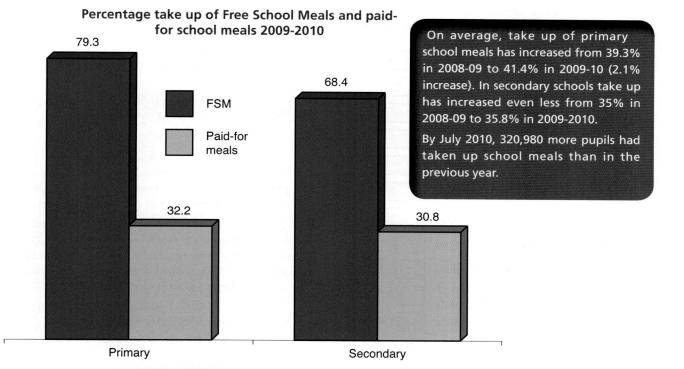

Percentage take up of Free School Meals and paid-for school meals 2009-2010

- 79.3 FSM
- 32.2 Paid-for meals
- 68.4
- 30.8

Primary

Secondary

On average, take up of primary school meals has increased from 39.3% in 2008-09 to 41.4% in 2009-10 (2.1% increase). In secondary schools take up has increased even less from 35% in 2008-09 to 35.8% in 2009-2010.

By July 2010, 320,980 more pupils had taken up school meals than in the previous year.

The average price for a school meal was **£1.83** in primary schools and **£1.94** in secondary – an increase of **3%** on the previous year.

Since not all students eligible for FSM take them up, Local Authorities have been taking steps to improve this by checking the numbers eligible, sending letters to parents to encourage take up and by changing arrangements so that FSMs are not as identifiable and embarrassing for students.

Local authorities tried to identify the main reasons for school meals not being in demand (excluding a reduction in the number of pupils in school). The top reasons mentioned by schools included:

In Primary schools:

Parents providing packed lunches **65.6%**, the provision of more healthy options resulting in pupils bringing packed lunches **42.7%** and an increase in prices **39.6%**.

In Secondary schools:

The provision of more healthy options resulting in pupils bringing packed lunches was mentioned by **58.6%**, while a massive **72.4%** said the healthy options meant pupils bought their meals elsewhere. Another significant factor was shorter lunch hours - **59.8%**

In both primary and secondary schools vegetables, healthier drinks, cakes and biscuits were chosen more frequently by pupils consuming a school meal whilst fruit, confectionery, savoury snacks and drinks not meeting the school food standards were chosen more often by pupils eating a packed lunch. The school meals showed a better nutritional balance, with more fibre and essential nutrients. Although packed lunches contained 100 fewer calories than the school meals, they were higher in fat, sugar and salt.

Source: School lunch take up in England 2009-10
www.schoolfoodtrust.org.uk/

Waste not, want not

Avoidable food waste damages the environment and our pockets

Total amount of food and drink waste by food group, tonnes per year

Food group	Tonnes per year
Fresh vegetables and salads	1,900,000
Drink	1,300,000
Fresh fruit	1,100,000
Bakery	800,000
Meals (homemade and pre-prepared)	690,000
Meat and fish	610,000
Dairy and eggs	580,000
Processed vegetables and salad	210,000
Condiments, sauces, herbs & spices	210,000
Staple foods such as rice and pasta	200,000
Cakes and desserts	190,000
Oil and fat	90,000
Confectionery and snacks	71,000
Processed fruit	30,000
Other	300,000

Food and drink waste fits into three groups:

Avoidable – thrown away because it is no longer wanted or has been allowed to go past its best. The vast majority of this is made up of material that was, at some point, edible.

Possibly avoidable – food & drink that some people eat and others do not (e.g. bread crusts), or that can be eaten when prepared in one way but not in another (e.g. potato skins). Again, this would have been edible at some point.

Unavoidable – waste that is not, under normal circumstances edible. This includes egg shells, meat bones, tea bags, etc.

Total cost of avoidable food and drink waste by food group, £ million per year

Food group	£ million per year
Meals (homemade and pre-prepared)	2,100
Meat and fish	1,600
Drink	1,600
Fresh vegetables and salads	1,400
Bakery	1,100
Fresh fruit	990
Dairy and eggs	870
Condiments, sauces, herbs & spices	700
Cakes and desserts	510
Staple foods such as rice and pasta	470
Processed vegetables and salad	360
Confectionery and snacks	330
Processed fruit	63
Oil and fat	37
Other	110

A total of 8,300,000 tonnes of food & drink waste is produced each year. Of this, **5,300,000 is avoidable,** 1,500,000 is possibly avoidable and **1,500,000** is unavoidable

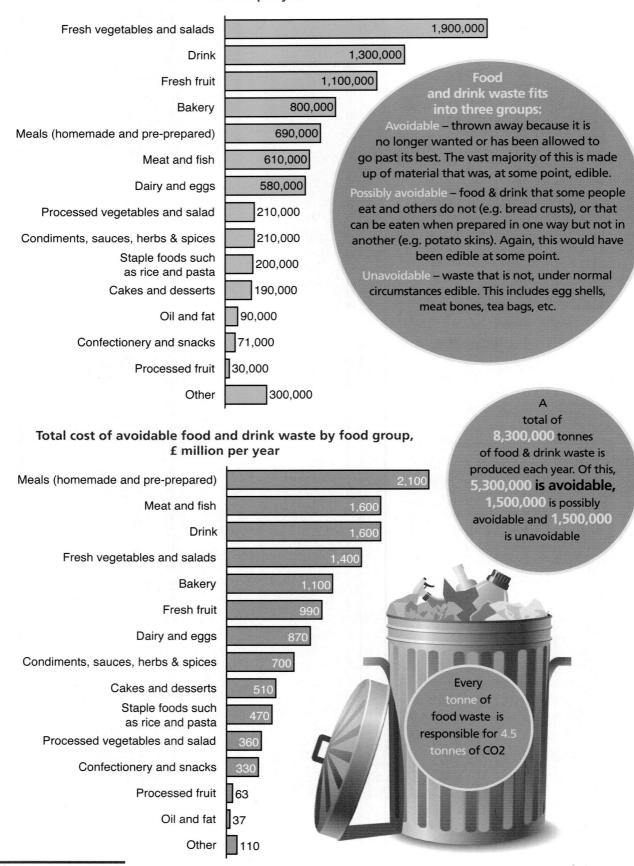

Every tonne of food waste is responsible for 4.5 tonnes of CO_2

We produce **8.3 million tonnes** of waste a year in the UK. Our population is over **60 million** people living within **25 million** households so in our 'average' household, **27kg** of food and drink waste is generated in a month. Of this, approximately **19kg** goes into the bin or food waste collections, **6kg** is poured down the sewer, and **2kg** is fed to animals or home composted.

For the average household, the retail price of the avoidable food and drink waste is **£40 per month**, or more than **£1 per day**.

This compares to an average monthly food and drink expenditure of **£260 per household.** Therefore avoidable food and drink waste accounts for approximately **15%** of the shopping budget.

Kilograms of food and drink waste per household, per month, by avoidability

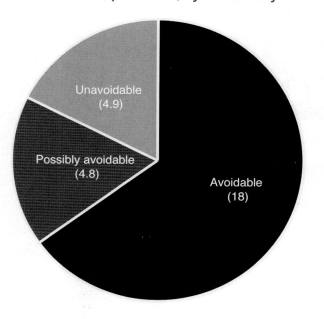

The **18kg** of food and drink waste which is **avoidable** could have been eaten if it had been better managed. This includes leftovers and food and drink that was disposed of because it was not used in time, either passing a use-by date, or going mouldy.

This corresponds to more than **half a kilogram every day per household.** This is a lot given that this does not include unavoidable or even possibly avoidable waste.

Cost of avoidable food and drink waste per household, per month, by food group

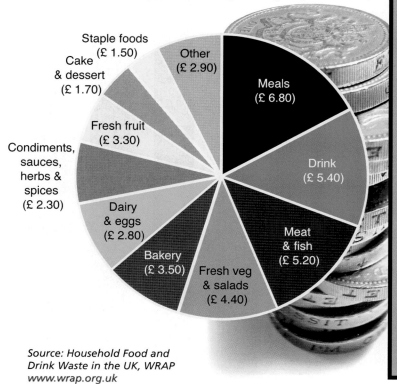

Source: Household Food and Drink Waste in the UK, WRAP
www.wrap.org.uk

The average household generates 210 kg of avoidable food and drink waste per year – roughly equivalent to 0.8 tonnes of CO_2. Total greenhouse gas emissions from consumption in the UK amount to approximately 33 tonnes CO_2 equivalent per household, per year.

So, food and drink waste accounts for 2.4% of the total greenhouse gas emissions. To illustrate the scale of these emissions, this is about the same amount of CO_2 as:

• All members of a household taking a return flight from London to Vienna every year

• The savings made by 270 mm of loft insulation in a house that previously contained none.

In other words, if we reduce our food and drink waste there would be an important cut in greenhouse gas emissions.

The Love Food Hate Waste campaign is having some success in encouraging people not to buy too much food, eat certain products a few days after the best before date and to be inventive with leftovers.

Fairer trade

Sales show that people are getting the Fairtrade message

What is FAIRTRADE?

The FAIRTRADE Mark is an independent consumer label which appears on UK products as a guarantee that they meet internationally agreed Fairtrade standards. It shares these standards with movements in 20 other countries.

The FAIRTRADE Foundation has licensed over 3,000 products for sale in the UK.

FAIRTRADE

Legend:
- Wine
- Bananas
- Honey Products
- Chocolate/Cocoa
- Tea
- Coffee

Sales of FAIRTRADE certified food and drink in the UK, £ Millions (Main products only)

The FAIRTRADE market

Sales of FAIRTRADE products continue to increase as people become more and more aware of the issues surrounding fair trade.

In 2000 the total value of the FAIRTRADE market was £32.9 million, by 2009 it had increased to £799 million, £499.5 million of which was from the main food and drink products.

As people become more aware of FAIRTRADE products, such as clothing and flowers, those sales are also increasing. Sales of FAIRTRADE cotton, for example, increased from £0.2 million in 2005 to £50.1 million in 2009. Flower sales rose from £5.7 million to £30 million in the same period. The remaining products increased their sales from £2.2 million in 2001 to £219.4 million in 2009.

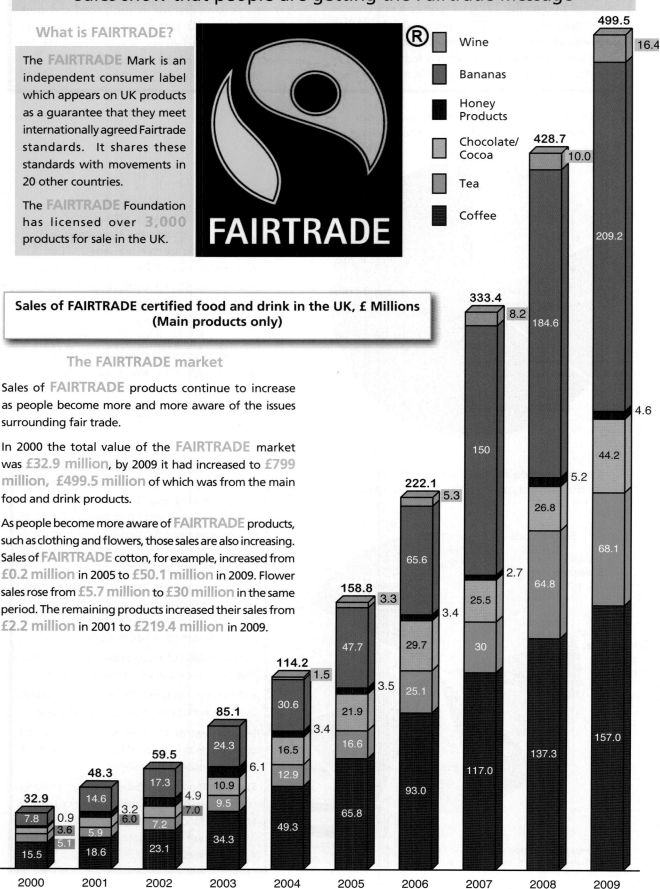

Sales of FAIRTRADE certified food and drink in the UK, £ Millions (Main products only)

Year	Total	Values
2000	32.9	7.8 / 0.9 / 3.6 / 5.1 / 15.5
2001	48.3	14.6 / 3.2 / 6.0 / 5.9 / 18.6
2002	59.5	17.3 / 4.9 / 7.0 / 7.2 / 23.1
2003	85.1	24.3 / 6.1 / 10.9 / 9.5 / 34.3
2004	114.2	30.6 / 1.5 / 3.4 / 16.5 / 12.9 / 49.3
2005	158.8	47.7 / 3.3 / 3.5 / 21.9 / 16.6 / 65.8
2006	222.1	65.6 / 5.3 / 3.4 / 29.7 / 25.1 / 93.0
2007	333.4	150 / 8.2 / 2.7 / 30 / 25.5 / 117.0
2008	428.7	184.6 / 10.0 / 5.2 / 64.8 / 26.8 / 137.3
2009	499.5	209.2 / 16.4 / 4.6 / 68.1 / 44.2 / 157.0

Source: The Fairtrade Foundation

www.fairtrade.org.uk

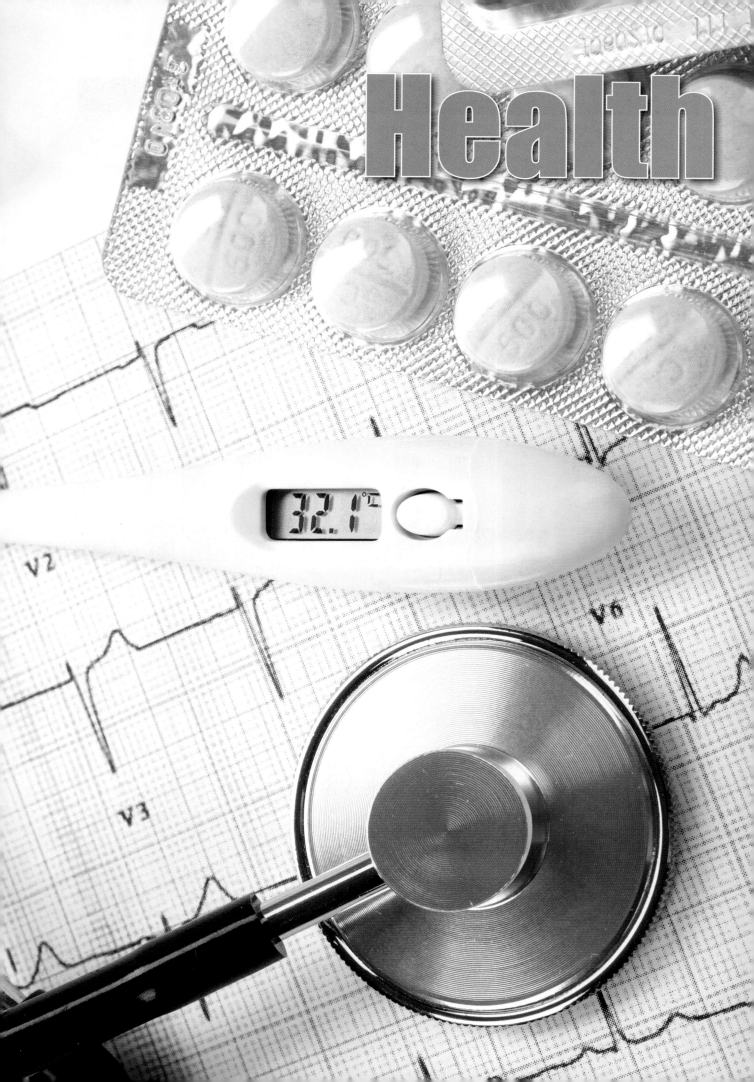

Health

Organ donation

The supply of organs is not keeping pace with demand

The UK active transplant waiting list is increasing by approximately **8%** each year. Our ageing population and increasing incidence of type 2 diabetes is likely to make this shortage of available organs worse.

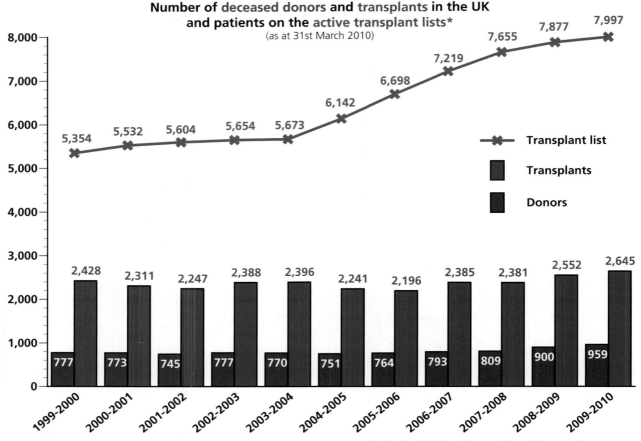

Number of deceased donors and transplants in the UK and patients on the active transplant lists*
(as at 31st March 2010)

Transplant list values: 5,354 · 5,532 · 5,604 · 5,654 · 5,673 · 6,142 · 6,698 · 7,219 · 7,655 · 7,877 · 7,997

Transplants values: 2,428 · 2,311 · 2,247 · 2,388 · 2,396 · 2,241 · 2,196 · 2,385 · 2,381 · 2,552 · 2,645

Donors values: 777 · 773 · 745 · 777 · 770 · 751 · 764 · 793 · 809 · 900 · 959

Years: 1999-2000 · 2000-2001 · 2001-2002 · 2002-2003 · 2003-2004 · 2004-2005 · 2005-2006 · 2006-2007 · 2007-2008 · 2008-2009 · 2009-2010

*A further 2,545 patients registered for transplants were not fit or not available and therefore not on the active list

Transplants are now so successful in the UK that a year after surgery the following are still functioning well:

94% of kidneys in living donor transplants

88% of kidneys from people who have died

86% of liver transplants

84% of heart transplants

77% of lung transplants and

73% of heart/lung transplants

At present the UK has an **informed consent** system in which individuals **opt in** if they are willing for their organs to be used after death. Donors carry a signed donor card, join the NHS organ donor register or fill in the relevant sections of a passport or driving licence. Only approximately **25%** of the UK population have done this.

Some campaigners suggest that a change in law to that of **presumed consent**, in which everyone is considered a donor unless they explicitly **opt out**, would increase donor rates.

Different systems do seem to affect donation rates in other countries.

Donation rates in selected countries, 2009
Deceased organ donors
(annual rate per million population)

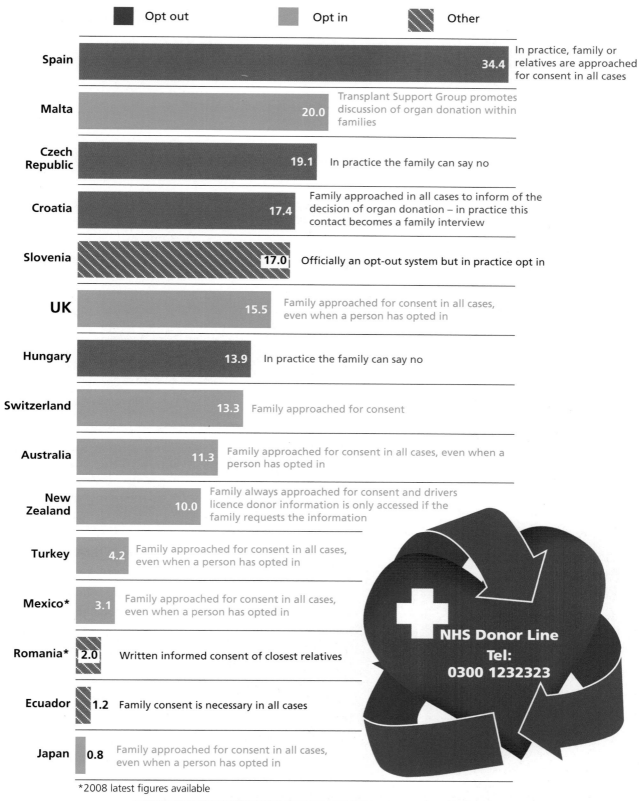

Legend: Opt out | Opt in | Other

Spain 34.4 — In practice, family or relatives are approached for consent in all cases

Malta 20.0 — Transplant Support Group promotes discussion of organ donation within families

Czech Republic 19.1 — In practice the family can say no

Croatia 17.4 — Family approached in all cases to inform of the decision of organ donation – in practice this contact becomes a family interview

Slovenia 17.0 — Officially an opt-out system but in practice opt in

UK 15.5 — Family approached for consent in all cases, even when a person has opted in

Hungary 13.9 — In practice the family can say no

Switzerland 13.3 — Family approached for consent

Australia 11.3 — Family approached for consent in all cases, even when a person has opted in

New Zealand 10.0 — Family always approached for consent and drivers licence donor information is only accessed if the family requests the information

Turkey 4.2 — Family approached for consent in all cases, even when a person has opted in

Mexico* 3.1 — Family approached for consent in all cases, even when a person has opted in

Romania* 2.0 — Written informed consent of closest relatives

Ecuador 1.2 — Family consent is necessary in all cases

Japan 0.8 — Family approached for consent in all cases, even when a person has opted in

NHS Donor Line
Tel:
0300 1232323

*2008 latest figures available

Essential Articles 13 pages 118-119 discusses the controversy about who should receive a transplanted organ

Sources: NHSBT, Health Technology Assessment – A systematic review of presumed consent systems for deceased organ donation, European Transplant Coordinators Organisation (ETCO), International Registry of Organ Donation and Transplantation (IRODaT)

www.uktransplant.org.uk
www.hta.ac.uk
www.europeantransplantcoordinators.org
www.tpm.org/
www.giveandletlive.co.uk

Private pain – Secret shame

"Self-harm is not an illness, it is an expression of personal distress"

"Self-harm is when someone damages or injures their body on purpose...
it is not usually an attempt at committing suicide [but does include suicide],
but a way of expressing deep emotional feelings, such as low self-esteem.
It is a way to cope with traumatic events, or situations, such as the death
of a loved one, or an abusive relationship"

NHS Choices

Admissions to hospital for intentional self-harm, England

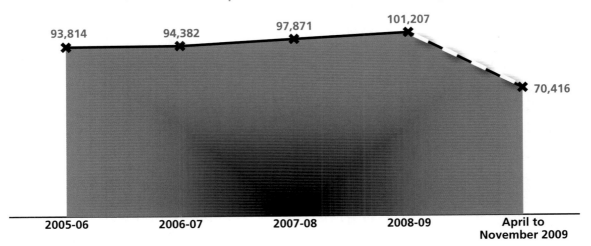

93,814	94,382	97,871	101,207	70,416
2005-06	2006-07	2007-08	2008-09	April to November 2009

"During my dark times the cutting never inflicted any pain. I was numb to it all but I wanted to feel – that was the whole point."
Laura, 21

Types of self-harm may include:

cutting and/or burning the skin and destructive, or dangerous, behaviour, such as misusing alcohol or drugs

In the year to November 2009 there were
102,527 admissions
for intentional self-harm –
an increase of **1.3%** on the previous year.
59% were female patients

The highest rate of admission was for patients living in the
North East
health authority area with
315 admissions per
100,000 population

Source: HES online, NHS
www.hesonline.nhs.uk

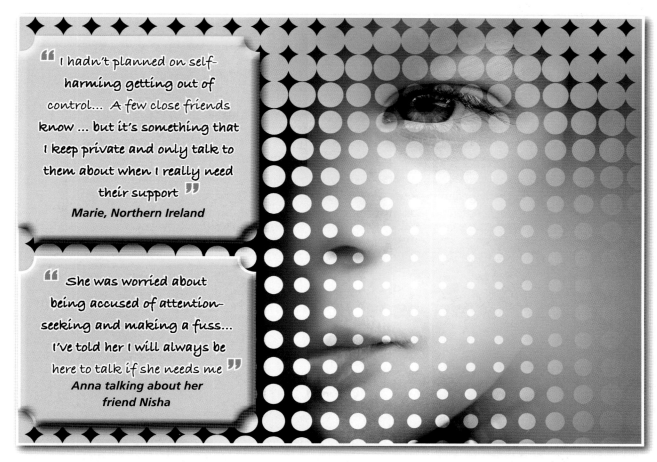

" I hadn't planned on self-harming getting out of control... A few close friends know ... but it's something that I keep private and only talk to them about when I really need their support "
Marie, Northern Ireland

" She was worried about being accused of attention-seeking and making a fuss... I've told her I will always be here to talk if she needs me "
Anna talking about her friend Nisha

In a survey of over 2,000 people aged 16 and over, the answers, particularly from 16-24 year olds, revealed that friends and family of people who self-harm may be giving well-intentioned but potentially harmful advice, because of a poor understanding of the best ways to provide support

21% of **16-24 year olds** have self-harmed

57% knew someone who had self-harmed in the past

43% cited the internet as their first port of call
15% said that a medical professional would be the first place they would go to for advice
38% of respondents over the age of 25 said that they would go to 'a medical professional' for advice and information first

"Usually, young people who self-harm do so as a way of coping with complex and difficult situations and although it's understandable that a parent, friend or carer's instinct would be to try and stop the person from self-harming, it's actually the issues behind [self-harm] that need addressing"

Paul Marriot, Chief Executive of Depaul UK

32% of **16 to 24-year-olds** and **18%** of those **aged 25 and over**
said that their first reaction to discovering that someone close to them was self-harming would be to ask them to stop – advice that experts say is understandable but could place unrealistic emotional demands on the person

42% of **16 to 24-year-olds** and **30%** of those **aged 25 and over**
agreed with the statement

"I am confident I could give good advice to someone I discovered was self-harming"

Source: YouGov survey for 42nd Street, Depaul UK and YouthNet, 2009
www.thesite.org/selfharm

Your life, your voice

A survey in 2009 researched the views of 3,850 15-24 year olds from 15 countries across Europe, Asia Pacific and the USA.

It assessed how communication between young people and those around them affects their sexual activity and their use of contraception. The 2010 survey covered 5,253 young people and looked at responsibility for use of contraception.

16
Average age when first had sex
2010 survey

Multi-national results in 2010 show:

- Over **80%** of young people acknowledge their responsibility for arranging contraception before having sex with a new partner.

- **51%** consider themselves to be very well informed about contraceptive options yet **32%** believe that the 'withdrawal method' is effective when it is actually highly unreliable.

- **44%** of young people give more thought to showering, waxing and applying perfume than to contraception when preparing for a date that may lead to sex.

- And more young people are having sex without contraception. **45%** of sexually active young people surveyed have had sex without contraception compared to **36%** in the 2009 survey.

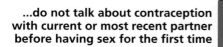

Key results from 2009 highlight that young people are NOT communicating effectively about contraception

Young people who said they...

...do not talk about contraception with current or most recent partner before having sex for the first time
 **35%**

...did not talk about contraception with first partner before having sex for the first time
31%

Why not talk about contraception?

17% said they were self-conscious

14% assumed their partner had arranged it

Responsibility for arranging contraception

■ Both ■ My partner's ■ Mine

85%

4%
11%

In both 2009 and 2010, the most common reason for not using contraception with a new partner was not having it available at the time. Other reasons included not liking it, forgetfulness and drunkenness. In Thailand, more than a third of young people said the main reason they did not use contraception is because "It's not cool".

In the UK and Norway, a fifth did not use contraception as they had "drunk alcohol and forgot".

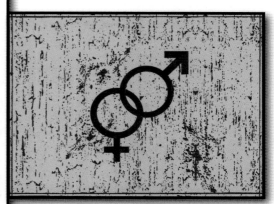

Rank	Best ways to remove barriers to talking about contraception	Rank	Trusted sources of contraception	Rank	Approachability of information source
1	Better sex education at school	1	Doctor	1	Partner
2	Having someone to talk to in confidence	2	Mother	2	Friends
3	Changing cultural attitudes	3	Partner	3	Doctor

But **13%** said they seek contraceptive advice from an anonymous source online

*** These results are alarming. They paint the real picture of what's happening in young people's lives, and are a necessary* wake up call *to us all... they are making decisions based on inaccurate information and 'guess work' ***

Jennifer Woodside, International Planned Parenthood Federation

*Source: Your Life – Talking Sex and Contraception, 2009 &
Contraception: Whose responsibility is it anyway? 2010*

www.your-life.com

Abortions

Early abortions are now more available

Abortion means choosing to end a pregnancy.

In England, Wales and Scotland abortion is **legal** if you are **less than 24 weeks pregnant** and if two doctors agree that it is necessary for one of the following reasons:

- having a baby would upset your mental or physical health more than having an abortion. This means you need to explain how you feel the pregnancy would affect your life to a doctor.

- having the baby would harm the mental or physical health of any children you already have.

An abortion is also legal at any time in pregnancy if two doctors agree that:

- an abortion is necessary to save your life
- an abortion would prevent serious permanent harm to your mental or physical health
- there is a high risk that the baby would be born with a serious disability.

Legal abortions for women resident in England & Wales, by age group, 2009

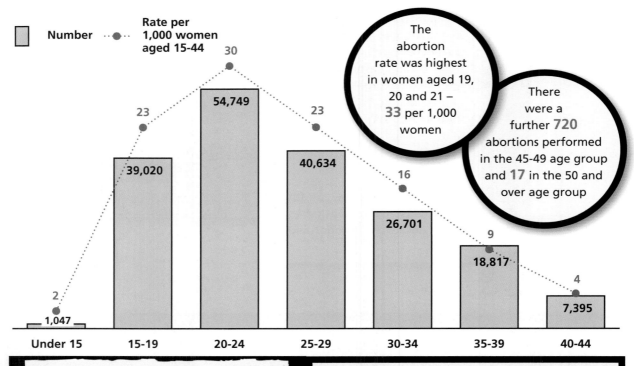

Number

Rate per 1,000 women aged 15-44

The abortion rate was highest in women aged 19, 20 and 21 – **33** per 1,000 women

There were a further **720** abortions performed in the 45-49 age group and **17** in the 50 and over age group

Age group	Number	Rate
Under 15	1,047	2
15-19	39,020	23
20-24	54,749	30
25-29	40,634	23
30-34	26,701	16
35-39	18,817	9
40-44	7,395	4

Pregnant? Who can I speak to?

England & Wales, 2009

The total number of abortions was **189,100** – a rate of **17.5** per 1,000 women aged 15-44. There were an additional **6,643** abortions performed for **non-residents**.

Scotland, 2009

The total number of abortions was **13,005** (including **60** abortions for **non-residents/unknown**) – a rate of **12.4** per 1,000 women aged 15-44. The rate was highest in women aged 16-19 – **22.3** per 1,000.

The rate was **16.5** per 1,000 in Scotland's most deprived areas, but only **8.8** per 1,000 in the least deprived areas.

Over **18,000** abortions were carried out on girls under the age of 18 and, for the first time, **more than a third** of terminations were performed on women who had ended at least one pregnancy.

Number of **previous** legal abortions, England & Wales, 2009	Age group*				Total
	under 18	18 - 24	25 - 29	30+	
None	16,486	55,086	23,817	30,321	125,710
1	1,341	17,746	12,392	16,561	48,040
2	..	..	3,262	4,933	11,602
3	..	..	828	1,243	2,637
4	..	..	242	382	779
5	..	..	70	127	214
6	..	..	..	48	70
7 or more	..	..	..	35	48
Total	17,916	76,900	40,634	53,650	189,100

28% of the women who had an abortion in **Scotland** in 2009, have had a **previous** abortion

* where age was not stated, numbers have been spread pro rata between the 18-24 age group
.. values less than 10 are not shown but are included in the total

% of legal abortions, England & Wales, by number of pregnancy weeks

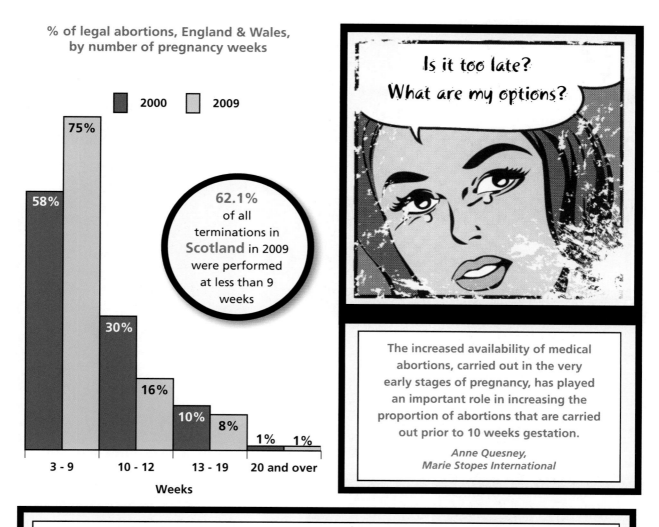

■ 2000 ☐ 2009

75%
58%
30%
16%
10%
8%
1% 1%

3 - 9   10 - 12   13 - 19   20 and over
Weeks

62.1% of all terminations in **Scotland** in 2009 were performed at less than 9 weeks

Is it too late?
What are my options?

The increased availability of medical abortions, carried out in the very early stages of pregnancy, has played an important role in increasing the proportion of abortions that are carried out prior to 10 weeks gestation.

Anne Quesney,
Marie Stopes International

Marie Stopes International
0845 300 80 90 **(24 hours)**
www.likeitis.org

Ask Brook 0808 802 1234
Confidential advice for under 25s
www.brook.org.uk

Sources: *Department of Health © Crown copyright 2010, Marie Stopes International, Brook*

www.dh.gov.uk

Repeated risk

Young people are most vulnerable to sexual infection

How many cases?

In 2009 a total of **482,696** new sexually transmitted infections (STI) diagnoses were reported. This is almost **12,000** more cases than were reported in 2008 continuing the steady upward trend over the past decade.

Who is affected most?

New figures released by the Health Protection Agency show that 15 to 24 year olds, particularly young women, continue to be the group most affected by STIs in the UK.

Number of new STI diagnoses, 2008 and 2009, UK

	2008	2009	% 2008-09 change
Gonorrhoea (complicated and uncomplicated)			
Male	10,860	11,663	7%
Female	5,591	5,696	2%
Total	16,451	17,385	6%
Chlamydial infection (complicated and uncomplicated)			
Male	81,696	85,828	5%
Female	120,730	130,333	8%
Total	203,773	217,570	7%
Non-specific genital infection (complicated and uncomplicated)			
Male	73,759	70,670	-4%
Female	22,394	22,700	1%
Total	96,153	93,456	-3%
Genital herpes simplex (first episode)			
Male	11,190	11,796	5%
Female	17,617	18,294	4%
Total	28,807	30,126	5%
Genital warts (first episode)			
Male	48,228	49,106	2%
Female	43,275	42,096	-3%
Total	91,503	91,257	0
All other new STI diagnoses (including syphilis)			
Male	20,749	20,542	-1%
Female	13,265	12,315	-7%
Total	34,014	32,902	-3%
Total STI diagnoses			
Male	246,482	249,605	1%
Female	222,872	231,433	4%
Total	470,701	482,696	3%

And...

In 2008 around **two thirds** of new STI diagnoses in women were in those under 25.

High rates of STI diagnoses have also been found among men who have sex with men.

Of all the 15-24 year olds diagnosed with an STI last year around **one in ten** will become re-infected within a year.

Why?

The increase is in part due to more sensitive tests and community based testing targeting the under 25s in England through the National Chlamydia Screening Programme.

However, according to Dr Gwenda Hughes, Head of the HPA's STI section

"We know that the rise in STIs is also due in part to unsafe sexual behaviour ...

... Young adults are more likely to have unsafe sex and often they lack the skills and confidence to negotiate safer sex.

"Re-infection is also a worrying issue ... this suggests teenagers are repeatedly putting their own, as well as others, long term health at risk from STIs"

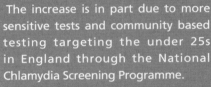

New Infections – % change 2000-2009

STI	Males	Females
Gonorrhoea	-23%	-15%
Chlamydia	+97%	+50%
Herpes	+75%	+69%
Genital warts	+32%	+27%

New episodes of STIs, UK, 2009 (total cases) by age and gender

Legend: ■ <16 ■ 16-19 □ 20-24 □ 25-34 ■ 35-44 ■ 45-64 □ >65

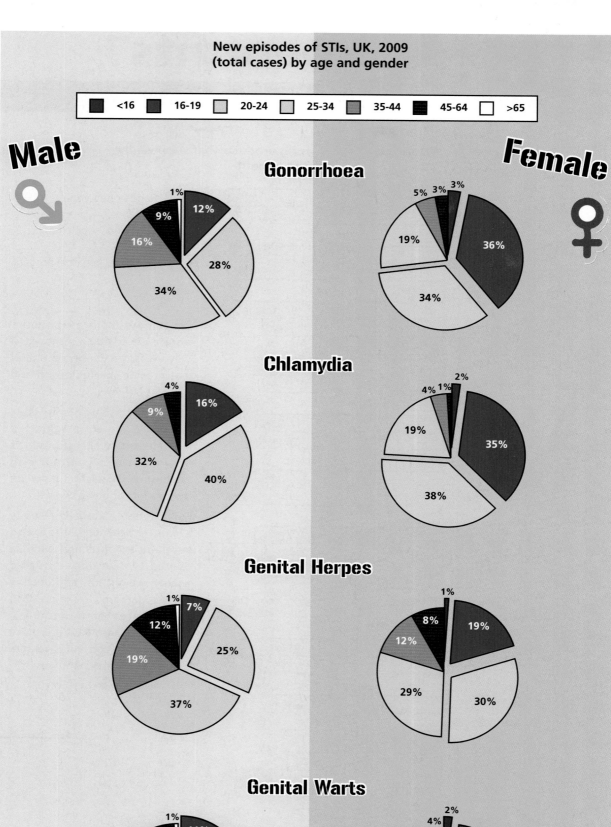

Male

Female

Gonorrhoea

Male: 12%, 28%, 34%, 16%, 9%, 1%

Female: 36%, 34%, 19%, 5%, 3%, 3%

Chlamydia

Male: 16%, 40%, 32%, 9%, 4%

Female: 35%, 38%, 19%, 4%, 1%, 2%

Genital Herpes

Male: 7%, 25%, 37%, 19%, 12%, 1%

Female: 19%, 30%, 29%, 12%, 8%, 1%

Genital Warts

Male: 11%, 35%, 34%, 12%, 7%, 1%

Female: 30%, 34%, 22%, 8%, 4%, 2%

Source: Health Protection Agency
www.hpa.org.uk

Buying benefits?

What would you buy to improve your health?

Percentage of consumers interested in using products that supposedly provide a specific health benefit

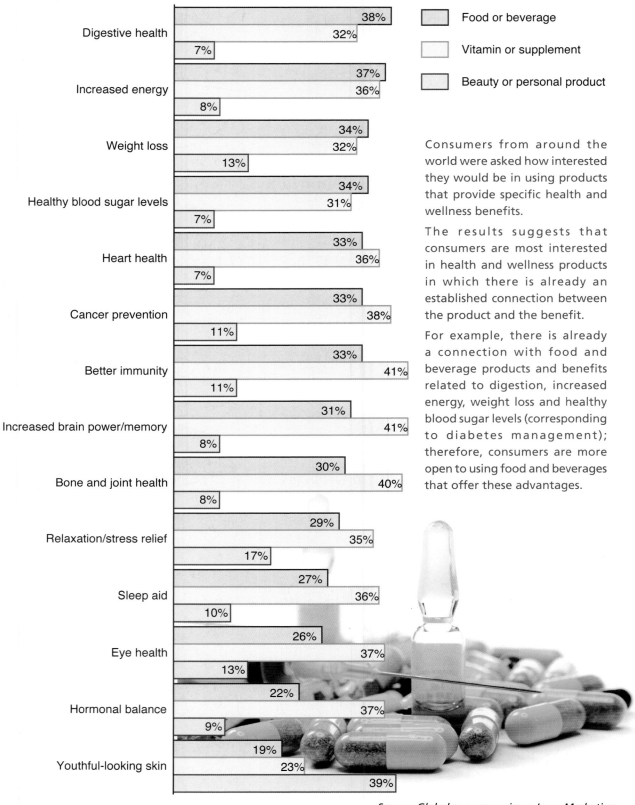

Legend:
- Food or beverage
- Vitamin or supplement
- Beauty or personal product

Digestive health
- 38%
- 32%
- 7%

Increased energy
- 37%
- 36%
- 8%

Weight loss
- 34%
- 32%
- 13%

Healthy blood sugar levels
- 34%
- 31%
- 7%

Heart health
- 33%
- 36%
- 7%

Cancer prevention
- 33%
- 38%
- 11%

Better immunity
- 33%
- 41%
- 11%

Increased brain power/memory
- 31%
- 41%
- 8%

Bone and joint health
- 30%
- 40%
- 8%

Relaxation/stress relief
- 29%
- 35%
- 17%

Sleep aid
- 27%
- 36%
- 10%

Eye health
- 26%
- 37%
- 13%

Hormonal balance
- 22%
- 37%
- 9%

Youthful-looking skin
- 19%
- 23%
- 39%

Consumers from around the world were asked how interested they would be in using products that provide specific health and wellness benefits.

The results suggests that consumers are most interested in health and wellness products in which there is already an established connection between the product and the benefit.

For example, there is already a connection with food and beverage products and benefits related to digestion, increased energy, weight loss and healthy blood sugar levels (corresponding to diabetes management); therefore, consumers are more open to using food and beverages that offer these advantages.

Source: Global consumer views, Ipsos Marketing
www.ipsos-mori.com/

Housing

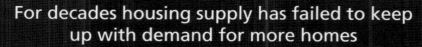

Supply...

For decades housing supply has failed to keep up with demand for more homes

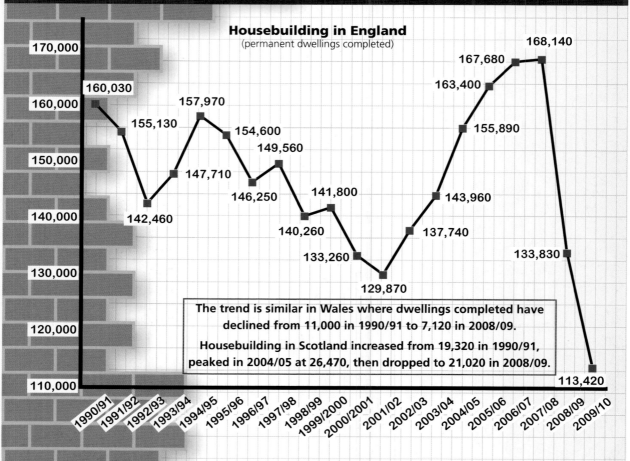

Housebuilding in England
(permanent dwellings completed)

- 160,030
- 155,130
- 157,970
- 154,600
- 147,710
- 149,560
- 146,250
- 142,460
- 141,800
- 140,260
- 133,260
- 129,870
- 137,740
- 143,960
- 155,890
- 163,400
- 167,680
- 168,140
- 133,830
- 113,420

x-axis: 1990/91, 1991/92, 1992/93, 1993/94, 1994/95, 1995/96, 1996/97, 1997/98, 1998/99, 1999/2000, 2000/2001, 2001/02, 2002/03, 2003/04, 2004/05, 2005/06, 2006/07, 2007/08, 2008/09, 2009/10

The trend is similar in Wales where dwellings completed have declined from 11,000 in 1990/91 to 7,120 in 2008/09.

Housebuilding in Scotland increased from 19,320 in 1990/91, peaked in 2004/05 at 26,470, then dropped to 21,020 in 2008/09.

New build completions in 2009 were **17%** lower than 2008.
Given this fall, it is likely that net housing supply will also fall in 2009-10.

Eight out of the nine English regions experienced a decrease in the number of additional dwellings supplied in 2008-09. The North East saw the largest decrease **(43%)** followed by the North West **(37%)**. London was the only region to experience an annual increase **(3%)**.

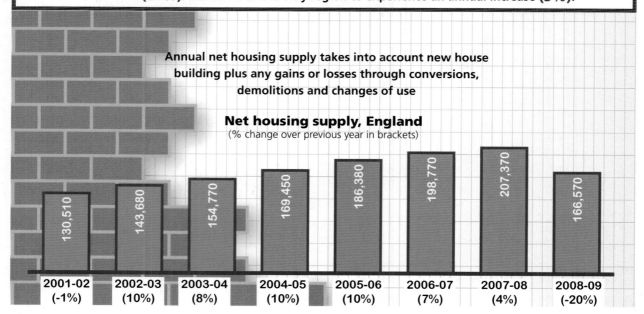

Annual net housing supply takes into account new house building plus any gains or losses through conversions, demolitions and changes of use

Net housing supply, England
(% change over previous year in brackets)

2001-02 (-1%)	2002-03 (10%)	2003-04 (8%)	2004-05 (10%)	2005-06 (10%)	2006-07 (7%)	2007-08 (4%)	2008-09 (-20%)
130,510	143,680	154,770	169,450	186,380	198,770	207,370	166,570

...and demand

More people are choosing to live alone and people are living longer – so demand for housing is growing

The number of households in England is projected to grow to **27.8 million** in 2031, an increase of **6.3 million (29%)** over the 2006 estimate.

One person households are projected to increase by **163,000** per year – two thirds of the overall increase in households by 2031.

18% of the population is projected to live alone, compared with **13%** in 2006.

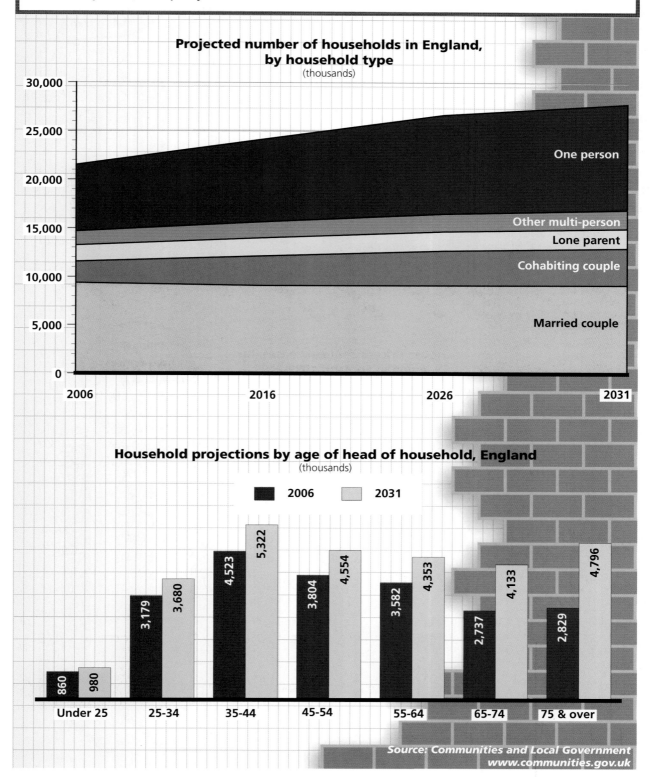

Projected number of households in England, by household type
(thousands)

One person
Other multi-person
Lone parent
Cohabiting couple
Married couple

Household projections by age of head of household, England
(thousands)

Legend: 2006 | 2031

Age	2006	2031
Under 25	860	980
25-34	3,179	3,680
35-44	4,523	5,322
45-54	3,804	4,554
55-64	3,582	4,353
65-74	2,737	4,133
75 & over	2,829	4,796

Source: Communities and Local Government
www.communities.gov.uk

Locked out

What chance does the next generation of young people have of finding a good quality home at a price they can afford?

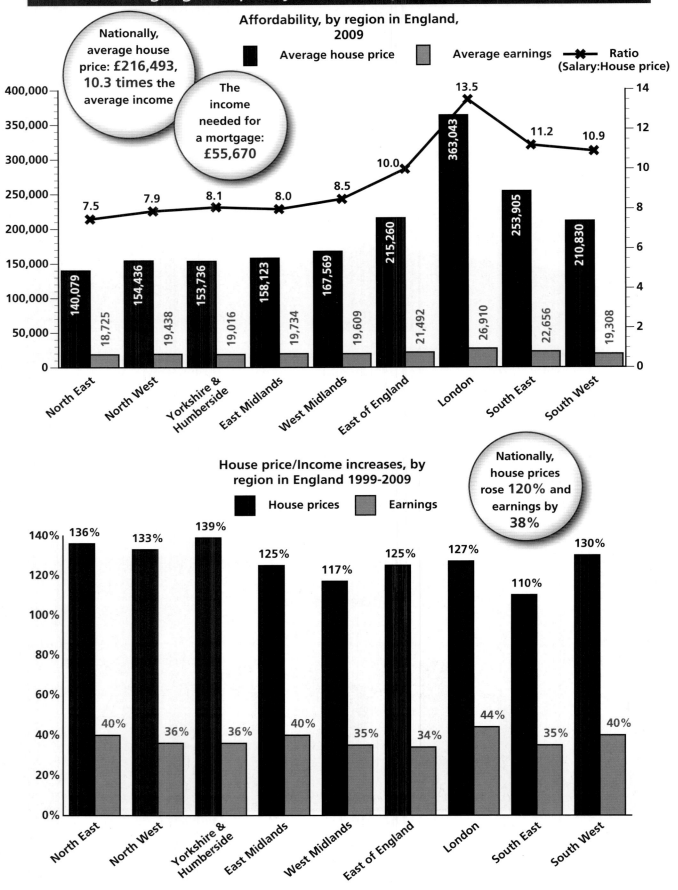

Affordability, by region in England, 2009

- Average house price
- Average earnings
- Ratio (Salary:House price)

Nationally, average house price: £216,493, 10.3 times the average income

The income needed for a mortgage: £55,670

Region	Average house price	Average earnings	Ratio
North East	140,079	18,725	7.5
North West	154,436	19,438	7.9
Yorkshire & Humberside	153,736	19,016	8.1
East Midlands	158,123	19,734	8.0
West Midlands	167,569	19,609	8.5
East of England	215,260	21,492	10.0
London	363,043	26,910	13.5
South East	253,905	22,656	11.2
South West	210,830	19,308	10.9

House price/Income increases, by region in England 1999-2009

- House prices
- Earnings

Nationally, house prices rose 120% and earnings by 38%

Region	House prices	Earnings
North East	136%	40%
North West	133%	36%
Yorkshire & Humberside	139%	36%
East Midlands	125%	40%
West Midlands	117%	35%
East of England	125%	34%
London	127%	44%
South East	110%	35%
South West	130%	40%

The Public Attitudes to Housing 2010 survey of 2,090 adults living in England found that many are relying on support from parents or other family members, either for a deposit or for a place in the family home while they save. There is concern that only those with parents who are able to support them financially into ownership are able to get on the housing ladder, further widening the gap between the housing haves and have-nots.

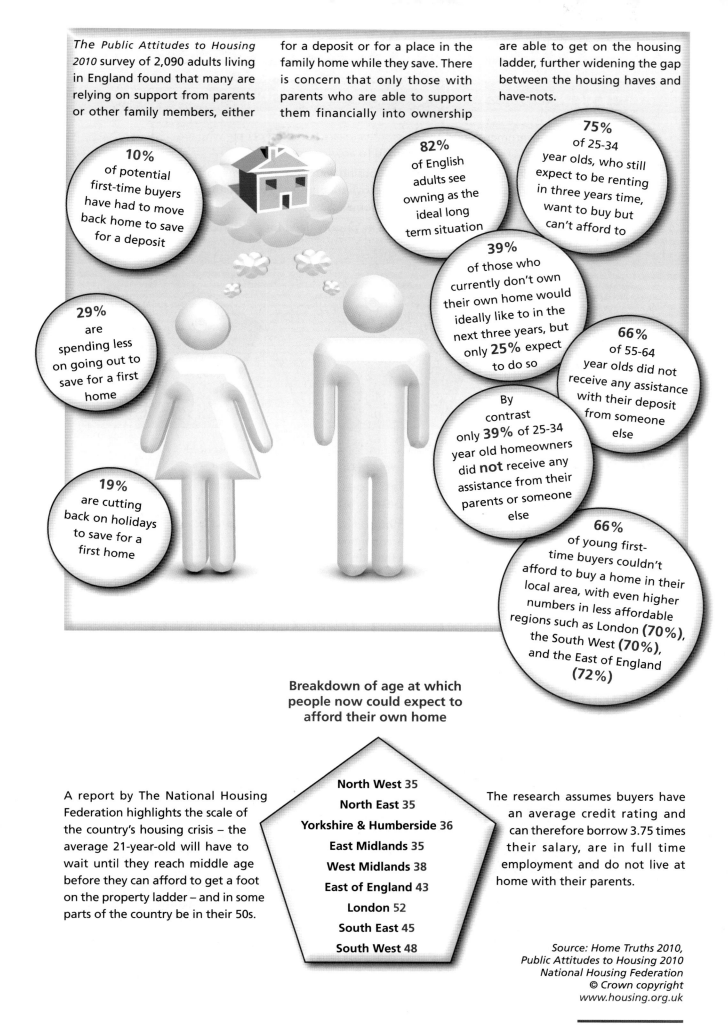

10% of potential first-time buyers have had to move back home to save for a deposit

82% of English adults see owning as the ideal long term situation

75% of 25-34 year olds, who still expect to be renting in three years time, want to buy but can't afford to

39% of those who currently don't own their own home would ideally like to in the next three years, but only **25%** expect to do so

29% are spending less on going out to save for a first home

66% of 55-64 year olds did not receive any assistance with their deposit from someone else

By contrast only **39%** of 25-34 year old homeowners did **not** receive any assistance from their parents or someone else

19% are cutting back on holidays to save for a first home

66% of young first-time buyers couldn't afford to buy a home in their local area, with even higher numbers in less affordable regions such as London (**70%**), the South West (**70%**), and the East of England (**72%**)

Breakdown of age at which people now could expect to afford their own home

A report by The National Housing Federation highlights the scale of the country's housing crisis – the average 21-year-old will have to wait until they reach middle age before they can afford to get a foot on the property ladder – and in some parts of the country be in their 50s.

North West 35
North East 35
Yorkshire & Humberside 36
East Midlands 35
West Midlands 38
East of England 43
London 52
South East 45
South West 48

The research assumes buyers have an average credit rating and can therefore borrow 3.75 times their salary, are in full time employment and do not live at home with their parents.

Source: Home Truths 2010, Public Attitudes to Housing 2010 National Housing Federation © Crown copyright www.housing.org.uk

Hidden homeless

Many people who apply for homelessness help aren't accepted

The Government's homelessness statistics are based on people who are accepted as entitled to accommodation.

To be eligible for local authority housing you must have some sort of connection to the local area and to prove that it is not your fault that you became homeless.

You then need to prove that you are in 'priority need for accommodation'.

England
In 2008/09 almost **113,000** households made a homelessness application. **47%** were accepted as entitled to housing.

Wales
In 2009/10 nearly **13,000** households applied for homelessness assistance. **49%** were accepted.

Scotland
In 2008/09, more than **57,000** households made an application for homelessness assistance. **71%** were accepted.

Most acceptances in all three countries were because the household included a pregnant woman or a dependent child.

Being accepted as homeless does not necessarily lead to getting a permanent home.

There are currently **over 50,000** households, mainly families, living in temporary accommodation in **England**, **2,500** households in **Wales** and **over 10,000** households in **Scotland**.

Households accepted by local authorities as owed a main homelessness duty, England
(2009/10 figures are provisional)

■ Number ——●—— Rate per 1,000 households

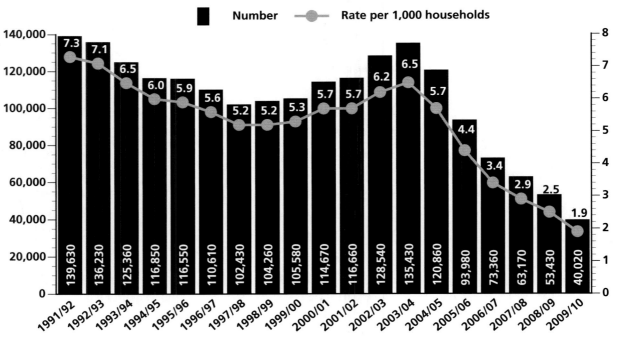

Year	Number	Rate per 1,000 households
1991/92	139,630	7.3
1992/93	136,230	7.1
1993/94	125,360	6.5
1994/95	116,850	6.0
1995/96	116,550	5.9
1996/97	110,610	5.6
1997/98	102,430	5.2
1998/99	104,260	5.2
1999/00	105,580	5.3
2000/01	114,670	5.7
2001/02	116,660	5.7
2002/03	128,540	6.2
2003/04	135,430	6.5
2004/05	120,860	5.7
2005/06	93,980	4.4
2006/07	73,360	3.4
2007/08	63,170	2.9
2008/09	53,430	2.5
2009/10	40,020	1.9

The majority of homeless people exist out of sight and are not included in official figures. The **'hidden homeless'** are those who have no accommodation or no reasonable place to stay and who have not been housed because they have not applied or because they are not counted as being 'in priority need'.

The hidden homeless include:

Rough sleepers

Bed and Breakfasts: People living in temporary boarded accommodation because they have no other option.

Hostels, night shelters or refuges: People usually only live here because they have nowhere else to live.

People living in severe overcrowding

People due for discharge from institutions – prison, hospital, etc who have no accommodation to go to.

Overcrowding in concealed households – people who are living with friends or family and where the housing is overcrowded – for example, this might mean always sleeping on the sofa.

Owner dissatisfaction in a concealed household – people who are living with friends or family but the owner or renter is unhappy with the situation.

People at risk of eviction with nowhere else to live.

Involuntary Squatting: those who have no right to stay in their accommodation but have nowhere else to go.

The charity Crisis estimates that there about **400,000** hidden homeless people in Great Britain at any one time and that about **60,000** young people aged 16-24 are living in concealed households – that is they are living within someone else's home but want a place of their own.

The largest proportion of people accepted for rehousing have become homeless because they can no longer stay with friends or relatives.

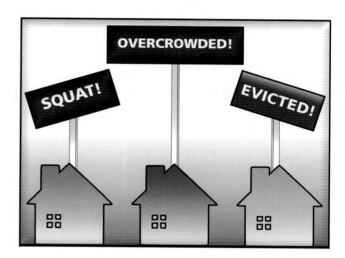

Why people accepted as homeless had lost their last home, England, 2009

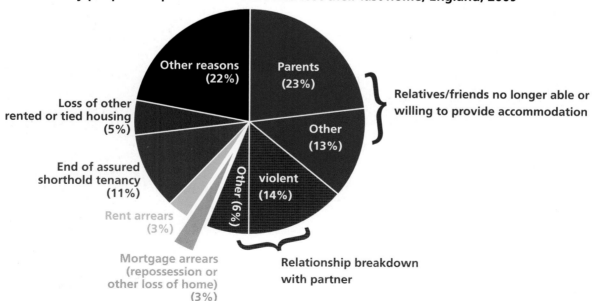

Other reasons (22%)

Parents (23%)

Loss of other rented or tied housing (5%)

Other (13%)

} Relatives/friends no longer able or willing to provide accommodation

End of assured shorthold tenancy (11%)

Other (6%)

violent (14%)

Rent arrears (3%)

Mortgage arrears (repossession or other loss of home) (3%)

} Relationship breakdown with partner

Source: Communities and Local Government © Crown copyright 2010, Crisis, Homeless Link

www.communities.gov.uk
www.crisis.org.uk
http://homeless.org.uk/facts

Internet & technology

Google earth

Where the world's internet users live

Top 20 countries with the highest number of internet users % of world users (% of that country's population in brackets) 2009

China 20.8% (26.9%)

US 13.1% (74.1%)

Japan 5.5% (75.5%)

India 4.7% (7.0%)

Brazil 3.9% (34.0%)

Germany 3.1% (65.9%)

Iran 1.9% (48.5%)

Italy 1.7% (51.7%)

UK 2.7% (76.4%)

Indonesia 1.7% (12.5%)

Russia 2.6% (32.3%)

Spain 1.7% (71.8%)

France 2.5% (69.3%)

South Korea 2.2% (77.3%)

Mexico 1.6% (24.8%)

Turkey 1.5% (34.5%)

Canada 1.4% (74.9%)

Philippines 1.4% (24.5%)

Vietnam 1.3% (24.8%)

Poland 1.2% (52.0%)

The top 20 countries make up 76.4% of the world total

Source: Internet World Stats

www.internetworldstats.com/top20.htm

Freedom on the net

Threats to internet freedom are growing

News and information can now flow around the world almost instantly thanks to the internet and other new media. It means millions of people are sharing opinions on a vast number of cultural, social and political issues.

However, some governments have tried to control and censor the content of blogs, websites and text messages.

The **Freedom on the Net Index** looks at internet and mobile phone freedom in a sample of 15 countries using three categories:

Obstacles to access:

Government blocks; problems with access caused by lack of systems, technology or lack of money; control of systems by owners or through laws.

Limits on content:

Filtering and blocking of some websites; censorship; controlling the content of websites; controlling online news from different groups; controlling use of the media for political or social purposes.

Violation of user rights:

includes legal protections and restrictions on online activity; surveillance and privacy violations; and repercussions for online activity, such as prosecution, imprisonment, physical attacks, and other forms of harassment.

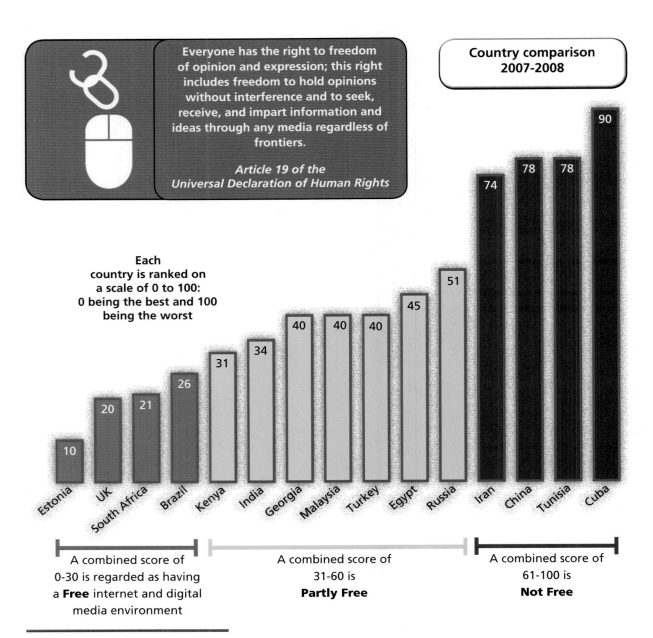

Everyone has the right to freedom of opinion and expression; this right includes freedom to hold opinions without interference and to seek, receive, and impart information and ideas through any media regardless of frontiers.

Article 19 of the
Universal Declaration of Human Rights

Country comparison 2007-2008

Each country is ranked on a scale of 0 to 100: 0 being the best and 100 being the worst

Country	Score
Estonia	10
UK	20
South Africa	21
Brazil	26
Kenya	31
India	34
Georgia	40
Malaysia	40
Turkey	40
Egypt	45
Russia	51
Iran	74
China	78
Tunisia	78
Cuba	90

A combined score of 0-30 is regarded as having a **Free** internet and digital media environment

A combined score of 31-60 is **Partly Free**

A combined score of 61-100 is **Not Free**

Country comparison: How the overall scores break down	Obstacles to access (Score 0-25)	Limits on content (Score 0-35)	Violation of user rights (Score 0-40)
Estonia	2	2	6
UK	0	6	14
South Africa	6	7	8
Brazil	5	8	13
Kenya	10	12	9
India	11	8	15
Georgia	13	15	12
Malaysia	8	12	20
Turkey	11	13	16
Egypt	8	11	26
Russia	11	17	23
Iran	19	24	31
China	18	27	33
Tunisia	20	27	31
Cuba	25	32	33

Estonia

Ranks among the most technologically advanced countries in the world. Limits on internet content and communication are among the lowest in the world. Freedom of speech and expression are strongly protected.

UK

While access to online content is extensive and free of significant barriers in the **UK**, some restrictions exist on terrorism-related content.

British law does not provide for blocking or filtering websites, blogs etc. Censorship systems focus on extreme pornography, racial hatred and material that is harmful to children. However, freedom of expression has been threatened by our libel* laws which would allow anyone in the world to sue for libel in a British court provided the material had been seen in Britain. This has led to people not writing about things in case they're sued.

Cuba

Cuba remains one of the world's most repressive digital environments despite the loosening of restrictions on the sale of computers and mobile phones in 2008. There is almost no access to internet applications other than email. Surveillance is extensive.

Cuban authorities rely heavily on lack of technology and prohibitive costs to limit users' access to information.

* libel is a published false statement that is damaging to someone's reputation.

STOP PRESS:

Google has stopped censoring its search results in China, ignoring warnings by the country's authorities. Google said its Chinese users would be redirected to the uncensored pages of its Hong Kong website.

BBC 23/3/10

For more information on individual countries see:
Freedom House – Freedom on the Net: A Global Assessment of Internet and Digital Media, 2009; Logo courtesy of Reporters without borders

www.freedomhouse.org
www.rsf.org

Digital world

Most internet growth is coming from the developing world

Estimated internet users
(millions)

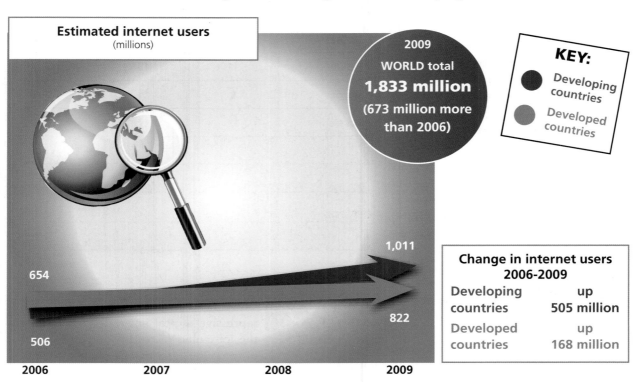

2009
WORLD total
1,833 million
(673 million more
than 2006)

KEY:
- Developing countries
- Developed countries

654

1,011

506

822

2006   2007   2008   2009

Change in internet users 2006-2009

Developing countries	up	505 million
Developed countries	up	168 million

Estimated internet users per 100 inhabitants, 2009

Developing countries	18.0
Developed countries	66.6

World estimated internet users per 100 inhabitants

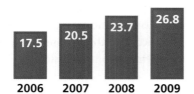

17.5	20.5	23.7	26.8
2006	2007	2008	2009

World internet usage, by region
% growth 2000-2009

Region	% growth
Africa	1,809.8%
Asia	568.8%
Europe	305.1%
Middle East	1,675.1%
North America	140.1%
Latin America/Caribbean	934.5%
Oceania/Australia	177.0%
WORLD TOTAL	**399.3%**

Source: Internet World Stats
http://www.internetworldstats.com

Fixed broadband internet prices are dropping sharply, but remain unaffordable in many developing countries

Broadband access remains the single most expensive and least affordable service in the developing world.

At less than **2%** of average monthly income, Europe has by far the cheapest fixed broadband services.

The affordability of services is crucial to building an inclusive information society.

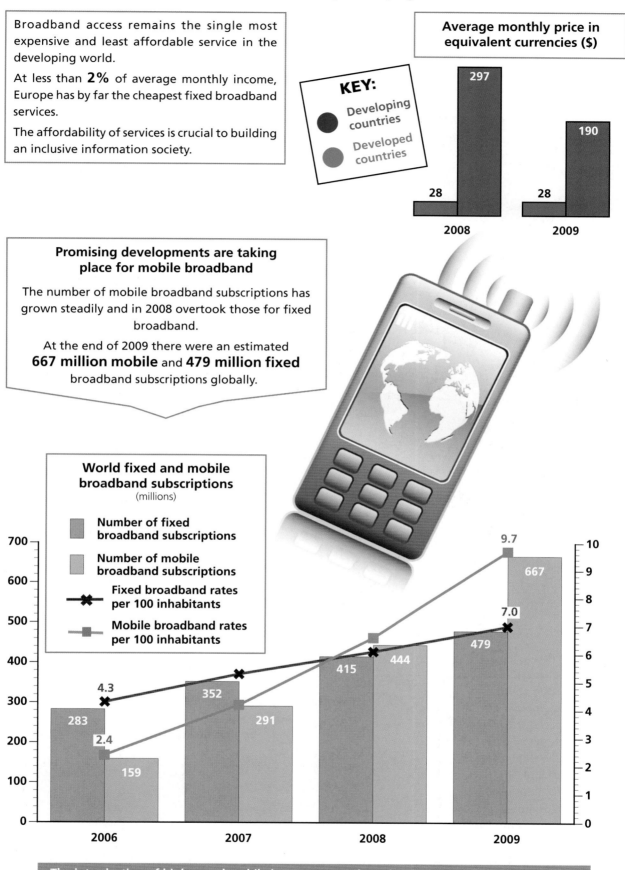

Average monthly price in equivalent currencies ($)

KEY:
- Developing countries
- Developed countries

	2008	2009
Developing	297	190
Developed	28	28

Promising developments are taking place for mobile broadband

The number of mobile broadband subscriptions has grown steadily and in 2008 overtook those for fixed broadband.

At the end of 2009 there were an estimated **667 million mobile** and **479 million fixed** broadband subscriptions globally.

World fixed and mobile broadband subscriptions
(millions)

- Number of fixed broadband subscriptions
- Number of mobile broadband subscriptions
- Fixed broadband rates per 100 inhabitants
- Mobile broadband rates per 100 inhabitants

Year	Fixed subscriptions	Mobile subscriptions	Fixed rate	Mobile rate
2006	283	159	4.3	2.4
2007	352	291		
2008	415	444		
2009	479	667	7.0	9.7

The introduction of high-speed mobile internet access in an increasing number of countries will further boost the number of internet users, particularly in the developing world.

Source: International Telecommunication Union
www.itu.int

Access all areas

In 2010, 19.2 million households in the UK had internet access

...this represented **73%** of households and an increase
of **0.9 million households** since 2009

In 2010 **38.3 million adults** – **77%** of the UK adult population – accessed the internet in the three months prior to interview.
Over **9 million (18%)** of adults had **never** accessed the internet, down from **10.2 million** in 2009.

There were **7 million** households without Internet access in 2010 – **39%** of adults said that they didn't need the internet; **21%** said a lack of skills prevented them from having it; **18%** said equipment costs were too high.

The proportion of households able to access the internet varied between UK regions.
The **highest** level of internet access was in London – **83%**, and the **lowest** was in the North East – **59%**.

The mobile phone was the most popular device used to access the Internet wirelessly, away from the home or workplace, with **31%** of internet users connecting this way. The adoption of mobile phone technology is being led by 16 to 24-year-old internet users, **44%** of them use a mobile phone to access the internet.

Percentage who use the internet every day
or almost every day
by age group

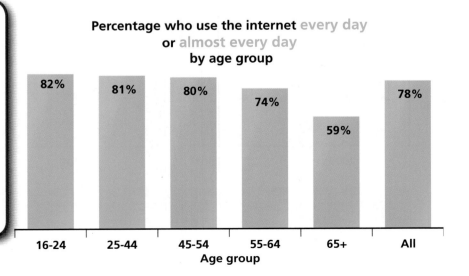

Age group					
16-24	25-44	45-54	55-64	65+	All
82%	81%	80%	74%	59%	78%

Where adults have accessed the internet from

(all UK adults who accessed the internet in the last three months)

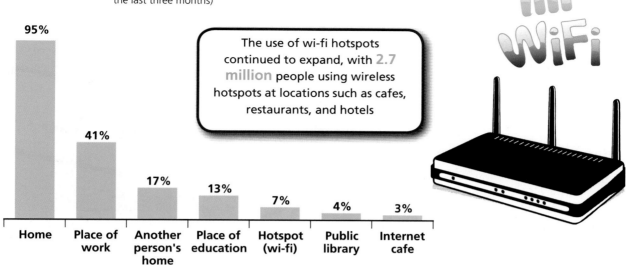

The use of wi-fi hotspots continued to expand, with **2.7 million** people using wireless hotspots at locations such as cafes, restaurants, and hotels

Home	95%
Place of work	41%
Another person's home	17%
Place of education	13%
Hotspot (wi-fi)	7%
Public library	4%
Internet cafe	3%

What the internet is used for

(all UK adults who accessed the internet in the last three months)

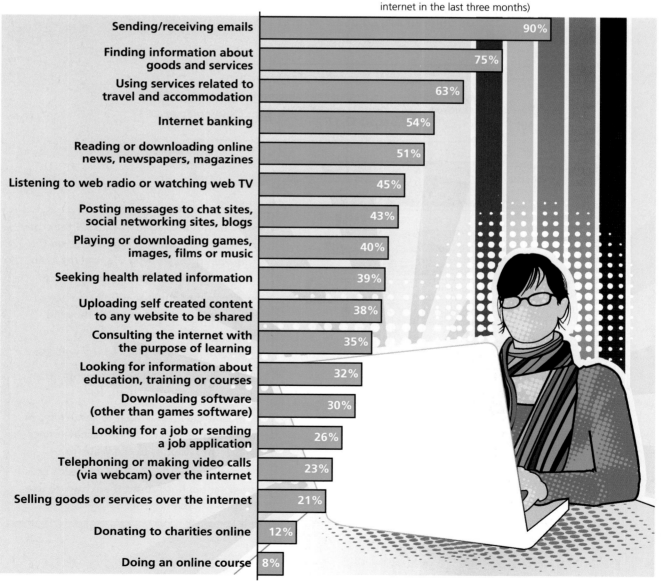

Sending/receiving emails	90%
Finding information about goods and services	75%
Using services related to travel and accommodation	63%
Internet banking	54%
Reading or downloading online news, newspapers, magazines	51%
Listening to web radio or watching web TV	45%
Posting messages to chat sites, social networking sites, blogs	43%
Playing or downloading games, images, films or music	40%
Seeking health related information	39%
Uploading self created content to any website to be shared	38%
Consulting the internet with the purpose of learning	35%
Looking for information about education, training or courses	32%
Downloading software (other than games software)	30%
Looking for a job or sending a job application	26%
Telephoning or making video calls (via webcam) over the internet	23%
Selling goods or services over the internet	21%
Donating to charities online	12%
Doing an online course	8%

Source: Office for National Statistics – Internet Access Households and Individuals © Crown copyright 2010

www.ons.gov.uk

Click clever click safe

95% of young people aged 12-17 said that their parents trusted them to use the internet safely...

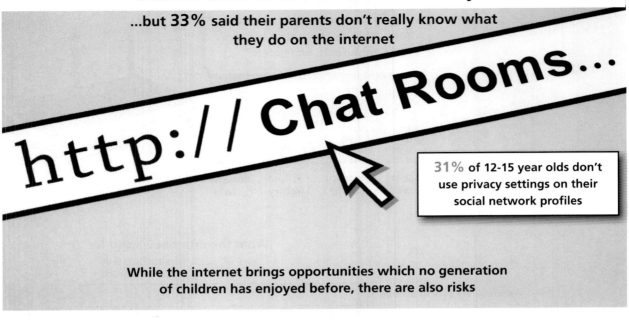

...but **33%** said their parents don't really know what they do on the internet

http:// Chat Rooms...

31% of 12-15 year olds don't use privacy settings on their social network profiles

While the internet brings opportunities which no generation of children has enjoyed before, there are also risks

Specific internet safety concerns

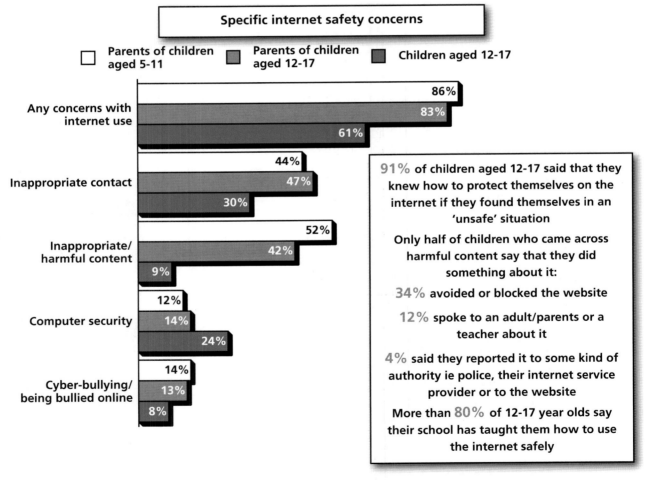

☐ Parents of children aged 5-11   ▨ Parents of children aged 12-17   ■ Children aged 12-17

Any concerns with internet use
- 86%
- 83%
- 61%

Inappropriate contact
- 44%
- 47%
- 30%

Inappropriate/harmful content
- 52%
- 42%
- 9%

Computer security
- 12%
- 14%
- 24%

Cyber-bullying/being bullied online
- 14%
- 13%
- 8%

91% of children aged 12-17 said that they knew how to protect themselves on the internet if they found themselves in an 'unsafe' situation

Only half of children who came across harmful content say that they did something about it:

34% avoided or blocked the website

12% spoke to an adult/parents or a teacher about it

4% said they reported it to some kind of authority ie police, their internet service provider or to the website

More than **80%** of 12-17 year olds say their school has taught them how to use the internet safely

Base: 1,076 parents of children/young people aged 5-17 and 833 children/young people aged 12-17 across the UK

Source: Staying Safe Survey 2009; Click Clever Click Safe – The UK Council for Child Internet Safety, Department for Education © Crown copyright
www.education.gov.uk

Living in a virtual community makes young people feel pressure to make personal information easily available

http:// Safe Place...

% agreeing to the following statements

Statement	%
On the internet you can never know if someone is who they say they are	77%
I think the internet is a safe place as long as you know what you are doing	76%
I often do my own research to see whether advice I have been given online is correct	71%
I feel more comfortable doing things online than I did a year ago	63%
I am wary of the information I find online	58%
I trust the opinions of people who give me advice on online forums and discussion boards	48%
I think buying things over the internet is more risky than buying them in the shops	45%
I would be happy to meet someone I had spoken to online in real life	44%
I know someone who has been the victim of an online scam	43%
I am concerned about coming across inappropriate websites by accident	42%
I never check who is behind a website or whether it has the correct accreditation	39%
I have good friends online who I have never met in real life	38%
I have been approached online by a person pretending to be someone else	31%

Young people are confident, yet cautious online...

...to a great extent they have the ability to see through posted information. They are well aware that people's profiles can just be a front.

The new 'Green Cross Code' for internet safety:

ZIP IT

Keep your personal stuff private and think about what you say and do online

BLOCK IT

Block people who send nasty messages and don't open unknown links and attachments

FLAG IT

Flag up with someone you trust if anything upsets you or if someone asks to meet you offline

clickcleverclicksafe.direct.gov.uk

Base: 994 young people in the UK aged 16-24

Source: Life support: Young people's lives in a digital age – Youthnet
www.youthnet.org

Life support

Q **Have you ever used the internet to...**

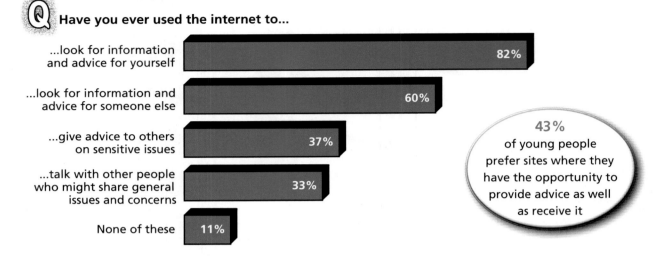

...look for information and advice for yourself **82%**

...look for information and advice for someone else **60%**

...give advice to others on sensitive issues **37%**

...talk with other people who might share general issues and concerns **33%**

None of these **11%**

43% of young people prefer sites where they have the opportunity to provide advice as well as receive it

Go http://www.

71% wanted as many opinions as possible but **53%** stated:

"there is so much information out there that it is impossible to know what is good advice and what isn't"

Q **If you had a problem that was worrying you, which of the following would make you look for advice on the internet rather than speaking to someone face-to-face?**

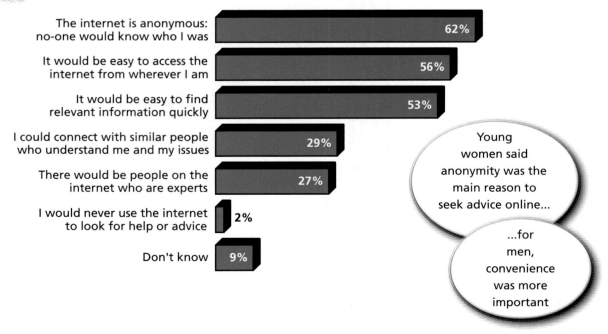

The internet is anonymous: no-one would know who I was **62%**

It would be easy to access the internet from wherever I am **56%**

It would be easy to find relevant information quickly **53%**

I could connect with similar people who understand me and my issues **29%**

There would be people on the internet who are experts **27%**

I would never use the internet to look for help or advice **2%**

Don't know **9%**

Young women said anonymity was the main reason to seek advice online...

...for men, convenience was more important

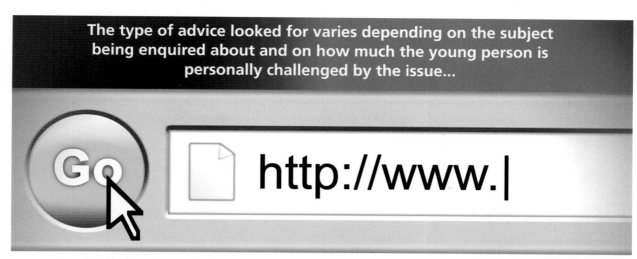

The type of advice looked for varies depending on the subject being enquired about and on how much the young person is personally challenged by the issue...

http://www.|

Go

...but the internet – including online forums/discussion groups and online help-sites – ranks in the top three **first sources of advice across all issues**

 Which one source of advice would you turn to first for information or advice about very sensitive concerns? (Top three answers)

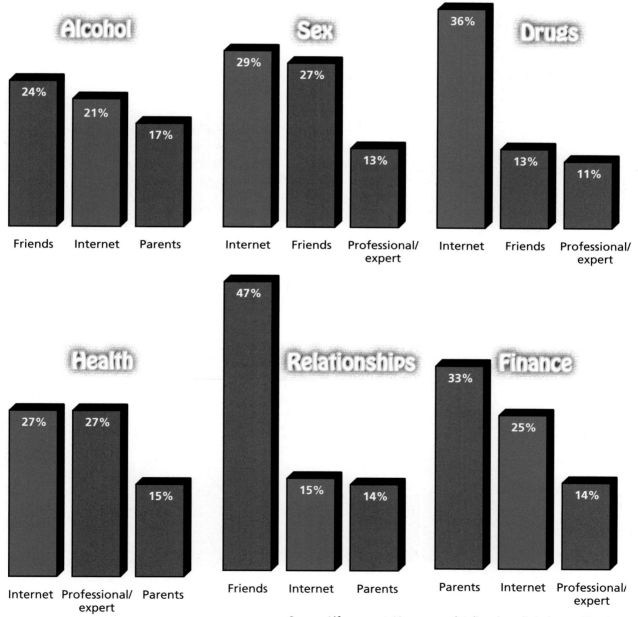

Alcohol
- Friends 24%
- Internet 21%
- Parents 17%

Sex
- Internet 29%
- Friends 27%
- Professional/expert 13%

Drugs
- Internet 36%
- Friends 13%
- Professional/expert 11%

Health
- Internet 27%
- Professional/expert 27%
- Parents 15%

Relationships
- Friends 47%
- Internet 15%
- Parents 14%

Finance
- Parents 33%
- Internet 25%
- Professional/expert 14%

Base: 994 young people in the UK aged 16-24

Source: Life support: Young people's lives in a digital age – Youthnet
www.youthnet.org

The writing's on the wall

49% of young people agree that writing is boring...

...but technology offers different writing opportunities

Over 3,000 pupils aged 9 to 16 from England and Scotland completed an online survey about their attitudes to writing – the key results showed that:

Most said they used computers regularly and believed that computers were helpful for their writing – overall nearly **60%** believe that computers allow them to be more creative, concentrate more and encourage them to write more often

56% of young people said they have a profile on a **social network site** **24%** said that they have their own **blog**

33% of girls but only **18%** of boys have a blog

Blog owners and social network site users had a more positive attitude to writing than those who didn't

Girls wrote in a greater range of formats than boys

Young people who do not own a blog were significantly more likely than blog owners to agree that writing is boring

75% of young people said they write regularly using technology eg **82%** wrote text messages, **73%** wrote instant messages such as MSN and **63%** wrote on a social network site

Writing for fun or family/friends **49.6%** of young people said that they use a computer **every day** and **22.2%** use it **2-3** times a week

Writing for schoolwork **18%** use a computer **every day** and **27%** use it **2 -3** times a week

For the full results see:
Young people's writing: Attitudes, behaviour and the role of technology, National Literacy Trust, 2009

www.literacytrust.org.uk

Online time

The average surfer spends almost a day a month online

Britons spent **65%** more time online in April 2010 than they did in April 2007 – **884 million hours** compared to **536 million hours**. The average time spent online each month is **22 hours and 15 minutes**. The way in which this time has been allocated across different sectors has changed dramatically.

In April 2007, Social Networks and blogs accounted for **less than 9%** of all UK internet time, but this has grown to almost **23%**.

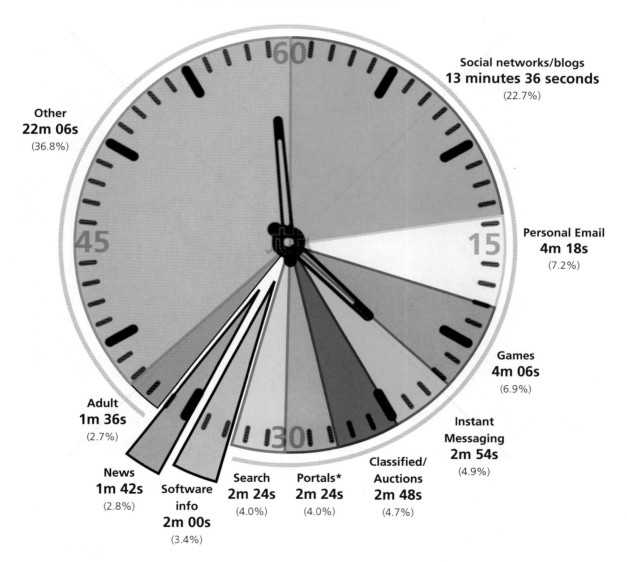

If all April 2010 UK Internet time was condensed into one hour, how would we spend that time?
(% share of UK internet time shown in brackets)

Social networks/blogs
13 minutes 36 seconds
(22.7%)

Other
22m 06s
(36.8%)

Personal Email
4m 18s
(7.2%)

Games
4m 06s
(6.9%)

Instant Messaging
2m 54s
(4.9%)

Adult
1m 36s
(2.7%)

News
1m 42s
(2.8%)

Software info
2m 00s
(3.4%)

Search
2m 24s
(4.0%)

Portals*
2m 24s
(4.0%)

Classified/ Auctions
2m 48s
(4.7%)

Instant Messaging was the most heavily used sector in 2007 but the rise in social networking has meant its share of UK internet time has fallen from 14% to 5%.

But personal email actually increased its share of online time. Britons spend **88% more** time on email sites than they did in 2007.

* such as Yahoo! and MSN
NB % do not add up to 100% due to rounding

Source: UKOM – UK Online Measurement Company
www.ukom.uk.net

Law & order

Police record

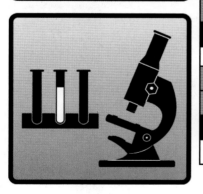

...but this may not be the full picture

Crimes recorded by the police in 2009/10

Offence group	Number of crimes in 000s	Percentage
Violence against the person	**8,871.7**	
with injury	*401.7*	20%
without injury	*470.0*	
Sexual offences	**54.5**	
most serious sexual crime	*43.6*	1%
other sexual offences	*10.9*	
Robbery offences	**75.1**	
of business property	*8.2*	2%
of personal property	*66.9*	
Burglary offences	**540.7**	
in a dwelling	*268.6*	12%
in a building other than a dwelling	*272.1*	
Offences against vehicles	**495**	11%
Other theft offences	**1,037.5**	
of which: theft from the person	*92.3*	24%
of which: taking of a pedal cycle	*109.9*	
Fraud and forgery offences	**152.3**	4%
Criminal damage offences	**806.7**	19%
TOTAL PROPERTY CRIME	**3,032.2**	
Drug offences	**235.0**	5%
Miscellaneous other offences	**70.1**	2%
TOTAL RECORDED CRIME – ALL OFFENCES	**4,338.6**	
of which: firearm offences	*8.0*	

Police recorded crime statistics are based on crimes reported to and recorded by the police and cover crimes against **individuals** and both **domestic and commercial property** and so-called **victimless crimes** (such as drug possession offences).

This isn't the only way that crime is recorded, see page 140, Crime survey, for a different way of presenting information about crime.

While police recorded crime has a wide coverage of offences and covers the entire population, it does not include those crimes **not** reported to the police.

Source: Home Office – Crime in England and Wales 2009/10 © Crown Copyright 2010
www.homeoffice.gov.uk

Unacceptable activity

Anti-social behaviour can ruin lives but do the police take it seriously?

The public see anti-social behaviour as blighting their neighbourhoods and leading to the decline of whole areas. It also influences the way people perceive the police – sometimes seeing them as ineffectual or unconcerned.

Anti-social behaviour (ASB) is a mixed bag of crime, disorder, and the activity that leads up to it, with rowdy/disorderly behaviour being the overwhelming majority of reported events – there were **2.1 million calls** to police in 2009-10.

The public do not see a difference between **crime** and **ASB** – they class both as bad or very bad behaviour. However, for some people in policing and some outside, dealing with issues that qualify as **crime** is **'real police work'**, but the **ASB** issue has now grown and evolved in intensity and harm.

Over recent years failure to tackle anti-social behaviour has led to tragic consequences in cases such as the murder of Garry Newlove, the suicide/murder of Fiona Pilkington and her daughter Francecca, who were harassed over 10 years, and the heart attack suffered by David Askew after years of bullying.

The most common forms of anti-social behaviour mentioned by respondents

Type	%
Problems relating to drunken behaviour and under age drinking	30%
Youths loitering in groups or gangs on the streets	29%
Vandalism and graffiti	25%
Rowdy or inconsiderate behaviour	23%
Noise and loud music	21%
Using/dealing drugs	13%
Intimidation/threats/harassment	11%
Verbal abuse/abusive behaviour	11%
Assault/violence/fighting	10%
Nuisance neighbours	10%

NB Because more than one type of anti-social behaviour can be mentioned, figures add up to more than 100%

Respondents were asked who they felt was responsible for dealing with anti-social behaviour in their local area
(Respondents could give more than one answer – Top ten mentions)

90% Police

36% Local council

16% Parents/family

15% Community as a whole

8% People themselves/individuals

7% Everyone

5% Housing association/ social landlord

4% Police Community Support Officer/ Community Support Officer

4% The government

4% Schools

Respondents were asked what action the police took
Base: All who said that the police took action
as a result of their call (2,129)

Attended the scene **56%**

Dispersed/separated the perpetrators **13%**

Stopped the noise/disruption **13%**

Came to see me **12%**

Made an arrest(s) **11%**

Cautioned the perpetrators **11%**

Spoke to me/reassured me over the phone **6%**

Got other public services/ agencies involved **4%**

Spoke to the offenders **3%**

Warning letter issued **3%**

> The police's role is seen to be multi-faceted: acting as a deterrent, responding to and dealing with incidents, and helping to foster positive relations within communities

41% of respondents said that they were told that the police **would** take action as a result of their call. This compares to **15%** who were told the police **would not** take any action.

When asked whether the police did eventually take action, **39%** said they are aware of **action** that the police took in response to their call. Equally, **39%** said the police ended up taking **no action**, while **22% did not know**.

See also Essential Articles 11 page 142 *Our criminal system is a persistent re-offender* which discusses the murder of Garry Newlove by three teenagers and raises questions about our criminal justice system

The number of police forces that have ASB as a force priority has grown from **20** in January 2010 to **all 43** in September 2010

Base: 5,699 telephone interviews were conducted in May-June 2010 with a random selection of people in England who had contacted the police to report anti-social behaviour during September 2009

Source: Ipsos MORI for HMIC – Policing anti-social behaviour: The public's perspective, HMIC – Anti-social behaviour: Stop the Rot
www.hmic.gov.uk

Cashpoint peril

As the number of cash machines increases, so does crime

Number of cash machines (ATMs) in Europe, by country
(as at 30/12/09)

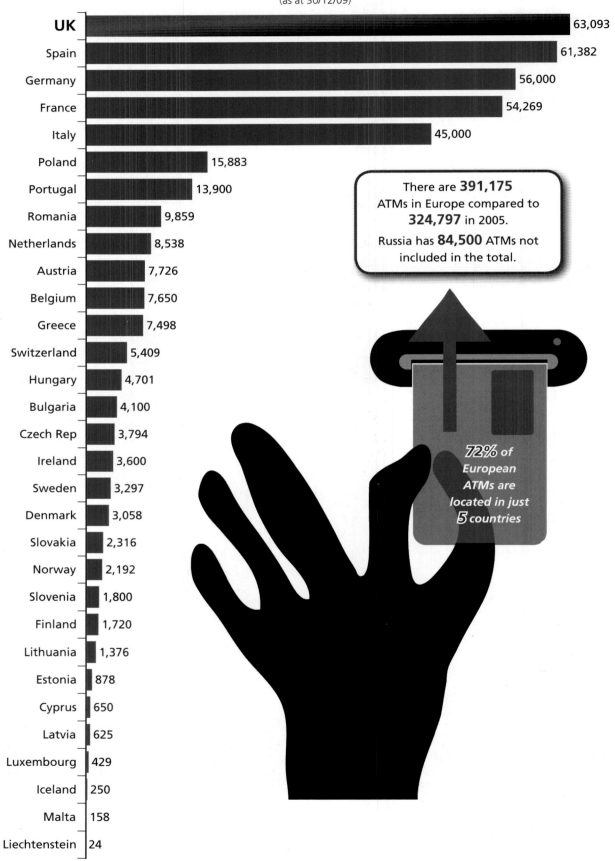

Country	Number
UK	63,093
Spain	61,382
Germany	56,000
France	54,269
Italy	45,000
Poland	15,883
Portugal	13,900
Romania	9,859
Netherlands	8,538
Austria	7,726
Belgium	7,650
Greece	7,498
Switzerland	5,409
Hungary	4,701
Bulgaria	4,100
Czech Rep	3,794
Ireland	3,600
Sweden	3,297
Denmark	3,058
Slovakia	2,316
Norway	2,192
Slovenia	1,800
Finland	1,720
Lithuania	1,376
Estonia	878
Cyprus	650
Latvia	625
Luxembourg	429
Iceland	250
Malta	158
Liechtenstein	24

There are **391,175** ATMs in Europe compared to **324,797** in 2005.

Russia has **84,500** ATMs not included in the total.

72% of European ATMs are located in just 5 countries

Although European ATM fraud losses are down 36%, overall ATM related fraud attacks rose 8% in 2009

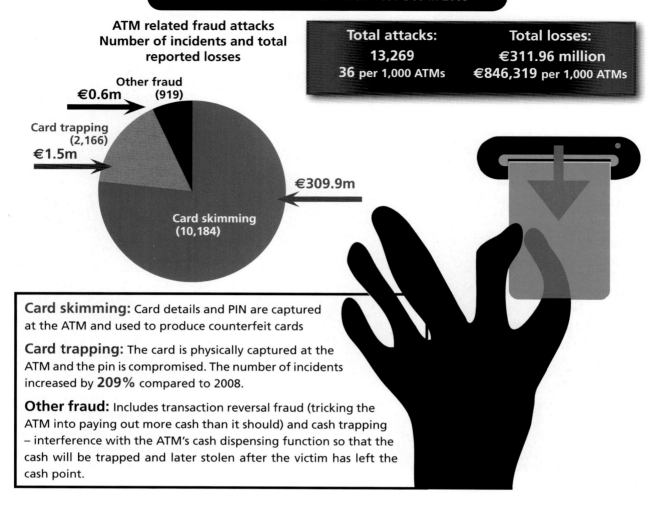

ATM related fraud attacks
Number of incidents and total reported losses

Total attacks:
13,269
36 per 1,000 ATMs

Total losses:
€311.96 million
€846,319 per 1,000 ATMs

Other fraud
(919)
€0.6m

Card trapping
(2,166)
€1.5m

€309.9m

Card skimming
(10,184)

Card skimming: Card details and PIN are captured at the ATM and used to produce counterfeit cards

Card trapping: The card is physically captured at the ATM and the pin is compromised. The number of incidents increased by **209%** compared to 2008.

Other fraud: Includes transaction reversal fraud (tricking the ATM into paying out more cash than it should) and cash trapping – interference with the ATM's cash dispensing function so that the cash will be trapped and later stolen after the victim has left the cash point.

Ram Raids/ATM burglary:
The ATM is attacked and ripped out/the safe is attacked in place. The attacks can be carried out by brute force or by using explosive or gas. Explosive/gas attacks have increased by **26%** compared to 2008.

Robbery: The people re-stocking the ATMs are attacked in their duties or when moving the cash.

Other:
Robbery (other than during cash re-stocking), vandalism or cash trapping.

ATM related physical attacks
Number of incidents and total reported losses

€3.4m
Other
(569)

€9.6m
Robbery
(510)

Estimated cash loss: €19,744 per incident

Ram Raids/
ATM
burglary
(1,389)

€17.7m

Estimated cash loss: €13,213 per incident

Total attacks:
2,468
6.7 per 1,000 ATMs

Total losses:
€27.62 million
€74,948 per 1,000 ATMs

NB Ram raids/ATM burglary does not take into account damage to equipment or property, which can be significant

Source: European ATM Security Team (EAST), European Payments Council (EPC)

www.european-atm-security.eu

Anonymous attacker

Identity fraud costs the UK economy more than £1 billion every year and is one of the fastest growing crimes

IDENTITY FRAUD

Someone uses your identity to commit a crime, by applying for credit, goods or services in your name (impersonation) OR by fraudulently using (taking over) your existing accounts.

In order to do this fraudsters often first commit ...

IDENTITY THEFT

Someone obtains your personal information without your permission

Proven instances of fraud identified by the UK Fraud Prevention Service (CIFAS) and % change on 2008

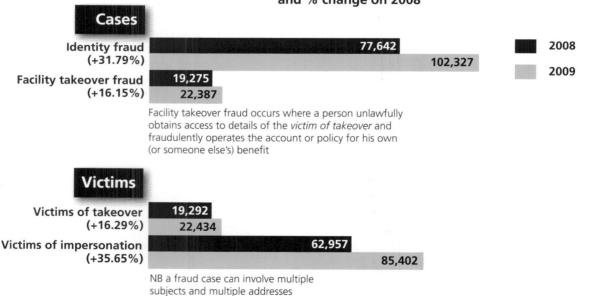

Cases

Identity fraud (+31.79%)
77,642 — 2008
102,327 — 2009

Facility takeover fraud (+16.15%)
19,275
22,387

2008
2009

Facility takeover fraud occurs where a person unlawfully obtains access to details of the *victim of takeover* and fraudulently operates the account or policy for his own (or someone else's) benefit

Victims

Victims of takeover (+16.29%)
19,292
22,434

Victims of impersonation (+35.65%)
62,957
85,402

NB a fraud case can involve multiple subjects and multiple addresses

> **The identity thief may be anonymous – but they are real and they are out there: don't make yourself a target!**
>
> *Sandra Peaston, CIFAS research manager*

During the first nine months of 2009...

Victims of impersonation, by age group

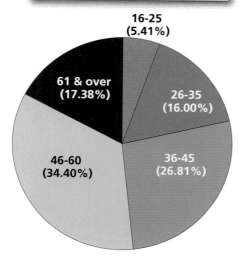

16-25 (5.41%)
26-35 (16.00%)
61 & over (17.38%)
36-45 (26.81%)
46-60 (34.40%)

Statistically, London and the South East are the hotspots for fraud

Top ten postcode areas involved in identify theft	Number of ID thefts (recorded by CIFAS members)
SE - South East London	2,680
B – Birmingham	2,111
N – North London	2,004
SW – South West London	1,905
E – East London	1,814
GU - Guildford	1,166
RG – Reading	1,148
KT – Kingston upon Thames	1,120
M – Manchester	1,103
CM – Chelmsford	1,096

Victims of impersonation, by gender

■ Male ▨ Female

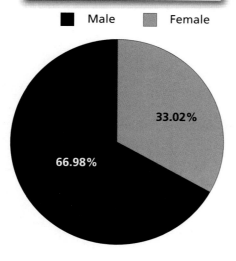

33.02%
66.98%

Number and type of accounts taken over by fraudsters

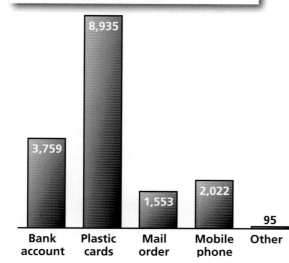

8,935
3,759
1,553
2,022
95

Bank account | Plastic cards | Mail order | Mobile phone | Other

identity theft

Don't become a victim

Criminals can find out your personal details and use them to open bank accounts and get credit cards, loans, state benefits and documents such as passports and driving licences in your name. If your identity is stolen, you may have difficulty getting graduate loans, credit cards or a mobile phone contract. To help avoid becoming a victim, visit:

www.identitytheft.org.uk

Home Office

"It has been very scary to know that someone has the majority of my personal details and will probably use them again"

Matthew Ash

*Source: The Anonymous Attacker, CIFAS –
The UK's Fraud Prevention Service 2009*

Focus on fraud

We are all victims of fraud in one way or another

The National Fraud Authority estimates that in 2008 alone, fraud cost the UK **£30.5 billion.** On average, it costs every adult member of the population **£621 per year** both through direct impacts of frauds and indirectly through taxation and increased costs of products and services.

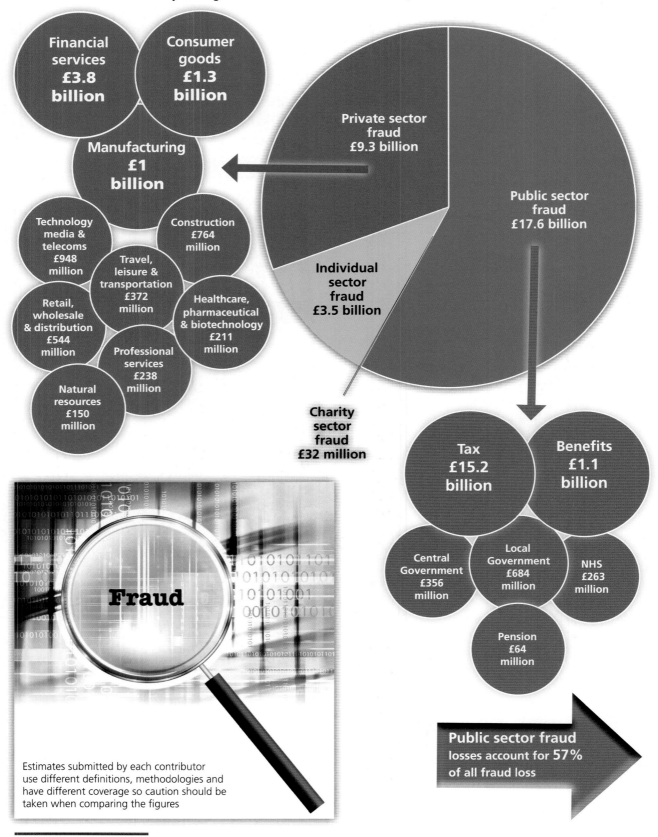

Financial services £3.8 billion

Consumer goods £1.3 billion

Manufacturing £1 billion

Technology media & telecoms £948 million

Construction £764 million

Travel, leisure & transportation £372 million

Retail, wholesale & distribution £544 million

Healthcare, pharmaceutical & biotechnology £211 million

Professional services £238 million

Natural resources £150 million

Private sector fraud £9.3 billion

Public sector fraud £17.6 billion

Individual sector fraud £3.5 billion

Charity sector fraud £32 million

Tax £15.2 billion

Benefits £1.1 billion

Central Government £356 million

Local Government £684 million

NHS £263 million

Pension £64 million

Fraud

Estimates submitted by each contributor use different definitions, methodologies and have different coverage so caution should be taken when comparing the figures

Public sector fraud losses account for 57% of all fraud loss

HM Revenue and Customs estimated the size of the UK **tax gap** (the difference between the amount of tax that is due and the amount that is collected) to be around **£40 billion** in 2007/08.

The tax gap arises from behaviours ranging from simple error to evasion: **Evasion** (including vehicle excise duty), **hidden economy** and **criminal attacks** equate to **fraud**. These fraudulent behaviours account for around **37.5%** of the tax gap – **£15 billion** for tax fraud in 2007/08.

Vehicle excise duty evasion figures are included within the tax fraud category – The Department of Transport estimate that **£79 million** of revenue was lost from unlicensed vehicles during 2007-08.

Focus on Tax Fraud

£15.2 billion

Focus on Benefit Fraud

£1.1 billion

Income support has represented the largest area of loss in previous years, however during 2008-09, housing benefit fraud **increased** by **£50 million** and is now the largest area of loss within the benefits system.

Figures may not add up to the sum due to rounding

For a full breakdown of all frauds see the Annual Fraud Indicator 2010, National Fraud Authority © Crown copyright 2010

Benefit fraud estimated losses in 2008-09

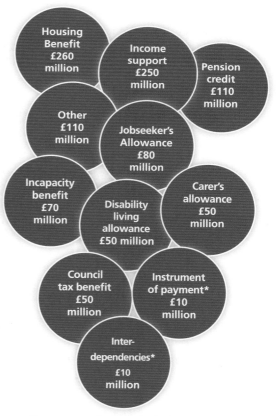

Housing Benefit £260 million

Income support £250 million

Pension credit £110 million

Other £110 million

Jobseeker's Allowance £80 million

Incapacity benefit £70 million

Disability living allowance £50 million

Carer's allowance £50 million

Council tax benefit £50 million

Instrument of payment* £10 million

Inter-dependencies* £10 million

*Instrument of payment – theft and forgery of payments such as Girocheques and benefit order books

Interdependencies – estimate of knock-on effects of overpayment of Disability Living Allowance which in turn gives access to other benefits

www.attorneygeneral.gov.uk

Crime survey

The British Crime Survey gives an insight into public attitudes to crime

The British Crime Survey (BCS) is a face-to-face victimisation survey in which people in England and Wales are asked about their experiences of crime in the 12 months prior to interview. It is based on nearly 45,000 respondents. It does not cover all offences or all population groups. For crime recorded by the police, see page 131, Police record.

British Crime Survey incidents of crime, 2009/10

- Burglary (7%)
- Vehicle-related theft (13%)
- Other thefts (33%)
- Vandalism (25%)
- All violence (incl robbery, excl sexual offences) (22%)

The BCS estimates a total of **9.6 million** offences

People in England and Wales were asked to select from a list the factors they thought were the **major** causes of crime in Britain today. If respondents selected more than one factor they were then asked which of the factors they believed to be the **main** cause of crime.

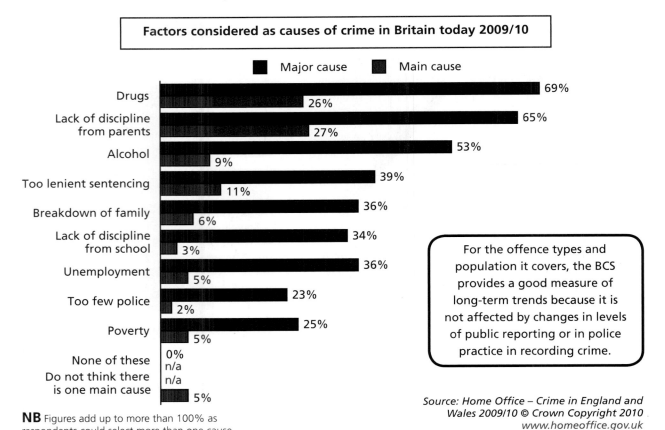

Factors considered as causes of crime in Britain today 2009/10

■ Major cause   ■ Main cause

	Major cause	Main cause
Drugs	69%	26%
Lack of discipline from parents	65%	27%
Alcohol	53%	9%
Too lenient sentencing	39%	11%
Breakdown of family	36%	6%
Lack of discipline from school	34%	3%
Unemployment	36%	5%
Too few police	23%	2%
Poverty	25%	5%
None of these	0%	n/a
Do not think there is one main cause	n/a	5%

For the offence types and population it covers, the BCS provides a good measure of long-term trends because it is not affected by changes in levels of public reporting or in police practice in recording crime.

NB Figures add up to more than 100% as respondents could select more than one cause

Source: Home Office – Crime in England and Wales 2009/10 © Crown Copyright 2010
www.homeoffice.gov.uk

Media

TV choice

How much TV do we watch? Where do we watch it? How is catch-up TV changing our viewing habits? A poll of Radio Times readers and statistics about catch-up from Ofcom tell us a lot about the British and TV...

How many? How much?

Our homes contain an average of **2.5** TV sets. People aged 18–24 own three TVs - more than any other age group. The average time spent watching TV each week is **19.58** hours. Contrary to what we might think, students watch on average **13.58** hours a week – **6** hours less than non-students.

What and where?

The digital revolution continues, with nearly half (**47%**) of us now with Freeview in our homes, while a total of **57%** pay for the two main subscription TV providers, Sky and Virgin.

Almost everyone (**93%**) spends time watching TV in their living rooms – but **43%** of us like to curl up in our bedrooms to watch, too.

Digital recording

More of us are 'time-shifting' our TV viewing – moving programmes to a time that suits us – especially with DVRs (Digital Video Recorders such as Sky+). The percentage of all TV viewing that was time-shifted through a recording device more than tripled between 2006 and 2009, from **1.7%** to **5.9%** People with a DVR record a higher proportion of their viewing – **15.1%**. But this is not the only way we time-shift programmes ...

Catch up

92% of us watch live TV, **49%** watch recorded programmes, **34%** use online catch-up or on-demand services, **17%** watch DVD boxed sets and **12%** use catch-up or on-demand services via their TVs. But a massive **56%** of students watch online catch-up or on-demand services.

In the last month, **42%** of us will have watched BBC iPlayer, **19%** ITV Player and **16%** Channel 4's 4oD service.

Proportion of adults with home internet who watch online catch-up TV, by age

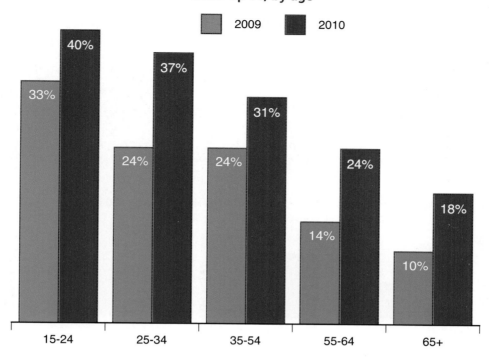

2009   2010

Age	2009	2010
15-24	33%	40%
25-34	24%	37%
35-54	24%	31%
55-64	14%	24%
65+	10%	18%

Which programmes?

Which programmes do we most like to watch? Top Gear, CSI and Doctor Who are our three favourite TV shows, with Doctor Who most likely to be watched on catch-up, ahead of Top Gear and Coronation Street.

And who?

And what about the people we like to see on TV? David Attenborough was named Britain's favourite presenter, with 20% of the vote, ahead of Stephen Fry on 12% and Ant and Dec on 9%. But more of us would invite Fry round for dinner, ahead of Attenborough, with Ant and Dec third. Bottom of our dinner party guest lists would be Jonathan Ross, followed by Gok Wan and Jeremy Clarkson.

Source: Ofcom communications market report; Radio Times/ seesaw.com TV nation 2010 Britain's Viewing Habits
www.ofcom.org.uk/
www.seesaw.com
www.radiotimes.com

Radio waves

90.6% of UK adults (46.8 million) were listening to the radio on a weekly basis in the first half of 2010

Total hours of radio listening fell by over **5%** in the five years to 2009.

Average hours listening to radio weekly, by age, 2010

Average listening per week

(all aged 15+) 20.1hours

20

10

0

| 10 | 15.5 | 17.7 | 20.4 | 22.2 | 23.2 | 22.3 | 20.1 |

| 4-14 | 15-24 | 25-34 | 35-44 | 45-54 | 55-64 | 65-74 | 75+ |

Despite more people listening, the time spent listening to radio services was down by **5.3%**. BBC Radio hours were down by **1.2%** during 2009 and down **2.2%** since 2004. By contrast, all commercial radio listener hours were stable over the year, but down **10.1%** over the five years since 2004.

Radio hours were down, particularly among younger listeners. Among 15-24 year olds, hours fell by **13%**; while among 25-34s they were down **11%**. Listening among older age groups was more stable; down by **2%** among listeners aged 65+, while among 45-54 year olds, hours were up by more than **1%**

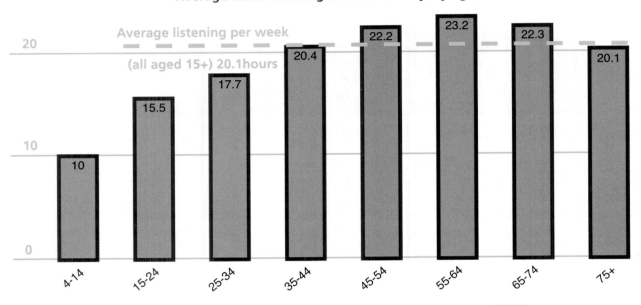

The average time spent listening to the radio was down by an hour and a half from five years ago. On average, men listened for **21.1** hours a week while women listened for **19.1** hours.

Changes in listening hours by age, 2004 - 2009

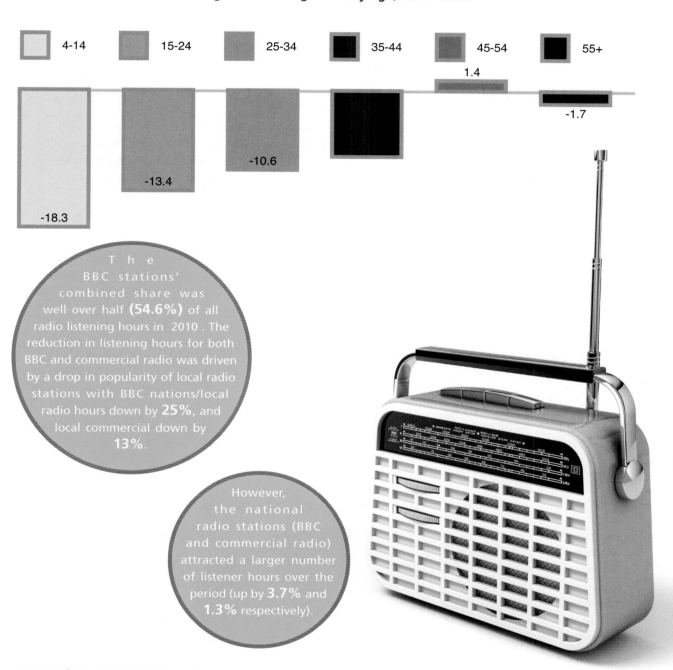

☐ 4-14   ▨ 15-24   ▨ 25-34   ■ 35-44   ▨ 45-54   ■ 55+

1.4

-1.7

-10.6

-13.4

-18.3

The BBC stations' combined share was well over half **(54.6%)** of all radio listening hours in 2010 . The reduction in listening hours for both BBC and commercial radio was driven by a drop in popularity of local radio stations with BBC nations/local radio hours down by **25%**, and local commercial down by **13%**.

However, the national radio stations (BBC and commercial radio) attracted a larger number of listener hours over the period (up by **3.7%** and **1.3%** respectively).

Source: Ofcom communications market report
www.ofcom.org.uk/

Bad news

Adults are often wary or afraid of groups of teenage boys...

...but so are the teenagers themselves

The Women in Journalism – Teenage Boys and the Media Report looked at the impact that negative media coverage has on teenage boys and their day-to-day lives.

The respondents were 1,000 boys aged 13-19 years old. The biggest single group were aged 17-19 years old – **43%**. The rest were evenly split between boys aged 15-16 – **29%**, and 13-14 – **28%**. Unsurprisingly given their ages, **95%** were in full time education.

They were drawn from five regions in the UK: nearly **39%** lived in the south, with **24%** living in the Midlands; **21%** in the north; **12%** in Scotland; and just **3%** in Wales.

When you're out on the street and you come across teenage boys that you don't know, do you feel wary?

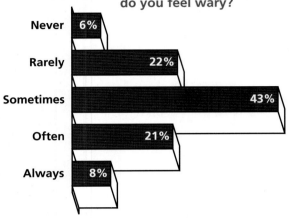

- Never 6%
- Rarely 22%
- Sometimes 43%
- Often 21%
- Always 8%

The **935** respondents who said they were wary of other boys were asked about the reasons for this – and the results suggest the media has a powerful effect on young people themselves.

What are the main reasons for your wariness?

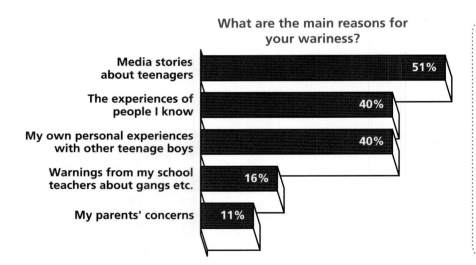

- Media stories about teenagers — 51%
- The experiences of people I know — 40%
- My own personal experiences with other teenage boys — 40%
- Warnings from my school teachers about gangs etc. — 16%
- My parents' concerns — 11%

The research identified a total of **8,269** stories in UK-wide newspapers involving teenage boys during the year – **4,374** were about crime (with boys either as victims or offenders). There were just **3,895** stories about boys and all other subjects, such as sport, fashion, education, entertainment, teenage fathers, etc.

Volume of coverage about teenage boys, by issue covered

The majority of stories about teenage boys seem to be about problems and their tone is likely to be negative

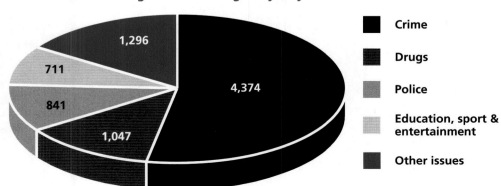

- 4,374
- 1,047
- 841
- 711
- 1,296

- Crime
- Drugs
- Police
- Education, sport & entertainment
- Other issues

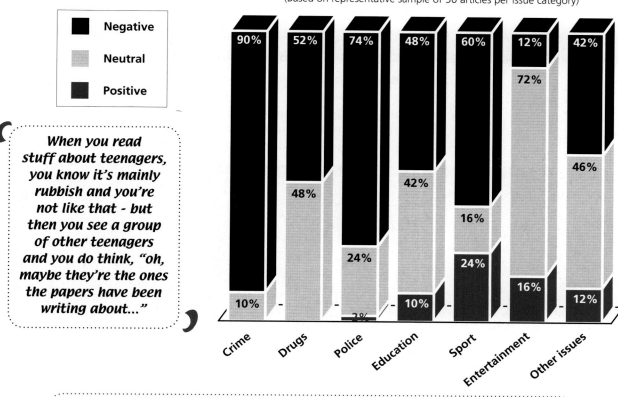

Tone of coverage for teenage boys, by issue
(Based on representative sample of 50 articles per issue category)

	Crime	Drugs	Police	Education	Sport	Entertainment	Other issues
Negative	90%	52%	74%	48%	60%	12%	42%
Neutral	10%	48%	24%	42%	16%	72%	46%
Positive			2%	10%	24%	16%	12%

> *When you read stuff about teenagers, you know it's mainly rubbish and you're not like that - but then you see a group of other teenagers and you do think, "oh, maybe they're the ones the papers have been writing about..."*

Analysis of **4,339** articles published about young people (boys and girls) during a one-week period in August 2009, found that only **4%** actually quoted a young person.

Terms used in stories about teen boys – top descriptors
(figures are indicative only)

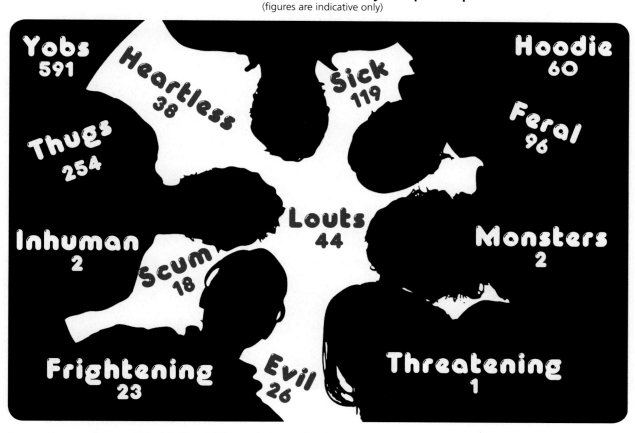

Source: *Teenage Boys and The Media – A Women in Journalism 2009 Report by Fiona Bawdon, WiJ committee member Research conducted by Echo*

www.leisurejobs.net/wijl
www.echoresearch.com

Multi-media

Despite all the new media available, TV still dominates our evenings...

... while radio is more popular in the morning

**Proportion of all media and communication activity
occurring each hour of the day, UK, 2009**
Base: all respondent days: 7,966

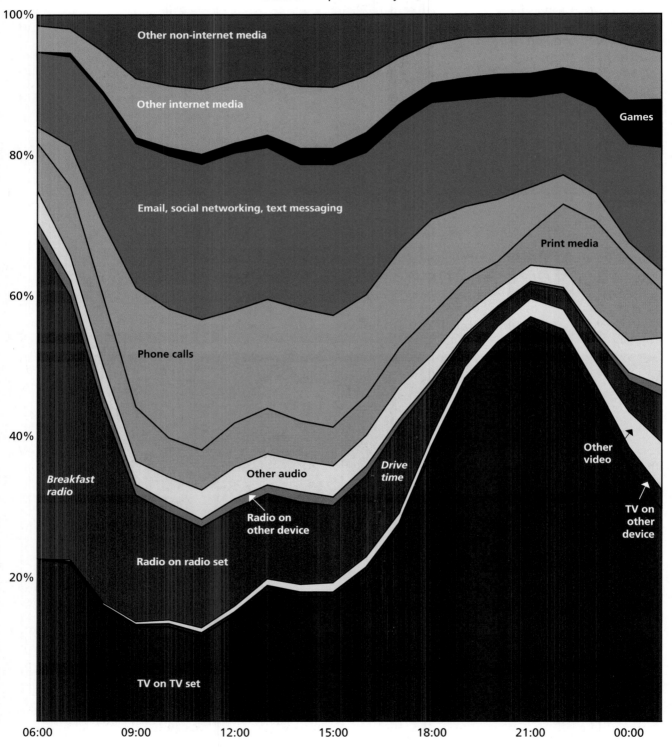

Source: Ofcom Communications Market Report 2010
www.ofcom.org.uk

Multi-tasking

People spend on average 7 hours a day using different media but they squeeze in 8 hours and 48 minutes' worth by using more than one at a time

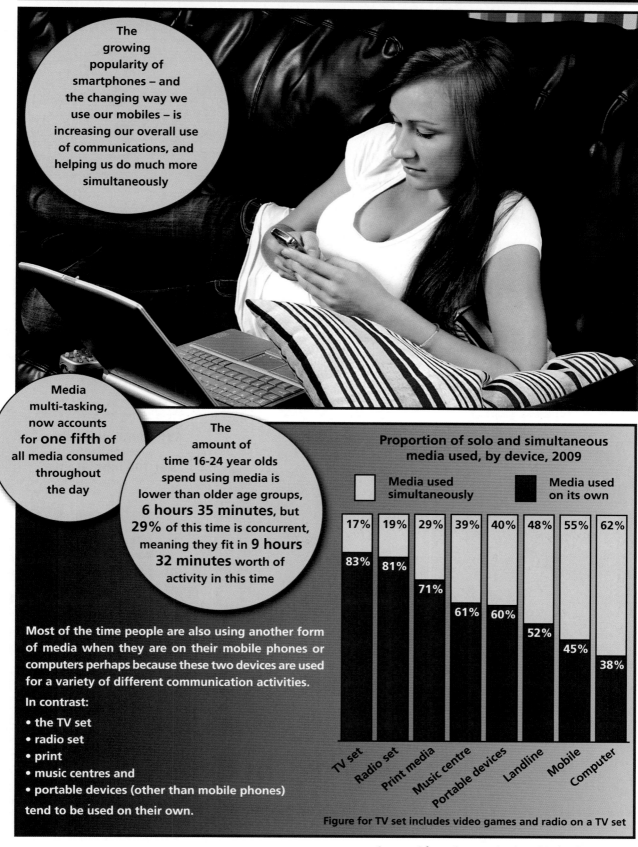

The growing popularity of smartphones – and the changing way we use our mobiles – is increasing our overall use of communications, and helping us do much more simultaneously

Media multi-tasking, now accounts for **one fifth** of all media consumed throughout the day

The amount of time 16-24 year olds spend using media is lower than older age groups, **6 hours 35 minutes**, but **29%** of this time is concurrent, meaning they fit in **9 hours 32 minutes** worth of activity in this time

Most of the time people are also using another form of media when they are on their mobile phones or computers perhaps because these two devices are used for a variety of different communication activities.

In contrast:

- the TV set
- radio set
- print
- music centres and
- portable devices (other than mobile phones)

tend to be used on their own.

Proportion of solo and simultaneous media used, by device, 2009

| | Media used simultaneously | | Media used on its own | |

Device	Simultaneous	On its own
TV set	17%	83%
Radio set	19%	81%
Print media	29%	71%
Music centre	39%	61%
Portable devices	40%	60%
Landline	48%	52%
Mobile	55%	45%
Computer	62%	38%

Figure for TV set includes video games and radio on a TV set

Source: Ofcom Communications Market Report 2010
www.ofcom.org.uk

Upwardly mobile

Despite the economic downturn, the use of mobile phones and the internet continues to grow worldwide

The number of fixed telephone lines worldwide continues to drop – but has been massively compensated for by the growth in mobiles

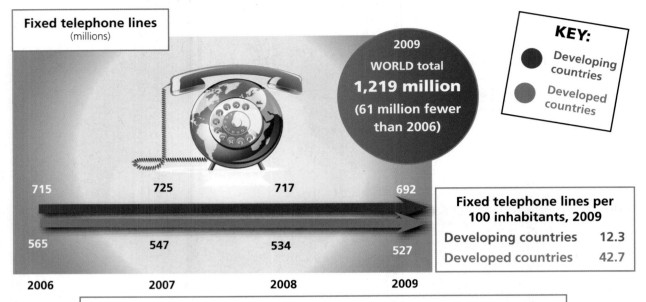

Fixed telephone lines
(millions)

2009
WORLD total
1,219 million
(61 million fewer than 2006)

KEY:
● Developing countries
● Developed countries

715   725   717   692

565   547   534   527

2006   2007   2008   2009

Fixed telephone lines per 100 inhabitants, 2009

Developing countries	12.3
Developed countries	42.7

Mobile penetration in **developing** countries has nearly doubled since 2006 when it was only **30** per 100 inhabitants. In 2009 it stood at **57.9** per 100 inhabitants.

Even though this remains well below the average in **developed** countries, **115.3** per 100 inhabitants, the rate of progress is remarkable.

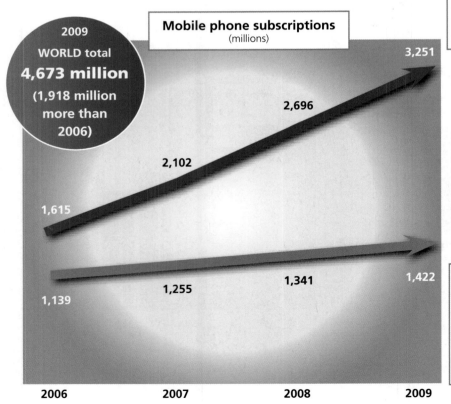

2009
WORLD total
4,673 million
(1,918 million more than 2006)

Mobile phone subscriptions
(millions)

3,251

2,696

2,102

1,615

1,255   1,341   1,422

1,139

2006   2007   2008   2009

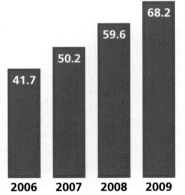

World mobile phone subscriptions per 100 inhabitants

41.7   50.2   59.6   68.2

2006   2007   2008   2009

Change in mobile phone subscriptions 2006-2009

Developing countries	up 1,636 million
Developed countries	up 283 million

Source: International Telecommunication Union
www.itu.int

Sport & leisure

Exhibiting an interest

More and more people are visiting museums and galleries

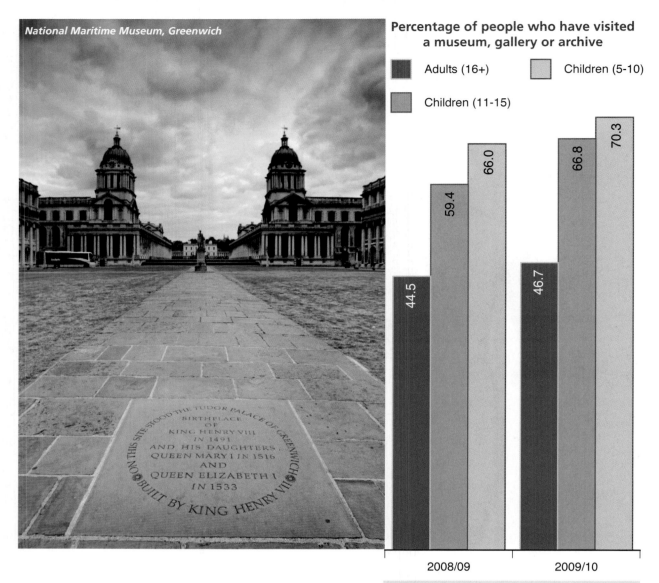

National Maritime Museum, Greenwich

Percentage of people who have visited a museum, gallery or archive

- ■ Adults (16+)
- ■ Children (11-15)
- ■ Children (5-10)

	2008/09	2009/10
Adults (16+)	44.5	46.7
Children (11-15)	59.4	66.8
Children (5-10)	66.0	70.3

Percentage who have visited a museum, gallery or archive in the last year, by age, 2009/10

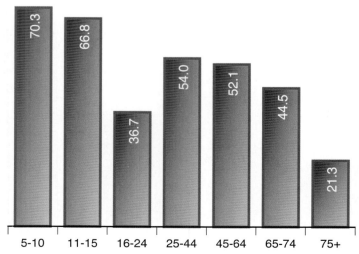

Age	%
5-10	70.3
11-15	66.8
16-24	36.7
25-44	54.0
45-64	52.1
65-74	44.5
75+	21.3

Regional difference

There has been a steady upward trend from 2005/06 when only **42.3%** of adults visited.

There was quite a difference regionally. Between 2005/06 and 2009/10, there was an increase in museum visits in the West Midlands (from **35.3%** to **42.4%**), the South East (from **43.8%** to **51.0%**) and Yorkshire and the Humber (from **38.8%** to **46.8%**).

Between 2005/06 and 2008/09, there was a significant increase in the proportion of people who had visited in the North West (from **40.4%** to **47.0%**). This may reflect the increase in activity in and around Liverpool as the city was the 2008 European Capital of Culture.

Deprivation difference

It is clear that school age people visit more than older people perhaps because of organised trips.

Visiting also varies according to where people live, and also the type of area they live in.

The effect of deprivation is particularly stark. In 2009/10, people who lived in the least deprived areas of England were twice as likely as those who lived in the most deprived areas to have visited a museum, gallery or archive in the last year (**63.8%** compared with **31.3%**).

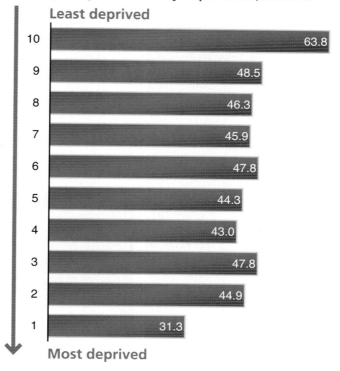

Percentage of adults who have visited a museum, gallery or archive by deprivation, 2009/10

Least deprived

10	63.8
9	48.5
8	46.3
7	45.9
6	47.8
5	44.3
4	43.0
3	47.8
2	44.9
1	31.3

Most deprived

Frequency of visits 54% of adults didn't visit any museum, gallery or archive in the year 2009/10, 27.9% visited 1-2 times in that year, 14.1% went 3-4 times that year, 3.6% went at least once a month and only 0.4% went at least once a week.

Birmingham Museum & Art Gallery

Source: Taking Part: The National Survey of Culture, Leisure and Sport, The Department of Culture, Media & Sport Crown copyright 2010
www.culture.gov.uk/

Arts alive!

There's an arts activity for (almost) everyone

75.7% of adults have attended an arts event at least once in the last year; along with **97.2%** of 5-10 year olds and **99.1%** of 11-15 year olds. Taking part in something active (e.g. dancing) is generally higher for the younger age groups while less active activities, such as reading, are more popular amongst the older age groups and attending plays/dramas are most popular among those aged 45-64.

Percentage of people who have attended an arts activities 2005/06 and 2009/10

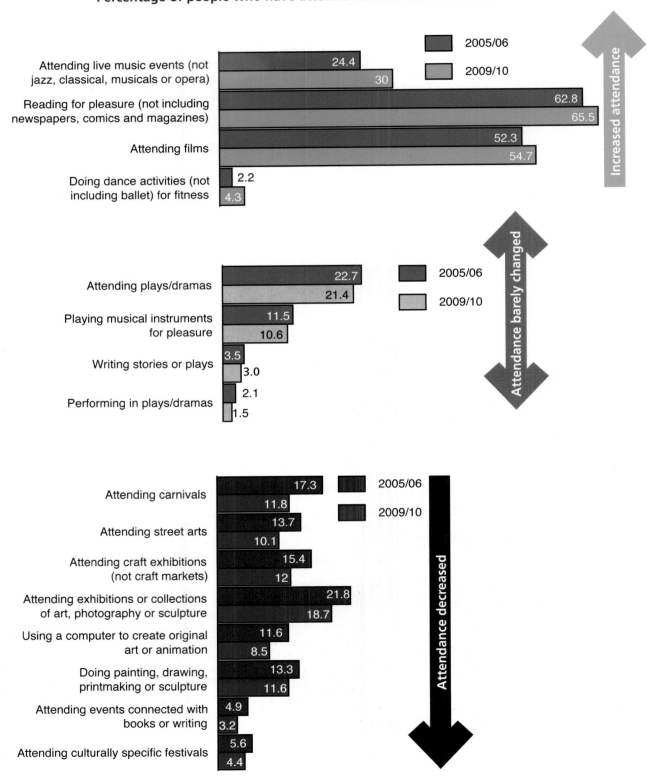

How often adults attended or took part in arts in 2009/10

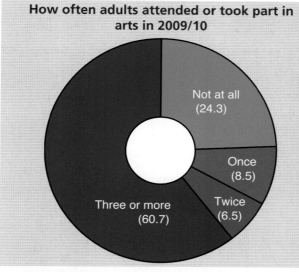

Not at all (24.3)

Once (8.5)

Twice (6.5)

Three or more (60.7)

Not surprisingly, the number of times people had taken part in arts activities over the past year varied considerably by activity. Of those adults who read for pleasure, **80%** had done this within the last week. Playing a musical instrument also had a high percentage of participants doing this regularly with **58.2%** of the adults who play a musical instrument for pleasure having done this in the past week.

% of people involved in arts activities, by gender, 2009/10

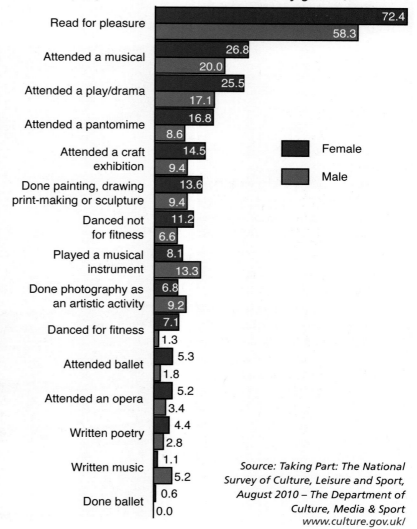

Activity	Female	Male
Read for pleasure	72.4	58.3
Attended a musical	26.8	20.0
Attended a play/drama	25.5	17.1
Attended a pantomime	16.8	8.6
Attended a craft exhibition	14.5	9.4
Done painting, drawing print-making or sculpture	13.6	9.4
Danced not for fitness	11.2	6.6
Played a musical instrument	8.1	13.3
Done photography as an artistic activity	6.8	9.2
Danced for fitness	7.1	1.3
Attended ballet	5.3	1.8
Attended an opera	5.2	3.4
Written poetry	4.4	2.8
Written music	1.1	5.2
Done ballet	0.6	0.0

Source: Taking Part: The National Survey of Culture, Leisure and Sport, August 2010 – The Department of Culture, Media & Sport
www.culture.gov.uk/

Library fine?

In 2009/10, **5.4%** of adults visited a public library at least once a week; **12.8%** of adults visited at least once a month; **10.9%** visited 3-4 times a year while **7.9%** visited 1-2 times a year.

- Adults (16+)
- Children (11-15)
- Children (5-10)

Percentage who have visited a public library in the last year, 2005/06 to 2009/10

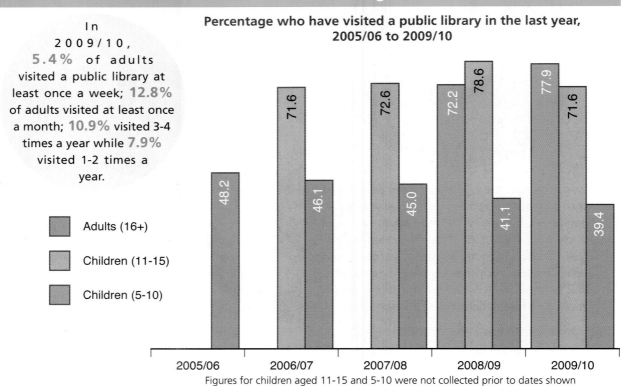

| 2005/06 | 2006/07 | 2007/08 | 2008/09 | 2009/10 |

48.2 | 71.6 | 46.1 | 72.6 | 45.0 | 72.2 | 78.6 | 41.1 | 77.9 | 71.6 | 39.4

Figures for children aged 11-15 and 5-10 were not collected prior to dates shown

Purpose of visit:

In 2009/10, among those people who had visited a public library, **93.8%** had done so in their own time, **10.3%** visited for academic study and **3.1%** for their job.

Deprivation:

People who lived in the least deprived areas of England were more likely than those in the most deprived areas to have visited a library in the past 12 months (**46.3%** compared with **37.6%**).

Age difference:

The difference between those aged 11-15 and those aged 16-24 is particularly noticeable. In 2009/10, **71.6%** of 11-15 year olds had visited compared with **40%** of 16-24 year olds. Some of this 'drop off' is likely to be a result of leaving school. It is also likely that a significant proportion of 16-24 year olds will use academic rather than public libraries once they go on to further education. Academic libraries are not included in these statistics.

Source: Taking Part: The National Survey of Culture, Leisure and Sport, The Department of Culture, Media & Sport © Crown Copyright 2010
www.culture.gov.uk/

Cup fever

History of the World Cup

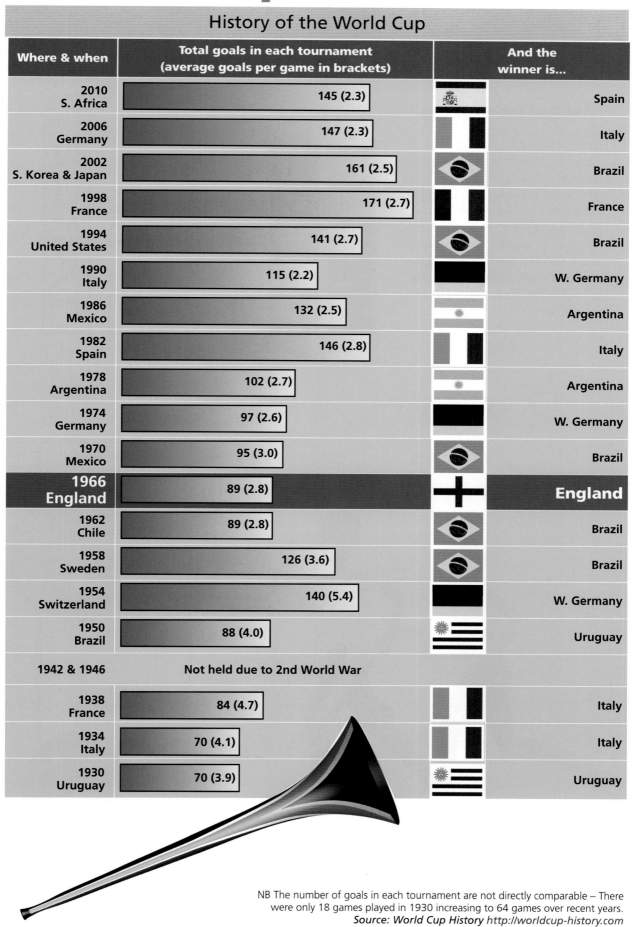

Where & when	Total goals in each tournament (average goals per game in brackets)	And the winner is...
2010 S. Africa	145 (2.3)	Spain
2006 Germany	147 (2.3)	Italy
2002 S. Korea & Japan	161 (2.5)	Brazil
1998 France	171 (2.7)	France
1994 United States	141 (2.7)	Brazil
1990 Italy	115 (2.2)	W. Germany
1986 Mexico	132 (2.5)	Argentina
1982 Spain	146 (2.8)	Italy
1978 Argentina	102 (2.7)	Argentina
1974 Germany	97 (2.6)	W. Germany
1970 Mexico	95 (3.0)	Brazil
1966 England	**89 (2.8)**	**England**
1962 Chile	89 (2.8)	Brazil
1958 Sweden	126 (3.6)	Brazil
1954 Switzerland	140 (5.4)	W. Germany
1950 Brazil	88 (4.0)	Uruguay
1942 & 1946	Not held due to 2nd World War	
1938 France	84 (4.7)	Italy
1934 Italy	70 (4.1)	Italy
1930 Uruguay	70 (3.9)	Uruguay

NB The number of goals in each tournament are not directly comparable – There were only 18 games played in 1930 increasing to 64 games over recent years.
Source: World Cup History http://worldcup-history.com

One Million?

Are enough of us doing our 30 x 3?

Number of adults participating in 3x30 mins sport a week (millions)

The Sport England Strategy

Sport England is committed to getting one million people taking part in more sport by 2012-13. The aim is to increase the number of adults (aged 16 and over) participating in at least 30 minutes of sport at moderate intensity at least three times a week. Sport England's progress towards this target is measured by the Active People Survey.

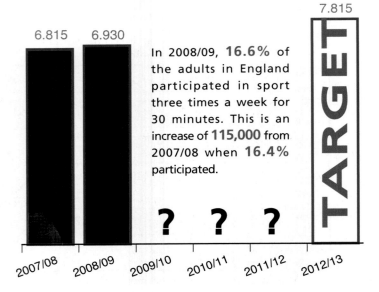

In 2008/09, **16.6%** of the adults in England participated in sport three times a week for 30 minutes. This is an increase of **115,000** from 2007/08 when **16.4%** participated.

6.815 — 2007/08
6.930 — 2008/09
? — 2009/10
? — 2010/11
? — 2011/12
TARGET 7.815 — 2012/13

2007/08
4.027m
20%
of adult men

2008/09
4.203m
20.6%
of adult men

Male numbers are slightly up

Men ↑

2007/08
2.788m
13.1%
of adult women

2008/09
2.727m
12.7%
of adult women

Female numbers are slightly down

Women ↓

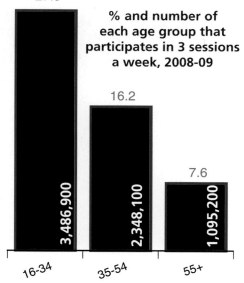

% and number of each age group that participates in 3 sessions a week, 2008-09

27.0 — 16-34 — 3,486,900
16.2 — 35-54 — 2,348,100
7.6 — 55+ — 1,095,200

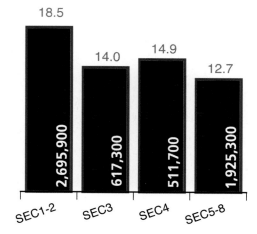

% of each socio-economic group that participates in 3 sessions a week, 2008-09

18.5 — SEC1-2 — 2,695,900
14.0 — SEC3 — 617,300
14.9 — SEC4 — 511,700
12.7 — SEC5-8 — 1,925,300

Socio-economic classifications:
1. Higher managerial and professional occupations; 2. Lower managerial and professional occupations; 3. Intermediate occupations; 4. Small employers and own account workers; 5. Lower supervisory and technical occupations; 6. Semi-routine occupations; 7. Routine occupations; 8. Never worked and long-term unemployed; 9.Full time students and occupations not stated or inadequately described.

Participation among white adults has increased by **16,000**, from **6.200 million** (16.49%) to **6.216 million** (16.54%).

Participation among non-white adults has increased by **98,800**, from **615,000** (16.1%) to **713,800** (17.0%).

Participation in seven regions (North East, North West, Yorkshire, East Midlands, East, South West and the South East) has not shown a significant change between 2007/08 and 2008/09. In the West Midlands, however, there are **35,800** more adults taking part in at least 30 minutes of sport at least three times a week, while in London there are **53,800** more adults taking part.

Source: Active People Survey 2008/09,
Sport England
www.sportengland.org

War & conflict

Snapshot

Journalists and their support workers faced serious dangers in reporting from Iraq during the conflict between 2003 and 2009

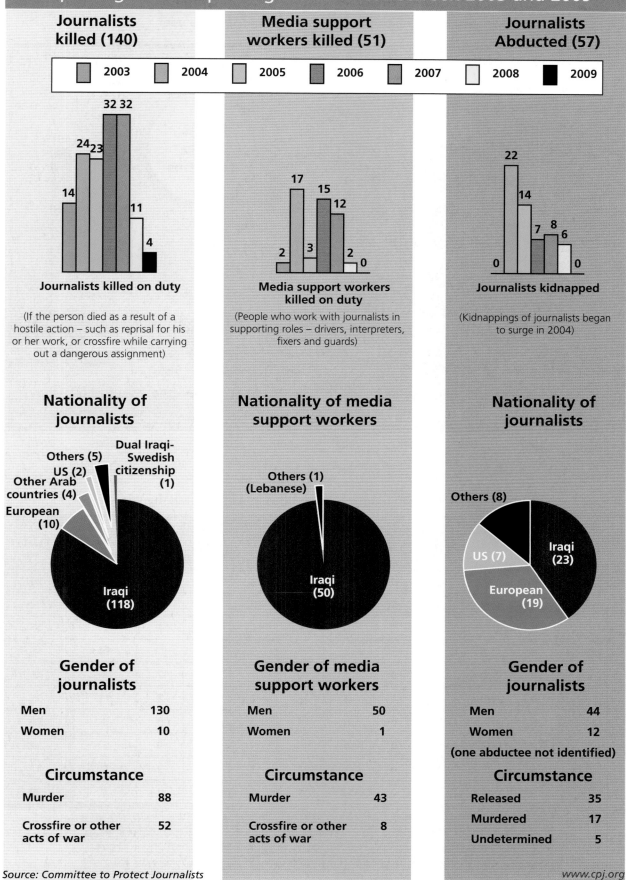

Journalists killed (140)

2003 **2004** **2005** **2006** **2007** **2008** **2009**

14 | 24 | 23 | 32 | 32 | 11 | 4

Journalists killed on duty

(If the person died as a result of a hostile action – such as reprisal for his or her work, or crossfire while carrying out a dangerous assignment)

Nationality of journalists

Others (5)
US (2)
Other Arab countries (4)
European (10)
Dual Iraqi-Swedish citizenship (1)
Iraqi (118)

Gender of journalists

| Men | 130 |
| Women | 10 |

Circumstance

| Murder | 88 |
| Crossfire or other acts of war | 52 |

Media support workers killed (51)

2 | 17 | 3 | 15 | 12 | 2 | 0

Media support workers killed on duty

(People who work with journalists in supporting roles – drivers, interpreters, fixers and guards)

Nationality of media support workers

Others (1) (Lebanese)
Iraqi (50)

Gender of media support workers

| Men | 50 |
| Women | 1 |

Circumstance

| Murder | 43 |
| Crossfire or other acts of war | 8 |

Journalists Abducted (57)

0 | 22 | 14 | 7 | 8 | 6 | 0

Journalists kidnapped

(Kidnappings of journalists began to surge in 2004)

Nationality of journalists

Others (8)
US (7)
European (19)
Iraqi (23)

Gender of journalists

| Men | 44 |
| Women | 12 |

(one abductee not identified)

Circumstance

Released	35
Murdered	17
Undetermined	5

Source: Committee to Protect Journalists

www.cpj.org

Mounting toll

A tally of deaths among those serving in Afghanistan – already the numbers will have risen

Coalition military fatalities in Afghanistan, by year

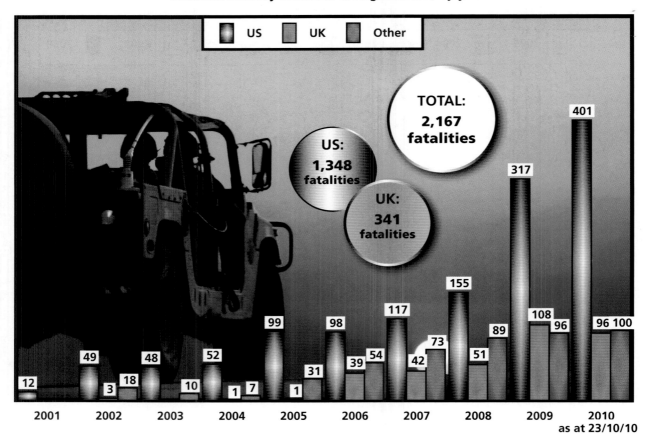

US | UK | Other

TOTAL: **2,167 fatalities**

US: **1,348 fatalities**

UK: **341 fatalities**

2001 2002 2003 2004 2005 2006 2007 2008 2009 2010 as at 23/10/10

'Other' countries sustaining troop fatalities in Afghanistan, by year

	2001	2002	2003	2004	2005	2006	2007	2008	2009	2010 as at 23/10/10	Totals
Australia	0	1	0	0	0	0	3	3	4	10	21
Canada	0	4	2	1	1	36	30	32	32	14	152
Denmark	0	3	0	1	0	0	6	13	7	7	37
France	0	0	0	3	2	6	3	11	11	14	50
Germany	0	10	6	0	4	0	7	3	7	8	45
Italy	0	0	0	1	2	6	2	2	9	11	33
Netherlands	0	0	0	0	0	4	8	6	3	3	24
Poland	0	0	0	0	0	0	1	7	8	6	22
Romania	0	0	2	0	1	1	1	3	3	6	17
Spain	0	0	0	0	18	1	4	2	1	4	30

Belgium, Czech Republic, Estonia, Finland, Georgia, Hungary, Jordan, Latvia, Lithuania, New Zealand, Norway, Portugal, South Korea, Sweden and Turkey have also sustained troop fatalities in Afghanistan, totalling a further **47**.

Overall military deaths, by gender
(as at 23/10/10)

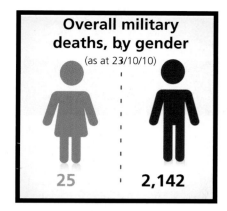

25   2,142

The overall death toll of 18 and 19 year olds troops in Afghanistan is 117 as at 23/10/10:

84 US troops

30 UK troops

2 from France and

1 from Estonia

UK military deaths, by age
(as at 23/10/10)

(There were **5** further deaths where ages are not known)

Their average age is 25.8

Age	18	19	20	21	22	23	24	25	26	27	28	29	30	31	32	33	34	35	36	37	38	39	40	42	43	48	49	51
Deaths	11	19	26	30	28	24	20	21	25	16	16	22	10	11	8	9	7	3	6	1	2	5	6	5	1	2	1	1

UK fatalities by service group
(as at 23/10/10)

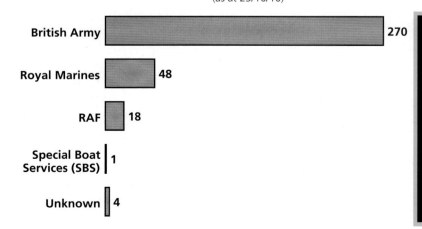

British Army — 270
Royal Marines — 48
RAF — 18
Special Boat Services (SBS) — 1
Unknown — 4

The UK death is rate more than double that of the US

Analysis by the University of Cambridge has suggested that in the period 3 May 2010 to 11 July, 2010 the estimated fatality rates per 1,000 personnel-years* were **6.8** for the US and **16.6** for the UK.

*4,000 troops in Afghanistan for 3 months contribute 1,000 personnel-years (pys). So too do 1,000 troops for one year.

Source: Operation Enduring Freedom, icasualties.org; Medical Research Council's biostatistics unit at the University of Cambridge

www.icasualties.org
www.mrc-bsu.cam.ac.uk

Caught in the cross-fire

The spread and intensification of the Afghanistan conflict continues to take a heavy toll on civilians

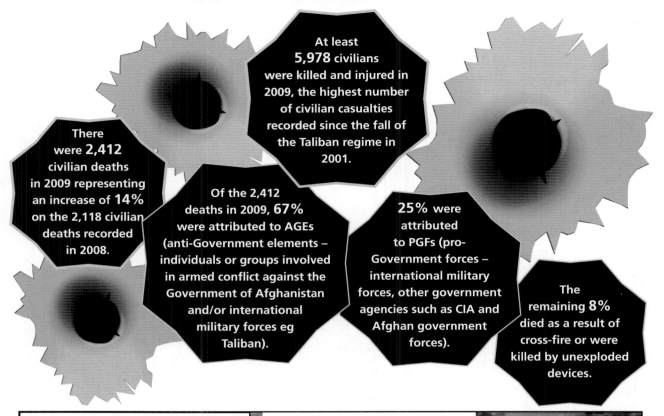

At least **5,978** civilians were killed and injured in 2009, the highest number of civilian casualties recorded since the fall of the Taliban regime in 2001.

There were **2,412** civilian deaths in 2009 representing an increase of **14%** on the 2,118 civilian deaths recorded in 2008.

Of the 2,412 deaths in 2009, **67%** were attributed to AGEs (anti-Government elements – individuals or groups involved in armed conflict against the Government of Afghanistan and/or international military forces eg Taliban).

25% were attributed to PGFs (pro-Government forces – international military forces, other government agencies such as CIA and Afghan government forces).

The remaining **8%** died as a result of cross-fire or were killed by unexploded devices.

Number of civilians reported killed, by year* and responsibility

■ 2009	■ 2008	■ 2007

*Collection of civilian fatality data only began in 2007

Anti-government elements	Pro-government forces	Undetermined/ other
1,630	596	186
1,160	828	130
700	629	194

Agencies who collect data are hampered by insecurity and lack of resources therefore estimates of the number of civilians killed vary widely and must be treated with caution.

Afghan children on their way to school

Number of civilian deaths attributed to AGEs and PGFs, by tactic used, 2009

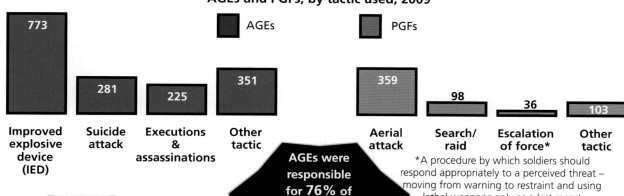

■ AGEs   ■ PGFs

| 773 | | | | 359 | | | |
| Improved explosive device (IED) | Suicide attack 281 | Executions & assassinations 225 | Other tactic 351 | Aerial attack | Search/ raid 98 | Escalation of force* 36 | Other tactic 103 |

*A procedure by which soldiers should respond appropriately to a perceived threat – moving from warning to restraint and using lethal weapons only as a last resort

AGEs were responsible for **76%** of these casualties mainly through their greater number of larger and more sophisticated IEDs throughout the country.

There were **3,268** civilian casualties including **1,271 deaths** and **1,997 injuries** in the first six months of 2010.

Women and children made up a greater proportion of those killed and injured than in 2009 – women casualties increased by **6%** and child casualties by **55%**.

Ongoing conflict, including threats and attacks on schools, deprives over **400,000** children of education in the most insecure and conflict affected areas.

About **106** incidents of attacks against schools were reported during the first four months of 2010.

A recent publication by Wikileaks of almost **90,000** military files on the war in Afghanistan reveals many more attacks on civilians.

Incidents in which civilians were killed – whether accidentally or deliberately – were often portrayed as attacks on enemy forces. Detailed data and analysis is available here: *www.guardian.co.uk/news/datablog/ 2010/jul/27/wikileaks-afghanistan-data-datajournalism*

Source: United Nations Assistance Mission in Afghanistan – Afghanistan Annual Report on Protection of Civilians in Armed Conflict. 2009; UNICEF Humanitarian Action 2010; Afghanistan conflict monitor

http://unama.unmissions.org
www.unicef.org/har2010
www.afghanconflictmonitor.org

Battle stations

The global financial crisis and economic recession had little impact on world military spending

The 15 countries with the highest military expenditure (at current prices) 2009, US$ billions

(% change 2000-2009 in brackets)

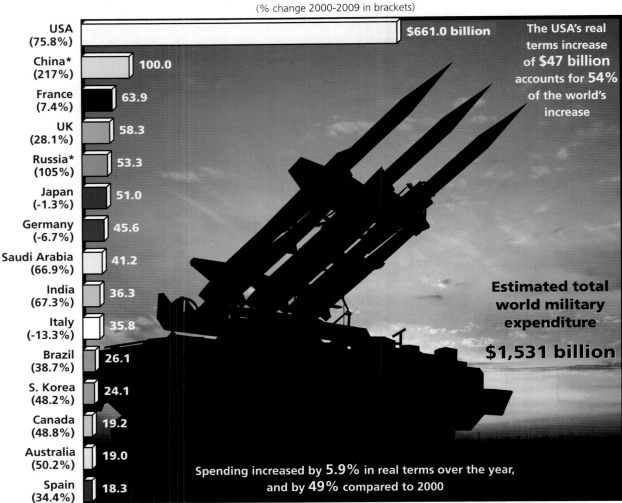

USA (75.8%) — **$661.0 billion**

China* (217%) — 100.0

France (7.4%) — 63.9

UK (28.1%) — 58.3

Russia* (105%) — 53.3

Japan (-1.3%) — 51.0

Germany (-6.7%) — 45.6

Saudi Arabia (66.9%) — 41.2

India (67.3%) — 36.3

Italy (-13.3%) — 35.8

Brazil (38.7%) — 26.1

S. Korea (48.2%) — 24.1

Canada (48.8%) — 19.2

Australia (50.2%) — 19.0

Spain (34.4%) — 18.3

The USA's real terms increase of **$47 billion** accounts for **54%** of the world's increase

Estimated total world military expenditure

$1,531 billion

Spending increased by **5.9%** in real terms over the year, and by **49%** compared to 2000

*Russia and China figures are estimates

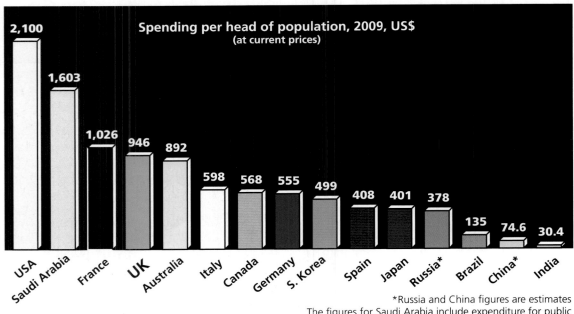

Spending per head of population, 2009, US$
(at current prices)

USA	Saudi Arabia	France	UK	Australia	Italy	Canada	Germany	S. Korea	Spain	Japan	Russia*	Brazil	China*	India
2,100	1,603	1,026	946	892	598	568	555	499	408	401	378	135	74.6	30.4

*Russia and China figures are estimates
The figures for Saudi Arabia include expenditure for public order and safety and might be slight overestimates

World nuclear forces. January 2010
(approximate estimates)

The USA, Russia, UK, France and China are legally recognised nuclear weapon states. They are either deploying new nuclear weapon systems or have announced their intention to do so. None appears to be prepared to give up their nuclear weapons in the foreseeable future

India, Pakistan and Israel continue to develop new missile systems capable of delivering nuclear weapons. North Korea is believed to have produced enough plutonium for a small number of nuclear warheads, but it is unknown whether it has operational weapons.

Country	Operational warheads	Other* warheads
USA	2,468	7,100
Russia	4,630	7,300
UK	160	65
France	300	-
China	-	200
India	-	60-80
Pakistan	-	70-90
Israel	-	80
Total	**7,560**	**14,900**

*Other – spares, warheads in both active and inactive storage, and intact warheads scheduled for dismantlement

It's about the oil: Natural resources help drive military spending and arms imports in the developing world

Some countries seem to have very large military spending in relation to their GDP.

This can seem puzzling – we might expect them to spend more in other areas such as health and education.

Often the reason for such spending is the income generated by oil or gas resources and the need to protect them.

In the Middle East, oil resources are one source of international tension. In Nigeria there is internal tension because of environmental damage caused by oil extraction and the fact that the regions where oil is found have not benefitted from it.

Conflicts such as this lead to higher military spending.

Countries also spend more to safeguard their resources. Brazil, for example, has justified its planned purchase of submarines in terms of the need to protect newly discovered underwater oil fields.

Oil- and gas-producing states with large military spending increases	
Country	Increase 2000-2009
Algeria	105%
Chad	663%
Nigeria	101%
Ecuador	241%
Timor-Leste[1]	255%
Viet Nam[2]	55%
Azerbaijan	471%
Kazakhstan	360%

[1] Increase 2003-2009
[2] Increase 2005-2009

Information from the Stockholm International Peace Research Institute (SIPRI)

www.sipri.org

Wider world

Malaria

"It is an appalling tragedy that every 30 seconds a child in Africa dies from Malaria"

Douglas Alexander, International Development Secretary

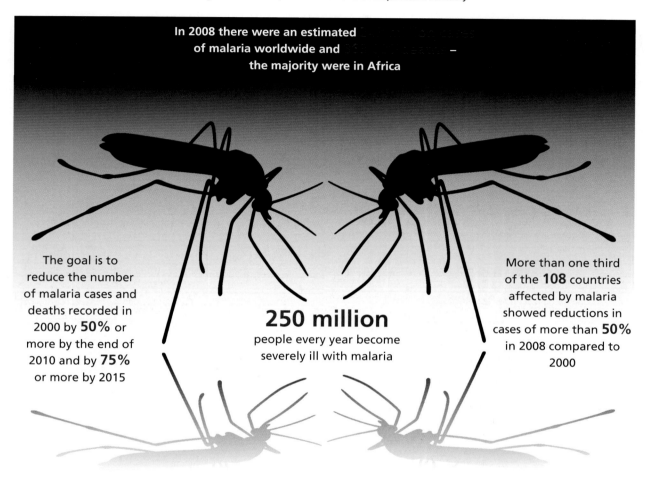

In 2008 there were an estimated of malaria worldwide and — the majority were in Africa

The goal is to reduce the number of malaria cases and deaths recorded in 2000 by **50%** or more by the end of 2010 and by **75%** or more by 2015

250 million
people every year become severely ill with malaria

More than one third of the **108** countries affected by malaria showed reductions in cases of more than **50%** in 2008 compared to 2000

Malaria is a wholly preventable disease – sleeping under a bednet is a simple and effective way of avoiding infection

In 2008, **23** countries in Africa and **35** other countries had adopted the World Health Organization's recommendation to provide bed nets for all age groups at risk of malaria, not just women and children.

In countries which have a high number of bed nets and treatment programmes, recorded cases and deaths due to malaria have **reduced by 50%**. This suggests that the Millennium Development Goals **can** be achieved.

Estimates show that **31%** of African households owned **at least one** Insecticide Treated Net (ITN), and **24%** of children under 5 years of age had used an ITN in 2008 but the percentage of children using a net is still below the World Health Assembly **target** of **80%**.

The **UK** is on track to have delivered **20 million** bednets to some of the world's poorest countries by the end of 2010, to help prevent **110,000** child deaths.

Bednets delivered by UKaid have prevented more than **80,000** child deaths in the developing world.

By helping to increase the number of people sleeping under a net, UKaid has helped to cut death from malaria by almost **50%** in some African countries.

Source: World Malaria Report 2009 – World Health Organization, Department for International Development
www.who.int
www.dfid.gov.uk

Child mortality

Although some progress is being made towards the Millennium Development Goal (MDG) to reduce child mortality, it is still falling short of the target

MDG 4: Reduce Child Mortality

Reduce the under-five mortality rate by two-thirds between 1990 and 2015

The MDG4 target has shifted the focus from tracking levels of child mortality to assessing whether countries are reducing child mortality at the **4.4%** rate per year needed to achieve the two-thirds reduction.

Worldwide mortality in children younger than five years has dropped from an estimated 11.9 million deaths in 1990 to 7.7 million deaths in 2010

Between 1970 and 2010, the number of deaths in children younger than 5 years has fallen by more than 52%, even though the total number of births has increased by 16% in the same period.

By 2010, estimated mortality was less than 200 per 1,000 in all countries, whereas in 1970, 40 countries had rates higher than this level.

Number of under-5 deaths, in millions, 2010

3.1	■ neonatal deaths (the probability of death before age 1 month)
2.3	■ postneonatal deaths (the probability of death between age 1 month and 1 year)
2.3	□ childhood deaths (probabilty of death from age 1 year to 5 years)

33% of deaths in children younger than 5 years occur in south Asia and **49.6%** occur in sub-Saharan Africa, with **less than 1%** of deaths occurring in high-income countries.

Child Mortality Illustration: © MDG Monitor

66 countries have decreased child mortality by more than **30% in just 5 years.**

Such remarkable declines provide hope that accelerated progress is possible.

In **13 regions** of the world, there is evidence of accelerating declines from 2000 to 2010 compared with 1990 to 2000.

In developing countries, mortality in children younger than 5 years declined by **35%** from 1990 to 2010, a yearly rate of **2·1%**.

This rate of decline is lower than the MDG4 target but represents substantial progress.

Estimated under-5 mortality rates per 1,000 births, 2010

Countries with highest rate of under-5 mortality

Equatorial Guinea	180.1
Chad	168.7
Mali	161.2
Niger	161.1
Guinea-Bissau	158.6

There were 38 countries in the world with under-5 mortality higher than 80 per 1,000 in 2010, **34** were in sub-Saharan Africa.

Countries lagging behind other high income countries

USA	6.7
New Zealand	5.8
UK	5.3
South Korea	5.1

The USA, UK, New Zealand and South Korea show rates of decline that are slower than expected and they lag behind other high-income countries, having failed to reach rates of under-5 mortality of less than five per 1,000 by 2010.

Countries with lowest rate of under-5 mortality

Luxembourg	2.9
Cyprus	2.8
Sweden	2.7
Iceland	2.6
Singapore	2.5

Source: Neonatal, postneonatal, childhood, and under-5 mortality for 187 countries, 1970–2010: a systematic analysis of progress towards Millennium Development Goal 4 – The Lancet, Vol 375 June 5, 2010
www.thelancet.com

Commitment to development

Reducing poverty in developing countries is about far more than giving money

The Commitment to Development Index (CDI) ranks 22 of the world's richest countries based on whether they are living up to their potential to help poorer countries. They are assessed under seven areas.

Within each area, a country receives points for policies and actions that support poor nations in their efforts to build prosperity, good government, and security.

Aid (quantity and quality)

Foreign aid is the first policy that comes to mind when people think of helping poorer countries. Most comparisons between donors are based only on how much aid each gives. The CDI assesses not only quantity but quality.

Norway would rank first on sheer aid quantity as a share of its wealth, but falls to third for funding smaller projects and being less selective.

Trade

Some goods that poor countries are best at producing such as crops, still face barriers in rich countries. Taxes on food imports and subsidies for farmers in rich countries lead to overproduction for example, which lowers prices and has a knock on effect for poor country farmers. Because access to rich country markets is crucial for developing countries the CDI ranks countries according to how open they are to these imports. Australia does best on trade.

Investment

The CDI rewards countries for policies that promote development-friendly investment. Many of East Asia's fastest growing countries benefitted from investment from abroad. But foreign investment can also breed instability, corruption and exploitation. Germany and the UK ranked best.

Migration

Around 200 million people – 1 in 33 – do not live in the country where they were born. The CDI rewards migration of both skilled and unskilled people. It also uses indicators of openness to students from poor countries and aid for refugees and asylum seekers. Austria takes first place for accepting the most migrants for its size.

Environment

Norway tops the environment category – its net greenhouse gas emissions are among the lowest per capita. Also near the top is the UK which has supported wind and other renewable energy sources and Finland which significantly reduced its net greenhouse gas emissions rate.

Security

Rich countries keep the peace in countries recently in conflict and keep vital sea lanes open to international trade but also supply developing countries with tanks and jets. The CDI penalises some arms exports especially to nations that are undemocratic and spend heavily on the military. Australia and New Zealand take the top spots on security.

Technology

The internet, mobile phones, vaccines and high-yielding grains were all invented in rich countries and exported to poorer ones where they improved – and saved – many lives. Spain is first on technology.

Sweden, although top, scores only about average (5) in four of the seven policy areas. Almost all countries score below average in at least one area and most are below average in at least three.

Legend: Aid (quantity and quality) · Trade · Investment · Migration · Environment · Security · Technology

CDI, by rank order of country, 2009

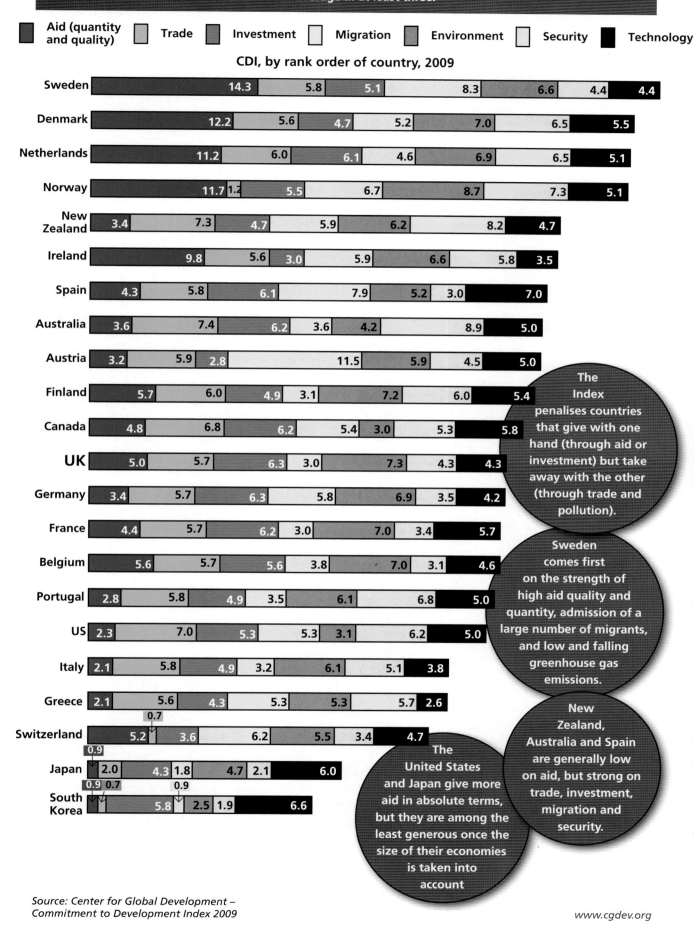

Country	Aid	Trade	Investment	Migration	Environment	Security	Technology
Sweden	14.3	5.8	5.1	8.3	6.6	4.4	4.4
Denmark	12.2	5.6	4.7	5.2	7.0	6.5	5.5
Netherlands	11.2	6.0	6.1	4.6	6.9	6.5	5.1
Norway	11.7	1.2	5.5	6.7	8.7	7.3	5.1
New Zealand	3.4	7.3	4.7	5.9	6.2	8.2	4.7
Ireland	9.8	5.6	3.0	5.9	6.6	5.8	3.5
Spain	4.3	5.8	6.1	7.9	5.2	3.0	7.0
Australia	3.6	7.4	6.2	3.6	4.2	8.9	5.0
Austria	3.2	5.9	2.8	11.5	5.9	4.5	5.0
Finland	5.7	6.0	4.9	3.1	7.2	6.0	5.4
Canada	4.8	6.8	6.2	5.4	3.0	5.3	5.8
UK	5.0	5.7	6.3	3.0	7.3	4.3	4.3
Germany	3.4	5.7	6.3	5.8	6.9	3.5	4.2
France	4.4	5.7	6.2	3.0	7.0	3.4	5.7
Belgium	5.6	5.7	5.6	3.8	7.0	3.1	4.6
Portugal	2.8	5.8	4.9	3.5	6.1	6.8	5.0
US	2.3	7.0	5.3	5.3	3.1	6.2	5.0
Italy	2.1	5.8	4.9	3.2	6.1	5.1	3.8
Greece	2.1	5.6	4.3	5.3	5.3	5.7	2.6
Switzerland	0.7	5.2	3.6	6.2	5.5	3.4	4.7
Japan	0.9	2.0	4.3	1.8	4.7	2.1	6.0
South Korea	0.9	0.7	0.9	5.8	2.5	1.9	6.6

The Index penalises countries that give with one hand (through aid or investment) but take away with the other (through trade and pollution).

Sweden comes first on the strength of high aid quality and quantity, admission of a large number of migrants, and low and falling greenhouse gas emissions.

New Zealand, Australia and Spain are generally low on aid, but strong on trade, investment, migration and security.

The United States and Japan give more aid in absolute terms, but they are among the least generous once the size of their economies is taken into account

Source: Center for Global Development – Commitment to Development Index 2009

www.cgdev.org

Where your money goes

In 2008/09 the UK Government gave £5.5 billion
in international development assistance

£3.3 billion went direct to developing countries

£2.2 billion went to international organisations, including charities, to support their activities within developing countries

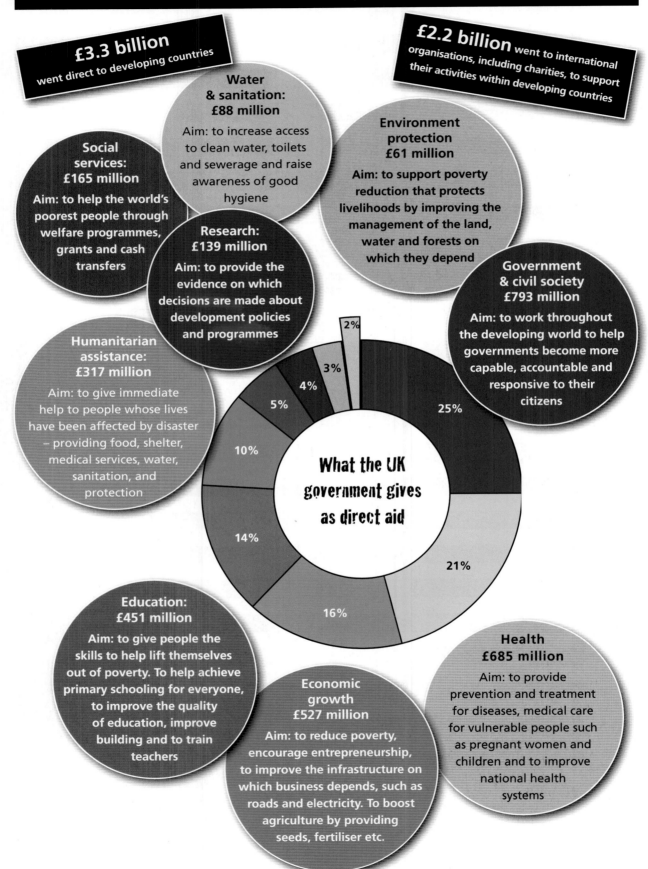

Water & sanitation: £88 million

Aim: to increase access to clean water, toilets and sewerage and raise awareness of good hygiene

Social services: £165 million

Aim: to help the world's poorest people through welfare programmes, grants and cash transfers

Environment protection £61 million

Aim: to support poverty reduction that protects livelihoods by improving the management of the land, water and forests on which they depend

Research: £139 million

Aim: to provide the evidence on which decisions are made about development policies and programmes

Government & civil society £793 million

Aim: to work throughout the developing world to help governments become more capable, accountable and responsive to their citizens

Humanitarian assistance: £317 million

Aim: to give immediate help to people whose lives have been affected by disaster – providing food, shelter, medical services, water, sanitation, and protection

What the UK government gives as direct aid

- 25%
- 21%
- 16%
- 14%
- 10%
- 5%
- 4%
- 3%
- 2%

Education: £451 million

Aim: to give people the skills to help lift themselves out of poverty. To help achieve primary schooling for everyone, to improve the quality of education, improve building and to train teachers

Economic growth £527 million

Aim: to reduce poverty, encourage entrepreneurship, to improve the infrastructure on which business depends, such as roads and electricity. To boost agriculture by providing seeds, fertiliser etc.

Health £685 million

Aim: to provide prevention and treatment for diseases, medical care for vulnerable people such as pregnant women and children and to improve national health systems

Five countries the UK supports directly
2008-09

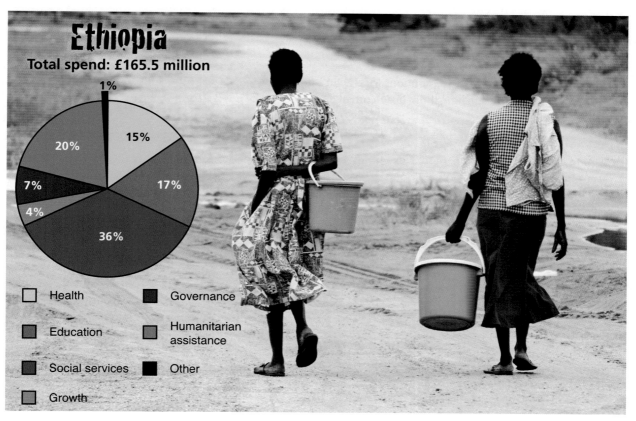

Ethiopia
Total spend: £165.5 million

1%
15%
17%
36%
4%
7%
20%

Legend:
- ☐ Health
- ☐ Education
- ☐ Social services
- ☐ Growth
- ■ Governance
- ■ Humanitarian assistance
- ■ Other

Afghanistan
Total spend: £147.5 million

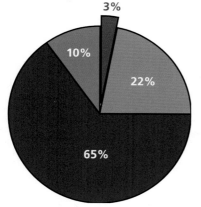

3%
10%
22%
65%

Bangladesh
Total spend: £132.9 million

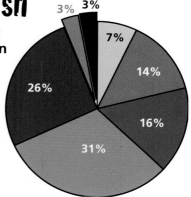

3% 3%
7%
14%
16%
31%
26%

Tanzania
Total spend: £132.7 million

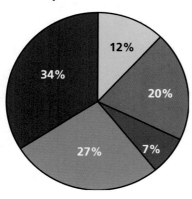

12%
20%
7%
27%
34%

Nepal
Total spend: £58 million

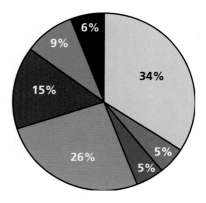

6%
9%
15%
26%
5%
5%
34%

Source: Department for International Development (DFID)
© Crown copyright 2010
www.dfid.gov.uk

Childhood decides

Spending more on **young** children increases wellbeing

> *"Spending early, when the foundations for a child's future are laid, is key especially for disadvantaged children and can help them break out of a family cycle of poverty and social exclusion"*
>
> *Angel Gurría – OECD secretary-general*

The *Doing Better for Children* report examines 21 different measures of children's living standards, education, health and protection from risks.

Public support for children is provided in different ways: family cash benefits and tax credits, education and childcare and other in-kind services.

Total public spending on children varies substantially between countries – obviously higher-income counties can usually afford to spend more. Education accounts for most spending on children in 23 out of the 28 countries for which data is available.

According to this report, governments should invest more on children in the first six years of their lives to reduce social inequality and help all children, especially the most vulnerable, have happier lives.

Total **public spending per child aged up to 17 years, OECD countries**

> Average public spending by OECD countries up to the age of six accounts for only a **quarter** of all child spending.

> Luxembourg (not shown) spends $380,000

				Iceland ($148,500)				
		Japan ($99,800)		United Kingdom ($145,800)				
	Czech Republic ($74,900)	Hungary ($90,900)	Italy ($121,500)	Germany ($144,500)				
	Greece ($71,600)	Spain ($89,800)	Australia ($121,200)	Finland ($140,400)			Denmark ($187,400)	
Poland ($43,700)	Korea ($53,200)	Portugal ($87,800)	Ireland ($114,900)	United States ($140,000)		France ($164,000)	Austria ($182,600)	
Mexico ($24,000)	Slovak Republic ($50,300)	New Zealand ($86,800)	Switzerland ($112,300)	Netherlands ($127,900)	Belgium ($155,000)	Sweden ($176,000)	Norway ($204,200)	

0    $25,000 $50,000 $75,000 $100,000 $125,000 $150,000 $175,000 $200,000 $225,000

The OECD consists of 31 democratic countries. This data is only available for 28 countries

There is most variation in the share of total spending at the early years stage

Public spending through childhood
(Totals do not add up to 100% due to rounding)

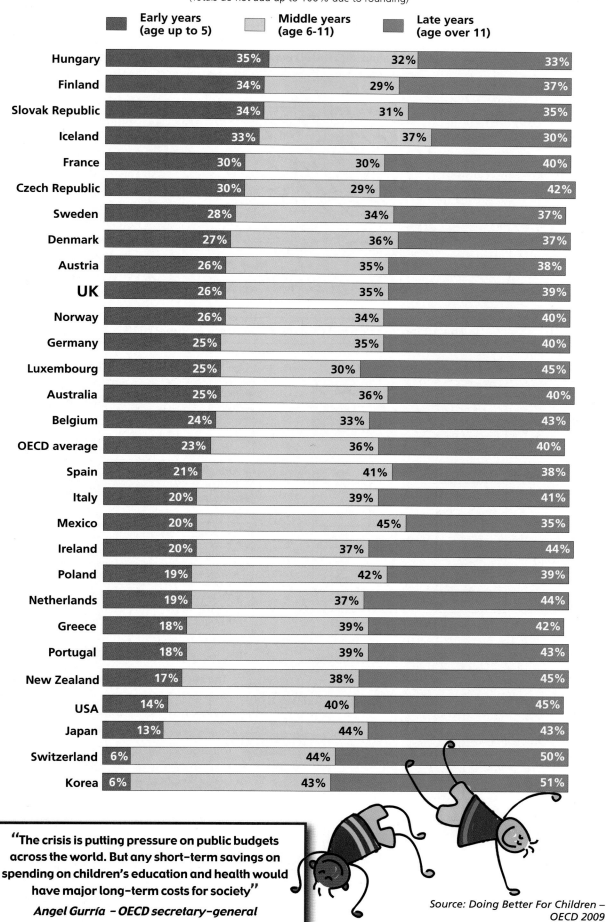

Legend:
- Early years (age up to 5)
- Middle years (age 6-11)
- Late years (age over 11)

Country	Early years (age up to 5)	Middle years (age 6-11)	Late years (age over 11)
Hungary	35%	32%	33%
Finland	34%	29%	37%
Slovak Republic	34%	31%	35%
Iceland	33%	37%	30%
France	30%	30%	40%
Czech Republic	30%	29%	42%
Sweden	28%	34%	37%
Denmark	27%	36%	37%
Austria	26%	35%	38%
UK	26%	35%	39%
Norway	26%	34%	40%
Germany	25%	35%	40%
Luxembourg	25%	30%	45%
Australia	25%	36%	40%
Belgium	24%	33%	43%
OECD average	23%	36%	40%
Spain	21%	41%	38%
Italy	20%	39%	41%
Mexico	20%	45%	35%
Ireland	20%	37%	44%
Poland	19%	42%	39%
Netherlands	19%	37%	44%
Greece	18%	39%	42%
Portugal	18%	39%	43%
New Zealand	17%	38%	45%
USA	14%	40%	45%
Japan	13%	44%	43%
Switzerland	6%	44%	50%
Korea	6%	43%	51%

"The crisis is putting pressure on public budgets across the world. But any short-term savings on spending on children's education and health would have major long-term costs for society"

Angel Gurría – OECD secretary-general

Source: Doing Better For Children – OECD 2009
http://www.oecd.org

Displaced by disaster

There were over 160 natural disasters in the first half of 2010...

...these events killed almost 230,000 people, affected 107 million others and caused over US $55 billion of damage

Earthquakes are the least predictable type of natural disaster and cause the most deaths.

The time between realising there is the threat of an earthquake and it actually happening is very short. Partly because of this, they cause most structural destruction and most deaths at the actual time of the disaster.

Haiti, one of the poorest countries in the world, was hit by an earthquake on 12th January 2010.

This was the worst disaster in a single country in the last decade in terms of the human impact it had, with at least 222,000 people killed and over 3 million people affected, 2 million of whom were displaced.

The 10 largest natural disasters – January to June 2010

...by number of people killed

Disaster	Month	Country	Number killed
Earthquake	January	Haiti	222,570
Earthquake	April	China	2,290
Earthquake	February	Chile	562
Landslide	February	Uganda	388
Flood	June	China	322
Hurricane Agatha	May	Guatemala	287
Flood	April	Brazil	256
Heat wave	March-May	India	250
Cold wave	January	Poland	212
Cold wave	January	Bangladesh	135

...by total number of people affected

Disaster	Month	Country	Number affected
Drought		China	51,000,000
Flood	June	China	29,000,000
Drought		Niger	7,700,000
Earthquake	January	Haiti	3,700,000
Earthquake	February	Chile	2,600,000
Landslide	May-June	China	2,100,00
Drought		Chad	2,000,000
Storm	January	China	1,500,000
Cold wave	Jan-May	Mongolia	769,000
Drought		Mali	600,000

...by estimated economic damages

Disaster	Month	Country	Total damage (million US$)
Earthquake	February	Chile	30,000
Earthquake	January	Haiti	8,000
Flood	June	China	6,300
Flood	May	Poland	3,200
Storm	February	United States	2,000
Flood	February	Portugal	1,800
Storm	February	France	1,650
Storm	March	Australia	1,380
Flood	May	Hungary	357
Drought		China	100

The earthquake in Chile in February 2010 was stronger (8.8) than that in Haiti (7.0), yet the number of deaths was much smaller.

Some reasons for the difference in impact are outside human control, such as how near an earthquake is to the surface, the different types of soil in the location, and whether it affects populated places.

On the other hand, the planning of cities, good governance and forward planning can be influenced by people.

Source: Centre for Research on the Epidemiology of Disasters – CRED CRUNCH August 2010
www.cred.be

The people of Pakistan face the largest humanitarian crisis in their history

The flooding in Pakistan has affected more people than the Asian Tsunami (2004) and Haiti earthquake combined.

Heavy monsoon rains started to hit Pakistan from 22nd July 2010.

This triggered both flash floods and several rivers breached their banks, resulting in loss of life, widespread displacement and damage.

Flood-affected people prepare food at a relief camp 27 August, 2010 in Hyderabad

Army officials rescue a man from the flood hit area via helicopter on 28 August, 2010 in Sukkur

Floods have caused widespread damage to public infrastructure, with roads submerged, tens of bridges swept away and many schools and hospitals severely damaged. Power and communication lines are down in many areas.

FLOOD DAMAGES IN FIGURES:

An estimated **20 million** people affected, of whom at least **8 million** are in need of humanitarian aid

Almost **1.9 million** homes have been destroyed or damaged

At least **10 million** people are currently without shelter

An area of at least **160,000km²** (larger than England) has been affected

An estimated **7,173** schools have been severely damaged

Over **2 million** hectares of crops have been lost

1.2 million pieces of livestock and **6 million** pieces of poultry have been lost

The **United Nations** and partners estimate **$459.7 million** will be required for the initial relief period – contributions of **$307 million** had been received at the time of going to press (**66.8%** of what was required) and there were pledges for **$21 million**

Source: United Nations Office for the Coordination of Humanitarian Affairs, Unicef

http://ochaonline.un.org
www.unicef.org.uk

Muslim population

Size and distribution of the world's Muslim population

The *Mapping the Global Muslim Population* study of more than **200 countries** finds that there are **1.57 billion** Muslims of all ages living in the world today, representing **23%** of the estimated 2009 world population.

More than **300 million** Muslims, or **one-fifth** of the world's Muslim population, live in countries where Islam is not the majority religion. These minority Muslim populations are often quite large. India, for example, has the third-largest population of Muslims worldwide **160.9m** making up **13.4%** of the Indian population. China's Muslim population is **21.7m** making up **1.6%** of the Chinese population.

Muslims live in all five inhabited continents, but the Middle East/North Africa region has the highest percentage of Muslim-majority countries. There are 20 countries and territories in that region and more than half of them have populations that are **95%** Muslim or even greater.

Number and percentage of all Muslims, by region

Asia-Pacific	Middle East/ North Africa	Sub-Saharan Africa	Europe	Americas
972.5m	315.3m	240.6m	38.1m	4.6m
61.9%	20.1%	15.3%	2.4%	0.3%

Focus on Europe

Estimated 2009 Muslim population in the EU and % of population that is Muslim

Sweden
149,000
2%

Denmark
88,000
2%

United Kingdom
1,647,000
2.7%

Netherlands
946,000   5.7%

Belgium
281,000
3%

Germany
4,026,000
5%

Luxembourg
13,000
3%

Austria
353,000
4.2%

France
3,554,000
6%

Slovenia
49,000
2.4%

Bulgaria
920,000
12.2%

Spain
650,000
1%

Greece
310,000
3%

Cyprus
198,000
22.7%

EU countries with less than 1% Muslim population	Estimated 2009 Muslim population	% of population that is Muslim
Finland	24,000	0.5%
Ireland	22,000	0.5%
Romania	66,000	0.3%
Hungary	24,000	0.2%
Malta	1,000	0.2%
Portugal	15,000	0.1%
Estonia	2,000	0.1%
Lithuania	3,000	0.1%
Poland	48,000	less than 1%
Italy	36,000	less than 1%
Latvia	2,000	less than 1%
Czech Republic	1,000	less than 0.1%
Slovakia	--	less than 0.1%

-- the number of Muslims is too small to be reliably estimated

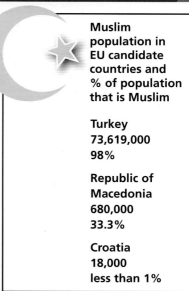

Muslim population in EU candidate countries and % of population that is Muslim

Turkey
73,619,000
98%

Republic of Macedonia
680,000
33.3%

Croatia
18,000
less than 1%

Source: Pew Forum on Religion & Public Life / Mapping the Global Muslim Population
www.pewforum.org

A woman's place...

... is in the home?

About half the world's workforce is women – they run companies and head governments, but a global survey of over **24,000** adults in 23 countries shows that **one in four** people, believe a woman's place is in the home.

Surprisingly, it was those aged between 18 and 34 who are most likely to hold that view, **not** those from the older, more traditional generation.

However, the majority , **74%**, of those polled, believe a woman's place is certainly **not** at home.

Generally there was little difference in opinion between the sexes.

A woman's place is in the home...

■ Agree ▢ Disagree

Country	Agree	Disagree
India	54%	46%
Turkey	52%	48%
Japan	48%	52%
China	34%	66%
Russia	34%	66%
Hungary	34%	66%
South Korea	33%	67%
Czech Republic	28%	72%
Australia	25%	75%
United States	25%	75%
Great Britain	22%	78%
Netherlands	20%	80%
Canada	20%	80%
Italy	19%	81%
Poland	18%	82%
Belgium	16%	84%
Germany	14%	86%
Spain	12%	88%
Brazil	10%	90%
Sweden	10%	90%
Mexico	9%	91%
France	9%	91%
Argentina	9%	91%

Source: Reuters/Ipsos

www.uk.reuters.com

Work

Below the breadline

The National Minimum Wage provides protection for the lowest paid

In 1998, a year before the National Minimum Wage (NMW) was introduced, nearly **1.3 million** employee jobs – **5.6%** – were paid below that rate.

The impact could clearly be seen as the percentage of employees being paid below the NMW fell to **2.1%** in the year of its introduction, by 2008 this had dropped to **288,000 – 1.1%**.

Today around **1%** of jobs are paid at below the NMW – **242,000** in April 2009.

Number of jobs paid below the national minimum wage, 2009

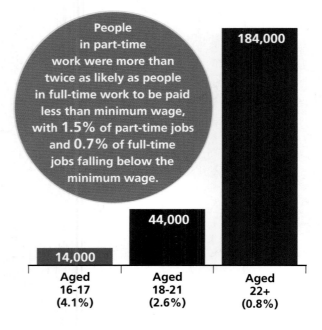

People in part-time work were more than twice as likely as people in full-time work to be paid less than minimum wage, with **1.5%** of part-time jobs and **0.7%** of full-time jobs falling below the minimum wage.

Aged 16-17 (4.1%)	14,000
Aged 18-21 (2.6%)	44,000
Aged 22+ (0.8%)	184,000

National minimum wage, hourly rates, UK

	Aged 16-17	Aged 18-21	Aged 22 +
Apr 1999 - May 2000		£3.00	£3.60
Jun 2000 - Sep 2000		£3.20	£3.60
Oct 2000 - Sep 2001		£3.20	£3.70
Oct 2001 - Sep 2002		£3.50	£4.10
Oct 2002 - Sep 2003		£3.60	£4.20
Oct 2003 - Sep 2004		£3.80	£4.50
Oct 2004 - Sep 2005	£3.00	£4.10	£4.85
Oct 2005 - Sep 2006	£3.00	£4.25	£5.05
Oct 2006 - Sep 2007	£3.30	£4.45	£5.35
Oct 2007 - Sep 2008	£3.40	£4.60	£5.52
Oct 2008 - Sep 2009	£3.53	£4.77	£5.73
Oct 2009 - Sep 2010	£3.57	£4.83	£5.80

October 2010

The government extended the adult minimum wage rate to 21-year-olds:

£3.64 an hour for workers aged 16 to 17

£4.92 an hour for workers aged 18 to 20

£5.93 an hour for workers aged 21 and over

The rise is around **2%** in each category.

Apprentices

The government also accepted a recommendation from the Low Pay Commission (LPC) to introduce an apprentice minimum wage of **£2.50** per hour.

The new rate applies to apprentices aged under 19 and to apprentices aged 19 and over, in the first year of their apprenticeship.

Sources: Office for National Statistics, Directgov, Low Pay Commission © Crown Copyright 2010

www.ons.gov.uk
www.lowpay.gov.uk
www.direct.gov.uk

Future imperfect

Jobs for young people are disappearing

Jobseeker's Allowance is the main benefit for people who are over 18 and actively seeking work. It is currently **£51.85** a week for under 25s

Using JSA data the TUC has found that the number of 18-24 year olds on the dole for over six months has increased in 142 local authorities across the UK since last year, compared to just 78 where it has fallen. The young people's unemployment rate is already over **17%** (more than twice the national unemployment rate).

Top 5 with a reduction in JSA claimants

Halton (-44)

Warrington (-43)

Knowsley (-43)

Bromley (-38)

Swindon (-35)

Changes in the number of 18-24 year olds claiming Job Seekers Allowance for over six months, best and worst by local authority (percentage change over the year)

Bottom 5 with an increase in JSA claimants

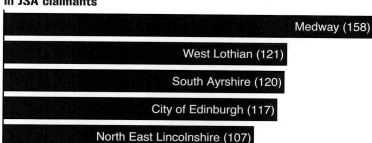

Medway (158)

West Lothian (121)

South Ayrshire (120)

City of Edinburgh (117)

North East Lincolnshire (107)

There were **103,230** 18-24 year olds claiming Job Seekers Allowance in June 2010. The total number of young people out of work for over six months reached **338,000** between March and May 2010.

Moves to reduce the budget deficit will have a particular effect on young people:

Between March 2009 and March 2011 the Future Jobs Fund had financed over **100,000** jobs mainly aimed at 18-24 year olds who had been out of work for 6 months and were claiming JSA. It was axed in May 2010 saving **£290m**. It was also part of the Young Person's Guarantee, which promised a job or training to everyone in this key group. Cutting this guarantee saves **£450m**.

A degree is no guarantee… Graduates are amongst those feeling the pinch

The number of graduate vacancies has fallen by nearly **7%** this year.

The average graduate starting salary hasn't risen and remains at the 2008 figure of **£25,000**.

The drop in vacancies has caused an increase in the number of applications for each graduate job – on average **69** applications for every vacancy. As a result

78% of people who employ graduates will only consider those with at least a 2.1 degree.

Source: TUC

www.tuc.org.uk
www.agr.org.uk

Cut backs

18% of us think it likely we could lose our jobs as a result of the recession

Job loss and recession

For the first time public sector employees are significantly more pessimistic over job security than staff in the private sector. 26% of public sector employees think it likely or very likely they could lose their jobs. In comparison, 17% of private sector workers think this is the case and 13% of voluntary sector staff think they could lose their jobs.

Q: How likely is it that you could lose your current main job as a result of the recession?

Legend:
- All
- Private sector
- Public sector
- Voluntary sector

Unlikely/Very unlikely
- 50%
- 51%
- 46%
- 59%

Neither/nor/ Don't know
- 32%
- 33%
- 28%
- 29%

Likely/Very likely
- 18%
- 17%
- 26%
- 13%

Finding a new job?

66% of respondents think it would be difficult or very difficult to find a new job.

Public sector staff are most pessimistic over their chances in the jobs market if made redundant. In all, 72% think it would be difficult or very difficult to find a new job. 64% of private sector employees think it would be difficult or very difficult to find a new job. 69% of voluntary sector employees are equally downbeat about their job chances, in comparison with 66% in the previous report.

Q: In which ways, if at all, has your organisation been affected by the downturn?

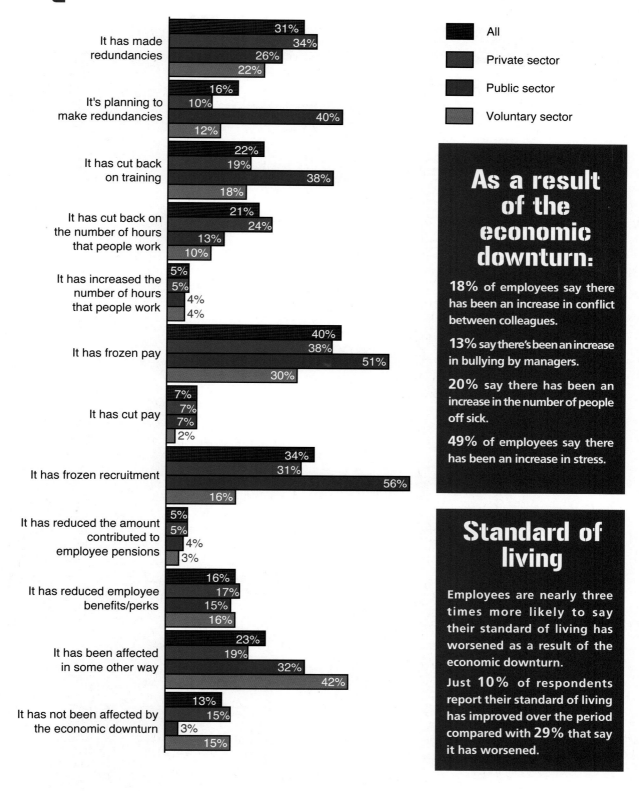

Legend:
- All
- Private sector
- Public sector
- Voluntary sector

It has made redundancies
- 31%
- 34%
- 26%
- 22%

It's planning to make redundancies
- 16%
- 10%
- 40%
- 12%

It has cut back on training
- 22%
- 19%
- 38%
- 18%

It has cut back on the number of hours that people work
- 21%
- 24%
- 13%
- 10%

It has increased the number of hours that people work
- 5%
- 5%
- 4%
- 4%

It has frozen pay
- 40%
- 38%
- 51%
- 30%

It has cut pay
- 7%
- 7%
- 7%
- 2%

It has frozen recruitment
- 34%
- 31%
- 56%
- 16%

It has reduced the amount contributed to employee pensions
- 5%
- 5%
- 4%
- 3%

It has reduced employee benefits/perks
- 16%
- 17%
- 15%
- 16%

It has been affected in some other way
- 23%
- 19%
- 32%
- 42%

It has not been affected by the economic downturn
- 13%
- 15%
- 3%
- 15%

As a result of the economic downturn:

18% of employees say there has been an increase in conflict between colleagues.

13% say there's been an increase in bullying by managers.

20% say there has been an increase in the number of people off sick.

49% of employees say there has been an increase in stress.

Standard of living

Employees are nearly three times more likely to say their standard of living has worsened as a result of the economic downturn.

Just **10%** of respondents report their standard of living has improved over the period compared with **29%** that say it has worsened.

Source: Employee outlook, CIPD
www.cipd.co.uk

Labour market snapshot

How has the recession affected job prospects?

The job market

The latest edition of the TUC's report on the state of the labour market shows a large increase in the number of people in employment indicating that employment recovery has strengthened.

But the recovery may still be fragile, with a high number of unemployed people for each vacancy and many people taking part-time, or temporary work or creating their own jobs.

Increase in unemployment

Unemployment

In March-May 2010 unemployment was 2,468,000 (according to the International Labour Organisation measurement), 34,000 lower than the December-February figure – the largest quarter on quarter fall since the start of the recession.

The number of unemployed people claiming benefits had also fallen – 1,460,100 people were on Job Seekers Allowance. The level fell 20,800 between May and June.

Long-term Unemployment

Although short-term unemployment (less than 6 months) had been falling for a year, long-term unemployment was still rising. The number unemployed for over 6 months climbed to reach 1,306,000 in July 2010. It was a similar story for even longer term unemployment – 787,000 people had been unemployed over 12 months, an increase of 61,000 on the previous quarter. 293,000 had been unemployed over 24 months, up 25,000 on the previous quarter.

Long term unemployment is usually the last statistic to show the end of a recession.

Employment

There were 28,984,000 people in employment in March-May 2010 – 160,000 higher than the figure for the previous three months. The month-on-month increase of 119,000 was the biggest increase since records began in 1971.

Increase in part-time and temporary jobs

Part time employment

However, nearly half the month-on-month increase in employment was due to a substantial increase in part-time employment, which was up 55,000. The number of people who said they were only working in part-time jobs because they couldn't find a full-time alternative had risen steadily during the recession.

Temporary employment

Temporary employment has also made a significant contribution to the employment increase. There are currently 1,539,000 temporary employees, the highest level since 2003. The increase, 78,000 on the quarter, was the second largest quarterly increase ever.

552,000 temporary workers stated that they would prefer a permanent job; this is the highest level since October 1999. This amounts to 35.9% of temporary workers, the highest proportion since April 1999.

Chances of employment

Between December 2009 and March 2010 there was only a 13,000 increase in the number of jobs (compared to an annual fall of 495,000). Industries that have in the past been drivers of job creation were doing badly. In construction the number of jobs fell by 63,000, in retail 36,000 and education 11,000. As with previous recessions, manufacturing jobs are also still being lost, with a fall of 51,000 over three months.

The number of jobs rose in some areas of employment. In administrative and support activities there was a 90,000 rise, and real estate (17,000) and electricity and gas (13,000) saw small increases.

Source: TUC Labour Market Report
www.tuc.org.uk

Work and play

40% of employees are under excessive pressure at work ...

The public sector provides and delivers services for local or national government e.g. social services, health

The private sector is run for profit and is under the control of individuals or groups rather than

government eg banks, shops

The voluntary sector consists of organisations which are not run for profit and are not government controlled but are usually of some benefit to society eg charities

Proportion of employees who reported being under excessive pressure at work...

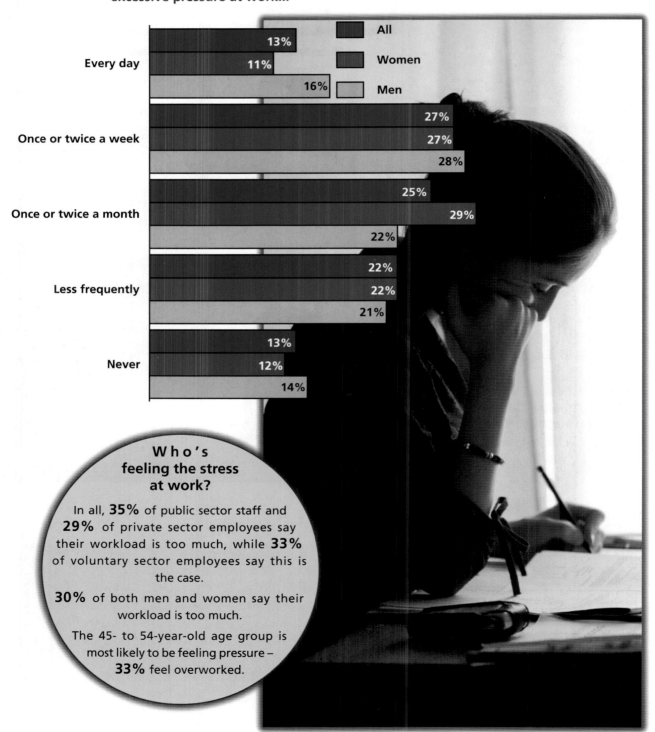

Legend: All / Women / Men

Every day
- 13%
- 11%
- 16%

Once or twice a week
- 27%
- 27%
- 28%

Once or twice a month
- 25%
- 29%
- 22%

Less frequently
- 22%
- 22%
- 21%

Never
- 13%
- 12%
- 14%

Who's feeling the stress at work?

In all, **35%** of public sector staff and **29%** of private sector employees say their workload is too much, while **33%** of voluntary sector employees say this is the case.

30% of both men and women say their workload is too much.

The 45- to 54-year-old age group is most likely to be feeling pressure – **33%** feel overworked.

Fact File 2011 · **www.carelpress.com**

Who's getting enough time at home?

58% of public sector staff feel they achieve the right work-life balance compared to **61%** in the private sector and **62%** in the voluntary sector.

65% of women compared with **56%** of men are happy with the balance between their work and home lives.

Employees aged between 18 and 24 are least happy in this respect. Just **53%** agree they have got this right, compared with **68%** of people aged 55 and over.

37% of respondents felt their organisation provides support to help them manage their work–life balance.

The proportion of employees agreeing they achieve the right balance between their work and home lives

Legend:
- All
- Women
- Men

	Agree/strongly agree	Neither/Nor/Not sure	Disagree/ stongly disagree
All	61%	15%	24%
Women	65%	14%	21%
Men	56%	17%	27%

Source: Employee outlook, CIPD
www.cipd.co.uk

Index

Entries in colour refer to main sections.

A

Abortion 34-35, 104-105

Addiction 8

Afghanistan 162-163, 164-165

Age restrictions 32-33

ALCOHOL & DRUGS 7-16 & 100-101, 126-127, 131, 132-133, 140

ANIMALS 17-24

Animal testing 18-19, 20

Arts & culture 152-153, 154-155, 156

Assisted suicide 34-35

B

BRITAIN & ITS CITIZENS 25-35 & 40-41, 60-61, 70-71, 79, 80-81, 114-115, 122-123, 132-133, 140, 142-143 (most charts contain UK information)

C

Censorship & freedom 118-119

CHARITY 36-43

Children 72, 170-171, 176-177

Class 52-53, 152-153, 154-155, 156, 158-159

Consumers & shopping 14-15, 84-85, 90-91, 92, 96, 108

Crime see LAW & ORDER 130-140

D

Death 10-11, 12-13, 14-15, 34-35, 98-99, 161, 162-163, 164-165, 170-171

Developing World 96, 169, 170-171, 172-173, 174-175

Disasters 178-179

E

EDUCATION 44-58 & 93, 102-103, 185

ENVIRONMENTAL ISSUES 59-68 & 94-95, 166-167, 172-173

Ethnicity 26-27, 52-53, 70-71

Euthanasia 34-35

F

FAMILY & RELATIONSHIPS 69-77 & 30-31, 34-35, 92, 112-113, 126-127, 140, 190

FINANCIAL ISSUES 78-87 & 56-57, 94-95, 112-113, 126-127, 134-135, 136-137, 138-139, 166-167, 172-173, 174-175, 176-177, 184, 185, 186 see also CHARITY 36-43

FOOD & DRINK 88-96 & 108

Football 157

Fraud 134-135, 136-137, 138-139

G

Gender 34-35, 74-75, 76-77, 146-147, 182

H

Haiti 178

HEALTH 97-108 & 8-9, 10-11, 12-13, 14-15, 16, 89, 90-91, 126-127, 158-159, 169, 170-171

Homeless 114-115

HOUSING 109-115

Human Rights 118-119

I

Identity theft 136-137

Immigration 26-27, 29

INTERNET & TECHNOLOGY 116-129 & 142-143, 148, 149

Iraq 161

L

Language 146-147, 58

LAW & ORDER 130-140 & 21, 32-33, 66-67

Libraries & reading 154-155, 156

M

Marriage & divorce 30-31, 34-35, 73, 76-77, 110-111

MEDIA 141-150 & 161

Mental health 10-11, 12-13, 100-101, 190

Mobile phones 118-119, 120-121, 122-123, 148-149, 150 see also INTERNET & TECHNOLOGY 116-129

N

News 146-147

P

Pakistan 179

Police see LAW & ORDER 130-140

Population 26-27, 28, 29, 30-31, 70-71, 110-111, 180-181

Poverty & debt 52-53, 86, 87, 114-115

Pregnancy & birth 26-27, 70-71, 72

R

Radio 144-145, 148, 149

Refugees 178-179

Religion 30-31, 34-35, 180-181

S

Salt 89, 90-91

Science 18-19, 20, 34-35

Self-harm 100-101

Sexual issues 30-31, 32-33, 34-35, 76-77, 102-103, 106-107, 126-127

Social networks 118-119, 148, 149 see also INTERNET & TECHNOLOGY 116-129

SPORT & LEISURE 151-159 & 142-143, 144-145, 148, 149, 150

T

Transplants 98-99

TV 142-143, 148, 149

U

University 54-55, 56-57

V

Violence 131, 132-133, 140

Volunteers 40-41, 42-43

W

Water 62-63

WAR & CONFLICT 160-167

Wealth 79, 80-81

WIDER WORLD 168-182 & 42-43, 45, 54-55, 56-57, 58, 64-65, 68, 72, 73, 98-99, 117, 118-119, 120-121, 134-135, 157, 161, 162-163, 166-167

WORK 183-190 & 29, 56-57, 182

World Cup 157

Y

Young people 8-9, 12-13, 32-33, 74-75, 92, 93, 100-101, 102-103, 104-105, 106-107, 112-113, 114-115, 124-125, 126-127, 128, 132-133, 146-147, 148, 149, 184, 185